THIS COMMON INHERITANCE

THE THIRD YEAR REPORT

BRITAIN'S ENVIRONMENTAL STRATEGY

Presented to Parliament by the Secretaries of State for the Environment and Foreign and Commonwealth Affairs, the Chancellor of the Exchequer, the President of the Board of Trade, the Secretaries of State for Transport, Defence, National Heritage and Employment, the Chancellor of the Duchy of Lancaster, the Secretaries of State for Scotland, Northern Ireland, Education and Health, the Minister for Agriculture, Fisheries and Food, the Secretary of State for Wales and the Minister for Overseas Development by Command of Her Majesty. May 1994.

Cm 2549   **LONDON: HMSO**   **£21.00 net**

FOREWORD
BY THE SECRETARY OF STATE FOR THE
ENVIRONMENT

With the publication of *This Common Inheritance* in 1990, the Government produced a comprehensive strategy for the environment. It included a wide range of commitments to further action, reflecting the high priority we attach to our stewardship of the environment. This is the third report on our progress in meeting those commitments.

We have made encouraging progress over the past 18 months; there is action to report on almost all commitments, and in many cases, promised action is now complete. We have, for example: ratified the Climate Change Convention; increased the energy efficiency budget; updated planning guidance; launched English Partnerships; finalised the UK's agri-environment programme; and introduced the ecolabelling scheme. But we are not standing still. Like previous reports, this one records further new commitments.

More particularly, sustainable development is now the touchstone of our policies. We published the UK's Sustainable Development Strategy on 25 January, together with documents on climate change, biodiversity and forestry that follow up the Earth Summit. This third year report incorporates the new commitments we made in those post-Rio documents. It therefore provides us with a new baseline for future monitoring.

But Government initiatives are not all. As we emphasised in both *This Common Inheritance* and the Sustainable Development Strategy, looking after our environment is not something the Government can do on its own. Local authorities, business, the voluntary sector and the individual all have an important part to play and many valuable initiatives have been taken recently by people outside government.

The Government's commitment to conserving our 'common inheritance' remains undiminished and we are determined to deliver our promises on the environment. The Sustainable Development Strategy gives fresh impetus to our policies and will help us chart our progress over the longer term.

THIS COMMON INHERITANCE

THE THIRD YEAR REPORT

THE GOVERNMENT'S COMMITMENTS TO ACTION ON THE ENVIRONMENT

The tables at the end of each chapter list all the commitments made in the previous three White Papers, except where the 1991 and 1992 White Papers indicated that action had been completed. The tables also set out new commitments.

The left hand column in each table lists commitments made in the earlier White Papers. The numbers in brackets refer to the place in which the commitment was first made or, in the case of some 1990 commitments, updated. The initials 'SYR' refer to the relevant commitment in the 1992 Second Year Report; the initials 'FYR' refer to the relevant pages of the 1991 First Year Report. All other references are to the appropriate paragraph in the 1990 White Paper.

The centre column shows what action has been taken to date to deliver those commitments, concentrating on action taken since the publication of the Second Year Report in October 1992.

The right hand column lists commitments to further action or new commitments.

Annex A contains a cross reference of commitments in the Second and Third Year Reports.

In Chapters 1-9 and 11-17, the lead Department for the action recorded in the tables is the Department of the Environment, unless otherwise indicated alongside the commitment. In Chapters 10, 18, 19 and 20, the lead Departments are the Department of National Heritage, the Welsh Office, Scottish Office and the Northern Ireland Office respectively. The key below refers to the abbreviations used in the tables.

KEY TO THE DEPARTMENTAL ABBREVIATIONS USED IN THE TABLES			
DOE	Department of the Environment	FCO	Foreign and Commonwealth Office
DFE	Department for Education	HMT	Her Majesty's Treasury
DH	Department of Health	HSE	Health and Safety Executive
DNH	Department of National Heritage	MAFF	Ministry of Agriculture, Fisheries
DOT	Department of Transport		and Food
DTI	Department of Trade and Industry	ODA	Overseas Development
ED	Employment Department		Administration
FC	Forestry Commission	MOD	Ministry of Defence

INTRODUCTION:
OBJECTIVES AND STRATEGIES

1 The last Environment White Paper was published in October 1992. During 1993, the co-ordination of environmental policy has focused on the production of the UK's Strategy for Sustainable Development, which was published in January 1994. While that document was in preparation it did not seem appropriate to publish another White Paper in the regular annual series reporting progress on targets and outlining new ones. But now that the strategy document is published, it is possible to bring forward this Third Year Report on *This Common Inheritance,* describing progress over the last year and outlining targets and proposals for the next year in particular, in the same way as its two predecessors.

2 The text briefly highlights some of the main policy developments, with cross references in some cases to fuller treatment in the Strategy for Sustainable Development or the other national plans on climate change, biodiversity and forestry, which were also published in January.

3 The tables in this report record progress on specific commitments from previous years, in many cases showing that the promised action is now complete; and they also record a number of new commitments, including some undertaken in the Strategy for Sustainable Development and the other national plans. Progress on these new commitments will in turn be reported on in next year's report.

OBJECTIVES

4 The Government's general objectives for protection of the environment and promotion of sustainable development have been set out in the earlier White Papers and, most recently, in the Sustainable Development Strategy. The overarching objective is:

The Government launched the UK's Sustainable Development Strategy and the other post-Rio documents in January 1994

"development that meets the needs of the present without compromising the ability of future generations to meet their own needs."
(The Brundtland Commission, 1987)

5 During 1993, three particular aspects of this general objective have received emphasis. The **preparation of the Sustainable Development Strategy** and the other post-Rio documents has required a sustained effort. The Sustainable Development Strategy reviews environmental problems, across the board and up to twenty years ahead, and identifies where changes and developments in the economy may give rise to problems for the environment and for the long term sustainability of development. In those areas, the Strategy has strongly identified the need to integrate environmental concerns and objectives into other policy areas, and policies and targets for such integration will need to be carried forward vigorously in 1994 and future years.

6 A second major emphasis during 1993 has been the need to reconcile environmental objectives with other major Government objectives of **promoting competitiveness and reducing the burden of regulation.** The Government is determined to maintain environmental standards. But wherever possible, it has sought, in the deregulation initiative and in the initiative to promote subsidiarity in relation to European legislation, to simplify and streamline the way in which regulation operates, and to seek non-regulatory means such as economic instruments to achieve environmental objectives. This report records progress in these directions during 1993, and indicates where further progress

can be looked for during 1994 and future years.

7 A third major emphasis during 1993 has been the **continuing drive to build partnerships** between Government, local government, industry, the voluntary sector and the public to promote environmental good practice and solutions to environmental problems. Very few of the problems confronting the environment can be resolved by Governments alone. This report records progress in co-operative working with the other actors and agencies, and indicates where more needs to be done to build such productive partnerships during 1994 and beyond.

8 This report records progress in a number of areas against specific targets for improvement of the environment in relation to climate change, the ozone layer, local air quality, water quality, the handling of wastes and recycling, and the protection of habitats and species. But more needs to be done to develop a fuller set of targets and indicators for sustainable development and the protection of our environment, and this will be an important challenge for 1994.

The Government's commitment to conserving our 'common inheritance' remains undiminished

1 WORLDWIDE ENVIRONMENTAL ISSUES

HIGHLIGHTS

Published UK Strategy for Sustainable Development, UK Climate Change Programme, UK Biodiversity Action Plan and UK Sustainable Forestry Programme

UK elected member of Commission on Sustainable Development

Ratified Climate Change Convention

Launched Darwin Initiative

Launched Technology Partnership Initiative

Hosted 'Partnerships for Change' conference

1.1 In the past year, the UK has taken forward the agenda set by the Earth Summit in Rio, ensuring that environmental concerns are fully integrated into Government programmes and policies. There have been some landmark events in the UK's follow-up to Rio. The Government ratified the Framework Convention on Climate Change in 1993. It launched the Darwin Initiative for the Survival of Species and the Technology Partnership Initiative, and hosted an international conference, 'Partnerships for Change', in 1993. It also published its Strategy for Sustainable Development and plans on climate change, biodiversity and forestry early this year. The UK has continued to fund a wide range of environmental projects in developing countries and to participate in international negotiations on environmental issues. The latter are considered below, or in the chapter appropriate to the subject under negotiation.

COMMISSION ON SUSTAINABLE DEVELOPMENT

1.2 The United Nations Commission on Sustainable Development (CSD) was set up in 1993 to monitor progress on Agenda 21, the international action plan for sustainable development agreed at the Earth Summit in 1992. Its first meeting was held in New York in June 1993. The UK, which has been elected to the CSD until the end of 1996, played an important role in that meeting.

1.3 One of the UK's major contributions to the work programme of the CSD is a joint Indo-British Initiative, forged through personal contacts between environment Ministers in the UK and India, to establish a bridge between the developed and developing nations on these issues. The UK Government believes that as many nations as possible should produce strategies for sustainable development, and published its own Strategy in January 1994 (see Chapter 3). A report on the Strategy has been submitted to the CSD.

CLIMATE CHANGE

1.4 In December 1993, the Government ratified the Framework Convention on Climate Change and, in January 1994, the UK was the first country to publish a Climate Change Programme under the Convention. Details of this programme are given in Chapter 4. The UK will continue to work with other countries on the details of interpretation and implementation of the Convention in the run-up to the first meeting of the Conference of the Parties to the Convention in 1995.

BIODIVERSITY

1.5 The UK intends to ratify the Convention on Biological Diversity, subject to achieving satisfactory safeguards on the financial provisions. Over 40 countries have now ratified the Convention, which came into force on 29 December 1993. The first meeting of an Inter-Governmental Committee to prepare for the implementation of the Convention was held in Geneva in October 1993. The Government published *Biodiversity: the UK Action Plan* in January 1994 (see Chapter 8), and is setting up a steering group to produce targets for species and habitats in 1995.

FORESTS

1.6 The Government published *Sustainable Forestry: The UK Programme* in January 1994, setting out policies to implement the Statement of Forest Principles agreed at the Earth Summit in 1992. In 1995, forests will be a key theme of the United Nations Commission on Sustainable Development, and the Forest Programme, part of which is concerned with forests overseas, will provide the basis for the UK's report to the CSD. The UK successfully pressed for the CSD to review the implementation of the Statement of Forest Principles. The first review will take place in 1995. The UK and India will host an international workshop in July 1994 to prepare for the review. This is one element of the Indo-British Forestry Initiative to promote the sustainable management of forests, signed in September 1993.

THE OVERSEAS AID PROGRAMME

1.7 The overall aim of the aid programme is to promote economic and social development in other countries and the welfare of their people. The Overseas Development Administration (ODA) has seven specific objectives which reflect the principles agreed at the Earth Summit as part of Agenda 21:
- to promote economic reform;
- to enhance productive capacity;
- to promote good government;
- to undertake direct poverty reduction activities and programmes;
- to promote human development, including better education, health and children by choice;
- to promote the status of women;
- to help developing countries tackle national environmental problems.

1.8 The ODA is reviewing its strategies in the five key areas of Agenda 21 identified by the Prime Minister at Rio: biodiversity; forest conservation; population planning; sustainable agriculture and energy efficiency. These were already important components of the UK's bilateral aid programme. In 1992-93, ODA had 320 projects under way whose principal or significant objective was one of the Earth Summit priorities; these spent over £100 million in that year.

1.9 In the area of biodiversity, activities currently supported through the aid programme include establishing nature reserves in Brazil, strengthening Kenya's wildlife service and providing conservation advisers to Indonesia and Nigeria. In November 1993, the Government prepared a revised strategy for support to biodiversity. Its objectives include helping targeted developing countries to implement the Convention by commissioning strategic research and by providing training and other bilateral assistance.

1.10 In October 1993, the Government prepared a strategy on forestry in support of actions that developing countries are taking to implement the Statement of Forest Principles agreed at the Earth Summit. This includes:

Over 40 countries have now ratified the Convention on Biological Diversity, which came into force on 29 December 1993

ENERGY EFFICIENCY IN INDIA

Economic growth in developing countries results in an increasing demand for energy, but this can lead to environmental damage. Using scarce energy resources more efficiently can go some way to reducing that damage.

For example, in India, limited financial resources and scarce energy supplies make it crucial that the available energy is used in the most efficient way. ODA concentrates its energy efficiency activities on the electrical power sector, where there is huge potential to make efficiency gains. ODA helps support projects which, directly or indirectly, reduce the level of damaging emissions to the environment and supports institutions which are following a reform programme, including energy price reform.

During 1993, ODA committed £86 million to energy efficiency projects in India. This includes a project to rehabilitate and uprate two generating units at a hydro-power station in Orissa, and a project which allows power to be shared between two regions, enabling total system efficiency improvements. The Indian institutions which manage these projects also receive technical assistance to improve their institutional performance.

In June 1993, ODA announced an additional £60 million environmental grant with energy efficiency as one of its main foci, and recently 13 projects were identified.

Aid is also used to finance advice and training in maintenance management systems and the planning of distribution projects. ODA is also currently preparing a programme of projects to improve industrial energy efficiency in India.

The UK Government has sought to make the Tropical Forest Action Programme more responsive to the needs of developing countries

The 'Partnerships for Change' Conference, held in September 1993, was attended by participants from 85 countries

- support to forest management, including agroforestry, for the sustainable supply of forest products;

- assistance to developing countries in maximising the economic and social benefits of forests and forest-based industries in a sustainable manner;

- sustaining the benefits of forests for the global environment as 'sinks' for carbon dioxide, as the richest repositories of biological diversity, and as a means of resisting and reducing desertification, through forest conservation and reforestation.

1.11 In 1989, the Government announced that it would commit a further £100 million to tropical forest activities over a three year period. This target was met. ODA has some 200 projects underway or being prepared in 45 developing countries, at a cost of over £150 million to the aid programme.

1.12 The UK participates in the Tropical Forest Action Programme (TFAP), which encourages co-ordinated funding and planning for forests in developing countries. The Government has sought to make the TFAP more responsive to the needs of these countries. The Government aims to enhance the International Tropical Timber Organisation's focus on its environmental objectives, particularly the target for all tropical timber to come from sustainably managed sources by 2000.

FINANCE FOR THE GLOBAL ENVIRONMENT

1.13 In recognition of the fact that some environmental issues affect our shared, global environment, the UK has a budget separate from and additional to the aid programme, the Global Environment Assistance (GEA) programme. From this, it contributes to the Montreal Protocol Fund and the Global Environment Facility (GEF). The Montreal Protocol fund meets the incremental costs to developing countries of phasing out substances that deplete the ozone layer. The GEF helps developing countries meet the incremental costs of protecting the global environment in four

areas: limiting emission of greenhouse gases; protecting biological diversity; reducing ozone depletion (in East European countries) and protecting international waters from pollution.

1.14 The UK has committed a total of £67 million from its GEA budget, of which £40.3 million is to the initial or pilot phase of the GEF. The GEF was restructured and replenished in March 1994. The Government believes the restructuring should enable the GEF to become a permanent funding mechanism for the Biodiversity and Climate Change Conventions. The UK has pledged £89.5 million of the agreed replenishment of over US $2000 million.

DARWIN INITIATIVE FOR THE SURVIVAL OF SPECIES

1.15 The Darwin Initiative, launched by the Prime Minister at Rio, provides funding for British organisations to assist conservation overseas and to help countries meet their obligations under the Biodiversity Convention. £9 million is available over the first four years of the Initiative. This is additional to the funding provided through the aid programme. In November 1993, the Secretary of State for the Environment announced the first thirty-one projects to receive support of over £3.7m under the Initiative. The projects include training, conservation and scientific study.

DESERTIFICATION

1.16 The UK is taking an active part in negotiations on a Convention to combat the effects of desertification, which have been initiated by the United Nations in response to Agenda 21. Negotiations are scheduled to be concluded by June 1994.

PARTNERSHIPS FOR CHANGE

1.17 The Government hosted an international conference, 'Partnerships for Change', for non-governmental organisations in Manchester in September 1993. The conference was attended by over

The Government supports action by developing countries to combat desertification

300 participants from 85 countries. Through case studies and workshops, participants considered the role of partnerships in developed and developing countries in enhancing sustainable development. A guide, *Partnerships in Practice,* drawing on discussions at the conference, is to be submitted to the CSD.

TECHNOLOGY CO-OPERATION

1.18 Technology co-operation is essential if developing countries in particular are to realise their economic potential in a way that responds to the needs of both local and international environmental threats and sustainable development. Business activity is responsible for the vast majority of this co-operation and should be encouraged.

1.19 The Technology Partnership Initiative was launched by the Prime Minister at a conference in Birmingham in March 1993. The conference was attended by over 250 senior businessmen and women, over half of whom came from the rapidly industrialising countries in the developing world. Speakers addressed the environmental challenges facing business, the role of technology co-operation from the point of view of suppliers and recipients, and the international help and funding available. The conference also included 36 individual workshops, aimed at exploring different technological approaches to familiar environmental problems. British and overseas business leaders went away with a much clearer picture of technology co-operation and the value of the transfer of skills and technology.

1.20 The Technology Partnership Initiative runs for three years. It will provide information to businesses in developing countries on the technologies and management techniques which can lead to significant improvements in performance and profits and at the same time reduce damage to the environment.

ANTARCTICA

1.21 The UK will ratify the Environmental Protocol to the Antarctic Treaty as soon as the legislative programme allows. A further Annex to the Protocol, on Environmental Liability, is under negotiation by the Antarctic Treaty Parties. A programme is under way which will either clean up or remove abandoned former UK bases in Antarctica or retain some as emergency refuges or Historic Sites.

1.22 In May 1993, the UK extended its maritime jurisdiction around South Georgia and the South Sandwich Islands to improve

ELEPHANT AND RHINO CONSERVATION

The 1992 CITES Conference recognised the importance of improving understanding and developing consensus on African elephants. The UK led a successful EC Mission to Africa in 1992 for this purpose, and has since taken the lead in promoting discussion to prepare the ground for the 1994 CITES Conference.

The Government provided £600,000 for African elephant conservation in addition to the £20 million which the UK is already providing for wildlife conservation projects in Africa.

The UK has also been at the forefront of international efforts to save the rhinoceros. Through CITES, the Government has supported steady pressure on the countries involved to crack down on the illegal trade in rhino horn. It also contributed some £200,000 to rhino conservation initiatives in 1992-93, including financial support for the work of the International Union for the Conservation of Nature and Natural Resources' African Rhino Specialist Group to improve the co-ordination of rhino conservation efforts throughout Africa. The UK also contributed towards the costs of sending a high-level CITES delegation to China and Taiwan to review progress in combatting illegal trade there.

the protection of the marine resources there, in line with the Convention on the Conservation of Antarctic Marine Living Resources.

WILDLIFE AND THE MARINE ENVIRONMENT

1.23 The Convention on International Trade in Endangered Species of Wild Fauna and Flora (CITES) conserves the world's endangered species and ensures that trade in other species does not exceed sustainable levels. The Government plays a prominent part under CITES (see Box).

1.24 The UK is an active participant in the UN Conference on Straddling Stocks and Highly Migratory Species, which seeks to persuade states to co-operate in conserving fish stocks in accordance with international law.

1.25 The UK ratified the Agreement on the Conservation of Small Cetaceans of the Baltic and North Seas in July 1993. The Government has provided funding for surveys of abundance and distribution of porpoises and dolphins in the North Sea and research into ways of preventing them from becoming caught in fishing nets. The

Government has also financed a scheme to investigate strandings of dolphins and other cetaceans.

1.26 Following measures agreed in 1992 by EC Fisheries Ministers, additional restrictions were introduced on the use of twin and multi-rig trawls in the Nephrops fishery in August 1993. In May 1993, the UK introduced a national measure to help lobster conservation. Following completion of the mid-term review of the Common Fisheries Policy in 1992, Fisheries Ministers may now consider longer term objectives for stocks where this is appropriate. As a result of pressure from the UK, the EC Commission is reconsidering the question of industrial fishing. A report is due later this year. (See Chapter 12 for further consideration of the North Sea and NE Atlantic.)

1.27 The Government continues to support the work of the International Whaling Commission, which met in Kyoto in May 1993. With UK support, the moratorium on commercial whaling was maintained; Japan and Norway were pressed to reconsider their scientific whaling; and Norway's planned commercial hunt was condemned.

The UK is at the forefront of international efforts to save the black rhino

REF NO	SUMMARY OF PREVIOUS WHITE PAPER COMMITMENTS	ACTION TO DATE	COMMITMENTS TO FURTHER ACTION
1	Ratify the Convention on Climate Change and prepare a national plan on implementation by end 1993 (SYR 1)	UK ratified the Climate Change Convention December 1993, and published the Climate Change Programme, the first report under the Convention, January 1994	
2	Establish basis on which UK can ratify Biodiversity Convention and prepare national Biodiversity plan by end 1993 (SYR 1,2)	UK Biodiversity Action Plan published January 1994	UK intends to ratify the Biodiversity Convention, subject to achieving satisfactory safeguards on financial provisions
3	Ensure that the Commission on Sustainable Development (CSD) establishes itself as an effective body assessing implementation of Agenda 21 (SYR 1)	First meeting of Commission held in June 1993. Programme of work and basis of national reporting to CSD agreed. UK elected member	
4			Report to CSD on issues to be considered at 1994 session. Contribute to the next CSD session and participate in preparatory working groups
5			Encourage Dependent Territories to pursue strategies for sustainable development (FCO)
6	Take an active role in producing an agreement to combat desertification which focuses on encouraging the countries affected to implement appropriate policies (SYR 1) (ODA)	UK taking part in negotiations. Commissioned several studies	
7	Assess implementation of Agenda 21 with NGOs, local government, business and UN bodies at UK conference in 1993 (SYR 1)	International conference, 'Partnerships for Change', held September 1993	
8			Produce a guide, *Partnerships in Practice*, for submission to CSD
9	Facilitate developing countries' access to information about environmental technologies. Launch Technology Partnership Initiative with Global Technology Partnership Conference in 1993 (SYR 1,11,113) (DTI)	Global Technology Partnership Conference in Birmingham in March 1993 saw launch of Technology Partnership Initiative and publication of guide to assist technology co-operation. Guide made available in most developing countries	Technology Partnership Initiative to run for three years
10	Assist developing countries to meet their obligations under the Biodiversity Convention, including continued financial and technical support for bilateral projects to conserve biodiversity (SYR 3) (ODA)	Funds provided through bilateral aid programme for projects, research, NGO activities and through UK contribution to the pilot phase of the GEF	Further support to be provided under Biodiversity Strategy
11	Work to ensure the improved operation of the Global Environment Facility (GEF), especially to help developing countries implement the Climate Change and Biodiversity Conventions (SYR 14,85) (ODA)	UK has been active in negotiations on GEF restructuring and replenishment, concluded in March 1994. UK pledged £89.5 million	

REF NO	SUMMARY OF PREVIOUS WHITE PAPER COMMITMENTS	ACTION TO DATE	COMMITMENTS TO FURTHER ACTION
12			Work towards GEF becoming permanent funding mechanism for Climate Change and Biodiversity Conventions
13	Work through the Darwin Initiative to assist in studies of natural resources, the development of inventories of the most important species and the promotion of the exchange of information about conservation (SYR 1,4)	First 31 projects to be funded under Darwin Initiative announced November 1993	Applications for funding from April 1994 now invited. Total funding over four years of £9m
14	Declaration of Forest Principles to be followed by a legal agreement (FYR p95, SYR 5) (ODA)		Negotiations unlikely to start until 1995
15	Press for an international review process for the Forest Principles agreed at UNCED (SYR 1,5) (ODA)	UK was instrumental in ensuring review of the implementation of Forest Principles included in the remit of CSD. Indo-British Forestry Initiative agreed in September 1993, under which UK and India will work jointly towards the success of the CSD's review of the Forest Principles in 1995	UK and India to host international workshop in 1994 to prepare for CSD review
16	Produce national plan to implement the Statement of Forest Principles by end of 1993 (SYR 1,5) (FC)	UK Sustainable Forestry Programme published January 1994	UK to report to CSD 1995
17	Further forestry programmes to develop principles of sustainable management and conservation (SYR 6) (ODA)	£11.3m commitments made to 47 new forestry projects between July 1992 and June 1993	
18	Conduct discussions with developing countries and donors on how to implement changes through the Tropical Forestry Action Programme at the country level. Develop country level capacity projects which will provide countries with the ability to analyse forest policy and prepare projects to strengthen sector activities (SYR 7) (ODA)	Continued follow-up action in countries following national forest action plans	
19	Develop forest accounting systems to monitor the condition of forests. Examine good incentives to the management and conservation of forests. Establish a database of trees used in timber trade production to identify any rare or endangered species (SYR 8) (ODA)	Initial phases of accounting system and identification of local incentives for sustainable forest management completed. Methodologies examined for identifying rare or endangered traded timber species	
20	In renegotiation of International Tropical Timber Agreement (ITTA), aim to strengthen ITTO's capacity to help its timber producing members achieve sustainable management of forests (SYR 8) (ODA)	Improved environmental and operational features promoted in negotiation of new ITTA	

REF NO	SUMMARY OF PREVIOUS WHITE PAPER COMMITMENTS	ACTION TO DATE	COMMITMENTS TO FURTHER ACTION
21	Support research to examine the organisation and management of forestry extension activities in the light of the reorientation of forest sector activities to the needs of rural people (SYR 9) (ODA)	Research supported into aspects of agroforestry and the organisation and management of forest extension services. Continued projects containing important agroforestry components	
22	Carry through project in Costa Rica for afforestation on livestock farms (SYR 9) (ODA)	Project currently under way	
23	Build on sustainable forestry research management programme by strengthening the uptake of and impact of commissioned research (SYR 10) (ODA)	Continued funding for research projects - £2.7m pledged for 1993-94. 57 projects under way	
24	Provide financial and technical assistance for the establishment of Centre for International Forestry Research (CIFOR) (SYR 11) (ODA)	Project worth £878,000 over three years agreed to assist CIFOR develop its information systems	
25			Maintain substantial programme of assistance to the sustainable development and conservation of forests in developing countries and review forestry research programme (ODA)
26	Help strengthen environmental institutions in developing countries through advice, training and education (4.48, SYR 12) (ODA)	Support being given to national environmental agencies in developing countries, including Egypt, Ghana and China	
27	Continue to support the work in developing countries of a wide range of voluntary organisations (4.54, SYR 13) (ODA)	Continued support through grants from the Joint Funding Scheme - £29m in 1993-94	
28	Ensure the adoption of procedures listed in the Overseas Aid Environmental Appraisal Manual, and encourage their use in developing countries (SYR 15) (ODA)	Continued training in use of the revised Manual for all ODA programme managers. Copies of Manual widely distributed	
29			Review Overseas Aid Environmental Appraisal Manual and its effectiveness in 1994 (ODA)
30	Consolidate and expand population work in Bangladesh, Kenya, Pakistan and Nigeria. Establish by August 1993 at least: - five projects to strengthen reproductive health services; - five contraceptive supply projects; and - five women's health and development projects (SYR 16) (ODA)	Population work increased in all eight priority countries. Targets for population initiatives met or exceeded New population strategy being prepared	Review priority countries with a view to increasing the number

REF NO	SUMMARY OF PREVIOUS WHITE PAPER COMMITMENTS	ACTION TO DATE	COMMITMENTS TO FURTHER ACTION
31	Maintain the poverty focus of aid programmes through dialogue on policies with recipient countries and finance direct poverty alleviation as appropriate (SYR 17) (ODA)	Social policy and planning on poverty policies supported in a number of African countries Participated in World Bank poverty assessments	
32	Continue to develop more effective methods for the participation of local people in planning and decision making (SYR 17) (ODA)	Supported projects to improve community management of resources in Africa and India	
33	Consider the specific links between poverty and environmental degradation (FYRp93, SYR 18) (ODA)	Work on relationship between poverty and environmental factors continues as part of two of ODA's main priorities (namely: poverty reduction; and helping developing countries tackle national environmental problems)	
34			Progress on research into relationship between poverty and environmental factors to be reported separately in ODA Departmental report for 1995 (ODA)
35	Directly fund projects to improve the health and education of women and reduce infant mortality (4.15, SYR 19) (ODA)	ODA continues to support projects aimed at improving the health and education of women and to reduce infant mortality	
36	Extend the involvement of women and encourage other donors and multilateral agencies to increase focus on women (SYR 19) (ODA)	Training in gender planning given to ODA staff. Implemented Women In Development policies with other donors. Seconded ODA social development advisers to the World Bank and EC	Extend gender training for field officers in all sectors
37	Implement new procedures for paying children's allowances to unaccompanied spouses attending UK training courses (SYR 19) (ODA)	New procedures implemented	
38			Review the impact of children's allowances to unaccompanied spouses attending UK training courses (ODA)
39	Continue to contribute to improvements in scientific understanding of the oceans and to support and fund research and environmental protection measures (SYR 20)	UK played a major part in preparation of 1993 Quality Status Report on the North Sea, and funded national programme of research which contributed to the QSR. Continued involvement with Group of Experts on Scientific Aspects of Marine Pollution (GESAMP) working groups and International Oceanographic Commission's Global Investigations for Protection of the Marine Environment (GIPME). Continued work through the London Convention 1972 for enhanced global controls on sea disposal of wastes	

REF NO	SUMMARY OF PREVIOUS WHITE PAPER COMMITMENTS	ACTION TO DATE	COMMITMENTS TO FURTHER ACTION
40			Participate in the second meeting of the London Convention 1972 Amendment Group in May 1994 and encourage the adoption of enhanced global measures for the protection of the marine environment (MAFF)
41	Work through International Whaling Commission to oppose the resumption of commercial whaling until it is clear that stocks can be safeguarded at a healthy level and methods used to take whales are humane; and urge the development and use of non-lethal research techniques for the study of whale populations and biology (4.34, SYR 21) (MAFF)	UK opposed any resumption of commercial whaling at 1993 meeting of the IWC. Secured IWC agreement for a workshop on improvements in humane methods of killing whales and for studies on whale watching; supported resolutions against Japanese and Norwegian programmes for lethal scientific whaling; commissioned non-lethal research on the impact on whale populations of global environment change	
42	Press IWC to agree similar measures for smaller cetaceans such as dolphins and porpoises (4.36, SYR 22) (MAFF)	Supported resolutions at 1993 IWC meeting calling for further protection for harbour porpoises and striped dolphins; for improvement in the conduct of the Faroese pilot whale drive fishery; and for progress in the consideration of mechanisms to address the conservation of other small cetacean species	
43	Ratify Agreement on Conservation of Small Cetaceans and encourage other states to do so; bring into operation by January 1993 (SYR 159)	UK ratified Agreement July 1993. 6th State ratified in December 1993 and agreement came into force in March 1994	Encourage other States to ratify Convention by end 1994
44	Finance interim secretariat to Agreement at Sea Mammal Research Unit (SYR 159)	£44,000 provided for interim secretariat	£128,000 to be contributed by UK to Small Cetacean Abundance in North Sea (SCANS) project in 1994-95
45	Help developing countries practise sustainable management of fish stocks (4.32, SYR 23) (ODA)	Support provided to 8 developing countries/regions for development of fisheries management institutions and management projects. Funded 15 fisheries management research projects in support of the assessment and management of aquatic resources. New projects supporting integrated coastal zone management identified and under appraisal in two developing countries	
46	Continue to oppose indiscriminate fishing practices such as large-scale ocean drift nets (4.33, SYR 24) (MAFF)	Indiscriminate practices opposed by UK at the inaugural session of the UN Conference on Straddling and Highly Migratory Fish Stocks	Support at 1994 sessions of the Conference on Straddling and Highly Migratory Fish Stocks the development of a Code of Responsible Fishing on the High Seas and in Exclusive Economic Zones

1. WORLDWIDE ENVIRONMENTAL ISSUES

REF NO	SUMMARY OF PREVIOUS WHITE PAPER COMMITMENTS	ACTION TO DATE	COMMITMENTS TO FURTHER ACTION
47	Continue work in the EC and internationally to conserve marine stocks by calling for action on fishing gear and take unilateral action where appropriate (12.40, SYR 253) (MAFF)	Additional unilateral measures introduced in May and August 1993. Mid-term review of Common Fisheries Policy completed	
48			Pilot projects to be carried out before June 1995 to evaluate costs and benefits of using satellites in fisheries enforcement (MAFF)
49	Continue to give strong support to the UN Convention on International Trade in Endangered Species of Wild Fauna and Flora (CITES) (4.28, SYR 26)	Financial support approved for delegates from poorer countries to attend 1994 conference. Helped to fund the CITES enforcement programme and pledged a further £65,000 over the next three years to rhino conservation initiatives arising from a UNEP conference in June 1993	
50	Carry through £0.6m ($1m) funding for support to developing countries to observe CITES and continue to support anti-poaching projects and the management of wildlife reserves (4.28, SYR 25) (DOE/ODA)	£0.6m supplied to a number of anti-poaching and wildlife management projects in four African elephant range states	
51	Continue to implement the provisions of the Environmental Protocol to the Antarctic Treaty, in advance of the Protocol's ratification (4.40, SYR 27-29) (FCO)	Guidance paper on Environmental Impact Assessment procedures for UK activities in the Antarctic drafted	Seek further Annex to the Protocol on Liability for Environmental Damage and determine appropriate means of regulating tourism in Antarctica
52	Provide strong support for polar research through the British Antarctic Survey and the International Arctic Science Committee (4.40, SYR 30) (FCO)	Strengthened UK science capability in the Antarctic by the purchase of a further aircraft	Participate in the review of Polar Sciences Strategy being undertaken by NERC. Consolidate marine biology work from RSS *James Clark Ross* and at Rothera. Introduce automated data collection systems at Faraday and at Signy
53	Clean up British bases in the Antarctic (4.40, SYR 31) (FCO)	Clean-up operation completed at four abandoned UK bases. Full survey of all accessible abandoned UK bases in Antarctica undertaken	

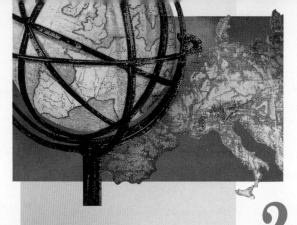

2 EUROPEAN ENVIRONMENTAL ISSUES

2.1 The European Community's environmental agenda remains busy, with measures to tackle a range of environmental problems being taken forward over the last year (see Box). The (Maastricht) Treaty on European Union, which came into force on 1 November 1993, will, in time, through the new procedures for working with the European Parliament, have a significant impact on the way the Community transacts its environmental business. All EC legislation will need to respect the subsidiarity principle, so that decisions are only taken at the European level when this is necessary to achieve the intended objectives. Elsewhere in Europe, Sweden, Finland, Norway, Austria and Iceland have become subject to much of the EC's environmental legislation, while the EC is playing a leading role in dealing with environmental problems in Central and Eastern Europe.

FIFTH ACTION PROGRAMME

2.2 EC Environment Ministers endorsed the Commission's Fifth Action Programme 'Towards Sustainability' in December 1992, and the UK has since played an active role in pursuing this. The Programme is the Commission's policy document on its environmental objectives and priorities, and builds on objectives in the Maastricht Treaty to promote sustainable development and integrate the needs of environmental protection in other Community policies.

2.3 In June 1993, the Commission adopted new internal procedures to enhance the integration of environmental concerns into other policy areas. These include:
- identifying and justifying proposals by the Commission which will have significant environmental consequences;
- reviewing annually progress on integration and designating a senior official in each Directorate-General to oversee progress;
- establishing a new unit to co-ordinate and monitor the implementation of the Fifth Action Programme;
- reporting on progress on integration in the Commission's annual report;
- adopting a code of conduct on 'green housekeeping'.

2.4 Integration is also currently being discussed by the newly established Environment Policy Review Group. In 1994, the Commission will prepare, with the Group, an interim report on the implementation of the Fifth Action Programme, and will undertake a full review in 1995. The Government expects to use the review to clarify the UK's priorities for future action.

2.5 The Fifth Action Programme proposes a large number of targets and objectives for national action. Many of these are already in hand in the UK, particularly those covered by the post-Rio climate change, biodiversity and forestry plans. In line with the Programme's spirit of 'shared responsibility', the Government will discuss with business, voluntary bodies and the Local Authority Associations the ways in which actions in the UK and at the European level can complement each other.

EUROPEAN ENVIRONMENT AGENCY

2.6 On 29 October 1993, the Special European Council, after long delays, agreed that the new European Environment Agency should be sited in Copenhagen. The UK is represented on the Agency's Management Board and is actively engaged in helping to formulate its work programme. The Agency's, and UK's, priority will be to improve the reliability and comparability of the environmental statistics actually collected in the various Member States.

Copenhagen, home to the European Environment Agency

ENFORCEMENT

2.7 The Government continues to emphasise the need for effective implementation and enforcement of EC legislation. The need to look more carefully at these issues is now finding wider support among the UK's partners and there are a number of initiatives afoot to improve enforcement across the Community:

• the UK hosted the first of a series of meetings of environmental enforcement authorities during its Presidency in 1992. A number of working groups have since been established and plenary sessions held in the two succeeding Presidencies. Now known as ECONET, this provides an opportunity for experts across the Community to exchange information and experiences and to develop common approaches to implementation;

• the Commission has undertaken to report annually on the implementation and enforcement of legislation in all the Member States. The first report was discussed in December 1992. The second report was published in July 1993 and discussed in December 1993;

• the Commission has begun to take action on the 1991 Directive on standardised reporting of data relating to Directives on water, air and waste pollution. Discussions are in progress on the questionnaires required by the Directive.

SUBSIDIARITY

2.8 Now that the Maastricht Treaty has come into force, all EC legislation, including environmental measures, must have regard to the principle of subsidiarity, which is that action should be taken by the Community only when it can be demonstrated that national action is not sufficient to achieve the intended objectives. Subsidiarity does not mean lower standards; it is merely about the level at which decisions are taken. The UK has played an active role in the Commission's review of the application of subsidiarity to all existing and proposed Community legislation. In December 1993, the Commission reported to the European Council, which took note of the report and asked for proposals as soon as possible to simplify and streamline Community legislation on water and air quality to make it consistent with the principle of subsidiarity, taking into account scientific progress and practical experience. The Government has welcomed this approach as a major step forward which offers a clear framework within which to achieve improvements in Community legislation without any lowering of standards in environmental protection.

RESEARCH

2.9 As outlined in the recent White Paper *Realising our Potential: A Strategy for Science, Engineering and Technology,* the Government attaches great importance to an outward-looking, global perspective in its science and

Ham Castle, Belgium. Venue for the third meeting of the EC Network of Environmental Enforcement Authorities

PROPOSED EC FRAMEWORK DIRECTIVE ON INTEGRATED POLLUTION PREVENTION AND CONTROL

The objective of integrated pollution control (IPC) is to prevent or solve pollution problems rather than transfer them from one part of the environment to another. IPC was introduced into England, Scotland and Wales in 1990 (see Chapter 3). In parallel, the concept of an integrated approach has grown in importance within the EC and beyond. This is a priority issue in the EC Fifth Action Programme.

In October 1993, the Commission published a proposal for an Integrated Pollution Prevention and Control (IPPC) Framework Directive. The Directive would establish a regime which balances environmental and economic considerations with a view to preventing or, where that is not practicable, to minimising harm to human health and pollution of all environmental media (air, water and land) from major industrial sources, in a way which offers the best practicable protection for the environment as a whole. During 1994, the UK will seek to negotiate early adoption of this important Directive in a form as consistent as possible with the current UK system.

Throughout Eastern Europe, uncontrolled growth has led to excessive industrialisation, with few pollution controls

technology policy. Such an approach is of particular importance in the environment arena and is assisted by the UK's participation in the EC's Research and Development Framework Programmes. The Europe-wide research collaborations generated by these programmes provide the UK with useful access to a wider and more varied group of partners than would usually be the case through domestic research programmes alone.

2.10 Specific programme areas within the Framework Programmes of greatest relevance to the environmental science research community include environment, marine science and technology, radioactive waste management, non-nuclear energy, industrial and materials technology, and measurement and testing. Between 1987 and 1991, British academics and industrialists secured just under 20 per cent, by value, of all the contracts, awarded under the Community Research and Development Framework Programmes.

2.11 Following the Third Framework Programme (1990-94), the European Commission submitted a proposal to the Council of Ministers in summer 1993 for a Fourth Framework Programme (1994-98). The Programme is likely to be formally adopted by a new co-decision procedure between the Council of Ministers and the European Parliament over the coming months. This will be closely followed by the finalisation and adoption of the specific programmes in each of the distinct areas of research. The Government attaches great importance to the need for effective co-ordination between the new environment research programme under the Fourth Framework Programme and the Commission's Fifth Action Programme.

EUROPE BEYOND THE COMMUNITY

2.12 Negotiations with Sweden, Norway, Finland and Austria over their accession to the EC are now complete. The decision to accede will be subject to the results of national referenda. In the meantime, these four countries, together with Iceland, have become subject to much of the Community's environmental legislation under the European Economic Area (EEA) agreement. The agreement entered into force on 1 January 1994, and will come into force in Liechtenstein as well, once matters relating to co-operation with Switzerland have been resolved.

2.13 The UK remains committed to the international effort to tackle the legacy of environmental problems in the countries of Central and Eastern Europe. The UK is assisting in this process through, for example: the EC's PHARE programme, to which the UK is contributing some 17% of expenditure; the World Bank and the European Bank for Reconstruction and Development; and the UK's own bilateral assistance programme - the Environmental Know How Fund (see Box).

2.14 The Ministerial Conference 'Environment for Europe', held in Lucerne in April 1993, endorsed an action programme setting out a strategy for environmental assistance. The priorities of the programme are policy reform, the strengthening of institutions, and investment. A Task Force and a Project Preparation Committee have been established to take the work forward. The UK is an active member of the United Nations Economic Commission for Europe (UNECE) Working Group, which will co-ordinate the process and prepare for the next Ministerial Conference in Sofia in 1995. The UK is working closely to ensure that the objectives of the programme are met.

THE ENVIRONMENTAL KNOW HOW FUND

The Environmental Know How Fund (EKHF) helps the countries of Central and Eastern Europe and the former Soviet Union tackle the environmental legacy of communism using British skills and expertise. The Fund is administered by the Foreign and Commonwealth Office and the Department of the Environment. Some £2 million a year is being made available through the Fund for technical assistance, help with legislation and planning, training, energy efficiency and nature conservation. Priority is given to projects which address problems identified in the action programme endorsed at the Lucerne 'Environment for Europe' conference in April 1993.

In Slovenia, formerly part of Yugoslavia, the EKHF has funded the preparation by UK consultants of a plan to reorganise the institutions responsible for the environment. It will be followed by a programme of investment funded by a loan from the World Bank. The

Slovenians asked the EKHF for help because of its reputation for giving assistance quickly and without excessive bureaucracy.

The plan, which has been worked out with key Slovenian officials, reviews the current environmental situation in Slovenia and identifies needs for Western finance and technical assistance. It sets out a blueprint for the expansion and restructuring of the Ministry of Environment and its agencies, whose task will be to develop a national environmental strategy based on EC standards.

The plan has identified air pollution from domestic sources, the quantity and quality of drinking water, waste management and the effects of industry on the environment as priority areas. The plan has been warmly received by the Slovenians, who are now following up its recommendations.

Rila Monastery, Bulgaria. The Environmental Know How Fund is supporting a major project to ensure the sustainable development of the unspoilt areas of Bulgaria

REF NO	SUMMARY OF PREVIOUS WHITE PAPER COMMITMENTS	ACTION TO DATE	COMMITMENTS TO FURTHER ACTION
54	Work for integration of environmental concerns into Community policy (SYR 33)	Fifth Action Programme calls for integration of environmental considerations into other policy areas. Discussion of environmental issues in 8 other specialist Councils during UK Presidency. Commission announced new internal procedures to aid integration in June 1993. Tighter provisions on integrating environmental protection requirements into definition and implementation of other Community policies came into force with Maastricht Treaty on 1 November 1993	
55			Put new requirements on integration into practice, especially through the Environment Policy Review Group
56	Aim to complete discussion of EC Fifth Environmental Action Programme during UK Presidency, for implementation at start of 1993 (SYR 34)	Council discussion of Fifth Action Programme concluded under UK Presidency in December 1992. Resolution formally adopted February 1993	Prepare input into Commission's 1995 review
57	Press the EC Commission to bring forward proposals for a Directive embodying Britain's approach to integrated pollution control and seek agreement by the Council during 1993 (SYR 35)	Commission's proposal presented to Council October 1993	Negotiate early adoption of IPPC Framework Directive
58	Ensure that enforcement of environmental legislation is discussed by the Council of Ministers during UK Presidency (SYR 36)	Enforcement of legislation discussed at December 1992 Council. Commission's second annual report on implementation published July 1993 and discussed at December 1993 Council	
59	Host the first meeting of environmental enforcement authorities from across the Community in 1992 (SYR 37)	Organised first meeting of environmental enforcement authorities (now ECONET) during UK Presidency, November 1992. Further meetings held under Danish and Belgian Presidencies	
60			Continue to develop work of ECONET and contribute positively to it
*61	Press for the establishment of the European Environment Agency as soon as possible (SYR 38)	Agreement reached that Agency will be sited in Copenhagen. Management Board set up	Work programme to be agreed by July 1994 and implemented from beginning of October 1994
*62	Seek regular and comparable published reports on Member States' records of compliance with EC obligations and financial sanctions taken against Member States which persistently fail to comply (SYR 39)	Maastricht Treaty, which entered into force on 1 November 1993, includes provision for Court of Justice to impose fines for failure to comply with its judgements

Discussion of questionnaires on water and air under Standardised Reporting Directive have taken place and are under way on waste | Complete discussion of questionnaires on waste by June 1994. Questionnaires to be completed in accordance with timetable laid down by Directive |

REF NO	SUMMARY OF PREVIOUS WHITE PAPER COMMITMENTS	ACTION TO DATE	COMMITMENTS TO FURTHER ACTION
63			Assist in preparations for, and participate in, the second European Conference on Environment and Health at Ministerial level, to be held in Helsinki in June 1994
64	Support appropriate international and Community action to help Central and Eastern Europe cope with environmental changes. Work for the success of the 1993 Conference of European Environment Ministers in follow-up to Dobris Castle (SYR 40-42)	1993 Lucerne Conference of European Environment Ministers endorsed action programme for environmental improvement and established arrangements to put it into effect	Pursue efforts to implement action programme, in collaboration with other signatories
65			Participate in follow-up conference to Lucerne, to be held in Sofia in 1995
66	European Energy Charter: work for a basic agreement and protocols on energy efficiency and nuclear energy (SYR 40)	Negotiations continuing on European Energy Charter Treaty, which will translate principles of Charter into a legally binding agreement. Charter has an Article on the environment and a supplementary Protocol on energy efficiency	
67	Carry through the £5m Environmental Exchange Programme with Eastern Europe (SYR 43)	Environmental Know How Fund in second year. Technical assistance programmes implemented	

Commitments reflecting the targets and objectives of the EC Fifth Action Programme are marked with an asterisk

3 UK ENVIRONMENTAL ISSUES

3.1 The UK has a key role to play in the environmental initiatives at the international and European levels outlined in the previous two chapters. These initiatives in turn impact significantly on UK environmental policy. The centrepiece of the UK's work over the past year has been the publication of the UK's Sustainable Development Strategy, the Biodiversity Action Plan, the Climate Change Programme and the Sustainable Forestry Programme. The UK is already active in promoting the key principles set out in the Strategy.

THE UK'S STRATEGY FOR SUSTAINABLE DEVELOPMENT

3.2 The UK's Sustainable Development Strategy builds on the targets and objectives of the 1990 White Paper *This Common Inheritance* and its successors, but it does not supplant this series of papers. The Strategy is distinguished by two features: first, its longer time horizon - it looks ahead 20 years from the Earth Summit, to 2012. The second characteristic is that it looks much more fundamentally at the rationale of the different sectoral policies, and at the opportunities which may be worth pursuing.

3.3 The Strategy also announced new follow up arrangements for carrying forward sustainable development in different sectors of society, including:

• **the Government's Panel on Sustainable Development.** A small group of individuals with wide knowledge and practical experience will advise the Government on strategic issues. The group will keep in view general sustainability issues at home and abroad, identify problems and opportunities, monitor progress and consider questions of priority. The Government will consult them on issues of major importance, and they will be able to offer the Government unsolicited advice;

• **a UK Round Table on Sustainable Development.** The Government is consulting widely on the membership and mode of operation of a UK Round Table on Sustainable Development, to be chaired by the Secretary of State for the Environment. The Round Table will be broadly based; it will include representatives from England, Wales, Scotland and Northern Ireland, and will have members drawn from different sectors, such as industry, local government, the scientific and academic community and the voluntary sector. It will discuss major issues of sustainable development and the way in which new policies and initiatives can be carried forward in the different sectors of society;

• **a Citizens' Environment Initiative.** The Government proposes to stimulate individuals and groups (including those not normally particularly active in environmental matters) to commit themselves to furthering sustainable development. An independent committee will publicise ideas and advice, and perhaps plan a year of activity, to increase people's awareness of the part they can play personally.

DEPARTMENTAL CO-ORDINATION

3.4 The co-ordination of the Government's environmental policies across Departments remains central to the process of promoting sustainable development. The formal machinery extends from the Ministerial Committee on the Environment (EDE), through the system of nominated 'Green Ministers' within each Department with responsibility for environmental aspects of Departmental policy, to the regular consultative arrangements with local government, business and voluntary groups.

MONITORING AND RESEARCH

3.5 The Government's commitment to a sound environmental policy based on scientific and economic knowledge has been emphasised repeatedly in *This Common Inheritance* and its anniversary reports. This commitment was reinforced in the Science, Engineering and Technology White Paper *Realising our Potential* and in the Sustainable Development Strategy. It is manifested in the substantial resources devoted by Departments, agencies, Research Councils and industry to monitoring and research on the state of the UK, European and global environments, and to the development and application of economic and technological measures to mitigate or avoid environmental problems.

Monitoring

3.6 Monitoring and surveillance are essential to determine the state and quality of the environment. The urban air quality monitoring system accessible to the public continues to be expanded. Air quality parameters are also measured at the terrestrial sites of the Environmental Change Network (ECN), co-ordinated by the Natural Environment Research Council (NERC), which now has environmental monitoring within its terms of reference. ECN also now includes two flagship sites

for NERC's Terrestrial Initiative in Global Environmental Research (TIGER), and has been expanded in conjunction with the National Rivers Authority (NRA) to include freshwater sites. The NRA has also expanded its monitoring for statutory purposes and has project tested the first combined air/sea surveillance in Europe of coastal waters for quality and related purposes. It contributes, along with Environment and Fisheries Departments, to increasing intensive monitoring of the quality of the North and Irish Seas. Remote sensing will play an increasing role in such work. The UK and Australia, for example, are funding the construction of the satellite-borne Advanced Along-Track Scanning Radiometer to monitor climate parameters, which will feed into the climate change prediction models of the Hadley Centre at the Meteorological Office.

3.7 The report of the Countryside Survey 1990 has been published. The extensive database is being developed into the Countryside Information System, and is being utilised in a range of studies, such as the determination of critical loads of sulphur and nitrogen, and the assessment of carbon sequestered from the atmosphere in terrestrial systems. The Government plans to repeat the Survey in 2000.

Research

3.8 The Government continues to support work aimed at understanding the environment, its problems, and how they might best be resolved.

3.9 The Research Councils now have mission statements which explicitly require them to support work aimed at wealth creation and improving the quality of life. They support a range of relevant research programmes, such as the Land Ocean Interface Study, a study of the movement of pollutants in soils and groundwaters, clean technology projects and a range of investigations into the processes and impacts of climate change (such as TIGER). These programmes often involve Departments and other bodies. The results of the Joint Agriculture and Environment Programme have been published and are

Advanced technology, such as satellites, will play an increasing role in environmental monitoring

Her Majesty's Inspectorate of
Pollution is responsible for
implementing integrated pollution
control

INTEGRATED POLLUTION CONTROL (IPC)

In England and Wales, Her Majesty's Inspectorate of Pollution (HMIP) is responsible for implementing IPC, which was introduced under Part 1 of the Environmental Protection Act 1990. The same system of control applies in Scotland, though the organisational arrangements are different. In Scotland, IPC is enforced by Her Majesty's Industrial Pollution Inspectorate and the river purification authorities. Similar arrangements to England and Wales will be introduced in Northern Ireland.

Authorisations granted by HMIP require the use of best available techniques not entailing excessive cost (BATNEEC) to prevent or, where that is not practicable, minimise and render harmless polluting releases; and where a process has the potential to release pollutants to more than one environmental medium (ie air, land or water), the BATNEEC requirement must ensure that the way in which the process is operated is the one with the least impact on the environment as a whole - the best practicable environmental option (BPEO).

During 1993, a further eight industry groups (in the minerals and chemical sectors) were brought within the IPC

system as part of a planned programme to cover existing industry by 1996, raising the number of processes controlled to 60% of the eventual total of around 5000. At the same time, there has been consultation on the scope of IPC and the local authority air pollution control system (LAAPC), which was also introduced by the Environmental Protection Act 1990, with a view to ensuring, in the light of experience so far, that each industrial sector is subject to the right level of control.

An important feature of the IPC system is the requirement that applications for authorisation and the authorisations themselves must be placed in public registers, which can be consulted at HMIP offices and in the appropriate local authority. Other relevant information is also required to be placed in the register, including monitoring data supplied to HMIP as a condition of authorisation to demonstrate compliance (or obtained by the Inspectorate itself as a result of check monitoring). During 1993, it was announced that this monitoring data would also be aggregated to provide a clearer picture of total releases and published in the form of an annual chemical release inventory.

being applied elsewhere (for instance in interpreting Countryside Survey data). New technologies are being developed, such as AUTOSUB, which will increase our capacity to monitor, survey and study the oceans. Departments and agencies continue to support more applied environmental research to meet their policy and statutory responsibilities. Details of all these activities can be found in the reports of each funding body and are summarized in the *Annual Review of Government-funded Research and Development, 1993*.

3.10 An overview of the UK's national research interests and strategies in certain sectors is provided by Inter-Agency Committees. The Committee on Global Environmental Change published its second *UK Research Framework* in 1993, and

oversaw the establishment of the Global Environmental Network for Information Exchange. It shares a common interest in data management with the Inter-Agency Committee on Marine Science and Technology. The UK was also involved in the work of the North Sea Task Force in completing North Sea quality status reports. The contributions of Departments and the NRA are likely now to shift towards the Irish Sea and North East Atlantic.

3.11 The UK's Sustainable Development Strategy emphasises the important roles that science, engineering and technology must play in making wealth creation sustainable. This means that research will be needed to address the difficult questions involved at one end and that the transfer and application of appropriate technologies will have to be enhanced at the other. The latter process is already apparent in the new emphasis given to technology transfer in the programmes of the Research Councils and Departments. Specific measures are being taken to help small and medium sized enterprises develop their technological expertise through UK and European programmes. The Government is also committed to assist developing countries wishing to meet their obligations under the Biodiversity Convention through technology transfer mechanisms. These include the Darwin Initiative, through which over 30 awards for training and research have already been made.

POLICY INSTRUMENTS

Regulation

3.12 The traditional method for protecting the environment from pollution or inappropriate development has been to make regulations, and an extensive framework of environmental legislation has been built up over many years. Today, much of its development stems from EC agreements, but enforcement and monitoring systems remain a national responsibility and those in the UK are among the best and most effective in Europe. In addition, in recent years, pollution control in the UK has been streamlined and improved with the introduction of a system of integrated pollution control (IPC) for industry with the greatest potential to cause harm to the environment (see Box). It is hoped that, during 1994, agreement will be reached on the introduction of this system throughout the European Community (see Chapter 2).

Deregulation and Environmental Protection

3.13 But there is always a risk that regulation will impose unnecessary costs on industry. In February 1993, the Government therefore launched a general review, to identify areas where administrative burdens on business can be reduced without sacrificing the aims and objectives of the regulations, and to reconsider whether those aims and objectives were still relevant and necessary.

3.14 Seven Deregulation Task Forces were set up to advise the Government on industry's priorities. A further Task Force was set up in September 1993 for the voluntary and charitable sector. The recommendations of the first seven Task Forces were published in January, when the Deregulation Bill was introduced. The eighth Task Force's recommendations are expected to be presented to Ministers in spring 1994.

3.15 DOE's own review looked at all aspects of regulatory systems; changes to existing environmental and water regulations are now in hand. The questions asked during the review are also being asked of all proposals for new or amending legislation. Every proposal affecting business is now accompanied by a compliance cost assessment, so that costs can be considered at an early stage alongside the benefits which the legislation is designed to produce.

3.16 Much of the gain to industry will come from administrative action to make enforcement simpler. Improvements have already been made and more are planned. Over the next year, central Government regulators, including HMIP and the National Rivers Authority, will implement the Codes of Practice which they have produced under the new Enforcer's Charter, which is linked with the Citizen's Charter Initiative. Local authorities are developing Local Partnerships with businesses in their areas and are looking for ways of improving enforcement locally.

3.17 Regulation will remain a key means of securing minimum standards. But regulation should be proportionate to the problem and should not be used where an alternative, such as an economic instrument, could be as effective. Over the longer term, improved environmental management by businesses should reduce further the need for regulation.

The proposed new environment agencies will further strengthen the effectiveness of pollution control

Environment Agencies

3.18 Paving provisions are being introduced to enable planning to go ahead for the proposed new independent Environment Agency in England and Wales and the Scottish Environment Protection Agency. By bringing together the existing agencies concerned with IPC, water regulation and waste regulation into single national bodies, these will further strengthen the effectiveness of pollution control whilst reducing the number of independent regulators with whom business must deal, and thus reduce the scope for overlap and conflict.

Economic Instruments

3.19 Economic instruments work by putting a price on the use of the environment and include emission charges, product charges and tradeable permits. They have several major advantages when compared with direct regulation:
* cost-effectiveness;
* innovation;
* flexibility;
* informational efficiency;
* public revenues.

The Second Year Report on *This Common Inheritance* established a presumption in favour of using economic instruments to deliver environmental goals; the Government is determined to make markets work for the environment and to honour the 'polluter pays principle'.

3.20 Existing instruments, or fiscal measures which have environmental effects, include:

* the tax differential between leaded and unleaded petrol, which has been very successful in stimulating sales of the latter;

* recycling credits to reflect the savings in disposal and collection costs which result from recycling domestic waste;

* VAT on domestic fuel and power, which should encourage energy efficiency in the home and contribute towards achieving the UK's CO_2 target;

* a commitment to raise fuel duty by at least 5% per annum in real terms, which should also help to meet the UK's CO_2 target;

* industrial rationalisation arrangements under the Montreal Protocol, to allow firms to trade quotas to reduce the cost of phasing out CFC production.

3.21 Proposals under consideration include:

* **water** - options are being looked at for controlling effluent discharges and conserving water;

* **air** - options for controlling SO_2 emissions are being examined;

* **waste** - a landfill levy is being considered and the principle of producer responsibility is being applied across a range of waste streams.

3.22 There is considerable potential for applying market based instruments of all kinds in delivering policies more effectively. However, their introduction needs careful preparation and to this end the Government published in November 1993 *Making Markets Work for the Environment,* which gives practical guidance about implementation. This guidance is intended to stimulate and help policy makers when considering the introduction of new instruments for the delivery of environmental, and perhaps other, policies. It should also assist others, in particular, those affected, to understand the rationale behind new policy instruments and to contribute effectively to their design.

REF NO	SUMMARY OF PREVIOUS WHITE PAPER COMMITMENTS	ACTION TO DATE	COMMITMENTS TO FURTHER ACTION
68	Prepare a national plan on the implementation of Agenda 21 by end 1993 (SYR 1)	UK Strategy for Sustainable Development published January 1994. Government has appointed small independent panel of experts to advise on strategic sustainable development issues	
69			UK Round Table on Sustainable Development, chaired by Secretary of State for the Environment, to be established in 1994
70			Citizens' Environment Initiative to be established in 1994 to encourage awareness of sustainable development amongst the general public
71	Retain a Ministerial Committee to co-ordinate the approach to environmental issues (18.3, SYR 44)	Implemented	
72			Review in 1994 the effectiveness of measures for the environmental appraisal of new policies and programmes put to Cabinet and Ministerial Committees
73	Give account of each Department's environmental performance in annual reports or elsewhere (18.5, SYR 47)	Environmental achievements included in 1993 reports	
74	Ensure the implementation and review use made of the guide *Policy Appraisal and the Environment* across Government. Build up case study material on particular applications. Publish further guidance by 1994 (18.8, SYR 48)	Conference organised in Durham in March 1994 to review the applicability of environmental evaluation methods Centre for Social and Economic Research on the Global Environment (CSERGE) producing a computerised database on environmental valuation for Government Departments	DOE to publish summary details of related guidance and relevant case study material in *Environmental Appraisal in Government Departments* in early 1994
75	Follow the *Environmental Action Guide* with additional guidance notes on specific topics and develop individual strategies for Departments' environmental performance by end 1992. Refine advisory notes for wider publication (18.7, SYR 49)	Notes published during 1993 on CFCs and halons, sources of information, premises management, water, lighting and grounds management. Green Housekeeping Statements prepared by all Departments. Individual environmental strategies prepared by nearly all Departments	
76			By end of 1994, Departments to assess the practicality of developing an environmental management system for their green housekeeping activities

REF NO	SUMMARY OF PREVIOUS WHITE PAPER COMMITMENTS	ACTION TO DATE	COMMITMENTS TO FURTHER ACTION
77	Discriminate positively as a consumer in favour of recycled products. Adopt strategies for every Government Department's environmental purchasing, including the use of recycled products (14.38, SYR 50)	Guidance on purchasing published 1993	
78	Review membership of committees and advisory groups with environmental aspects to ensure that they have appropriate environmental expertise (SYR 51)	Continued to ensure that environmental expertise is taken into account during reappointments	
79	Consider increasing the capacity of the Royal Commission on Environmental Pollution. Announce new membership for the Royal Commission and discuss with the Commission its future role and objectives (18.38, SYR 53)	New Chairman and one new member appointed. Commission's future role and objectives clarified, together with financial responsibilities of Commission's Secretary	Fill outstanding vacancy and others as they become vacant
80	Publish guidance on environmental management for local authorities in early 1993 (SYR 54)	Guidance published in October 1992	
81			Develop arrangements for national voluntary Eco-Management and Audit schemes for local authorities by 1995
82			Review whether new initiatives are required to encourage more voluntary groups to become involved with sustainable development
83	Publish environmental statistics annually and more detailed reports periodically (SYR 55)	Improved the coverage of environmental statistics in the *Digest of Environmental Protection and Water Statistics*. Published a new statistical report on the environment in October 1992	
84	Issue regulations and guidance on access to information by end of 1992 (SYR 57)	Regulations made and guidance for public and local authorities issued in late 1992	
85			Set up user group, including representatives from central and local government and non-government bodies, to develop and improve future statistical publications on the environment

REF NO	SUMMARY OF PREVIOUS WHITE PAPER COMMITMENTS	ACTION TO DATE	COMMITMENTS TO FURTHER ACTION
86	Increase environmental monitoring (17.20, SYR 56)	UK committed to construction of Advanced Along-Track Scanning Radiometer Results of Countryside Survey published November 1993. Countryside Information System being developed for wider use Urban air quality monitoring strategy strengthened National Monitoring Plan established for UK estuaries and coastal waters. Uses of data from the Harmonised Monitoring Scheme for inland water currently being reviewed. NRA monitoring strategy announced NERC mission statement modified to include long term monitoring of the natural environment. Environmental Change Network established, covering 9 terrestrial sites. NERC co-ordinating expansion of ECN	Channel Quality Status Report to be published in 1994 Further terrestrial as well as freshwater sites to be established
87			Establish working group to produce a preliminary set of environmental indicators for the UK by 1996
88	Develop proposals for an annual inventory of releases of pollutants (2.14, SYR 57)	Consultation paper on releases from IPC processes issued November 1992. Announcement of decision to proceed and scope of inventory made April 1993	First data will be published in 1994
89	Increase expenditure on environmental research in economic and social research programmes (17.9, SYR 59)	Continued funding for Centre for Social and Economic Research on the Global Environment and reports on the implications of greenhouse gas control policies	
90	Establish Environment Agency as soon as Parliamentary time allows (SYR 60,61)	Paving Bill to be introduced in 1993-94 Parliamentary session	Substantive Bill to be introduced as soon as Parliamentary time allows
91	Implement integrated pollution control across all relevant processes and publish criteria. Consider division of processes between IPC and Local Authorities' systems by spring 1993 (10.4, 10.9, SYR 62)	Amending regulations relating to definition of chemical process made in October 1993. Wider consultation on scope of regulations and division of processes between IPC and LAAPC also undertaken during 1993	Further amending regulations, following wide-ranging consultation, to be made in spring 1994
92	HMIP will publish process guidance notes to Inspectors on implementation of IPC. Notes to be published before each industry sector comes within the scope of IPC (10.12, SYR 64)	59 guidance notes have now been published, dealing with processes within the fuel and power, waste, minerals and chemicals sectors	Further notes will be published in advance of remaining sectors being brought within IPC

REF NO	SUMMARY OF PREVIOUS WHITE PAPER COMMITMENTS	ACTION TO DATE	COMMITMENTS TO FURTHER ACTION
93	HMIP to require stringent environmental standards to be met and the use of BATNEEC and to review and update standards and guidance as appropriate (10.12, SYR 65,66)	Authorisations to require application of best available techniques not entailing excessive cost (BATNEEC) as a minimum	HMIP will follow developments in techniques and update BATNEEC requirements as appropriate
94	HMIP will recover the bulk of the costs of IPC by charging for authorisations under IPC (10.20, SYR 67)	Consultation papers issued in autumn 1993 on charging schemes for 1994-95 and on basis of future charging	Implement in response to consultation exercise

4 GLOBAL ATMOSPHERE

4.1 In December 1993, the Framework Convention on Climate Change reached the 50 ratifications needed to bring it into force. Many of the other 150 countries who signed the Convention are at an advanced stage in preparing to ratify.

SCIENCE OF CLIMATE CHANGE

4.2 The ultimate objective of the Convention is to avoid dangerous man-made interference with the climate system within a time frame which will allow natural ecosystems to adapt and ensure that food production is not threatened. The scientific assessment underpinning the global response to man-made climate change is provided by the UNEP/WMO Inter-Governmental Panel on Climate Change (IPCC). The IPCC has, to date, produced two reports, with two more due in 1994 and 1995. The UK will continue to give support through funding and the Chairmanship of the science working group.

4.3 The Hadley Centre's General Circulation Model (GCM) is simulating current climate well and work is under way revising predictions of global climate change and the assessment of potential effects. These results are currently being compared with other GCMs in an international comparison project being conducted by the IPCC. In addition, a regional model has been developed and used to predict the likely climate expected over Western Europe during the middle of the next century.

4.4 Because of the influence that man-made aerosols and non-CO_2 greenhouse gases may have on the rate of climate change, the Hadley Centre GCM is being modified to include their direct and indirect effects with the intention of carrying out a full interactive experiment. Development is continuing on land and ocean carbon cycle models.

CLIMATE CHANGE PROGRAMME

4.5 The publication on 25 January 1994 of the Climate Change Programme makes the UK the first country to set out in full how it intends to meet the Convention commitments. The Programme is based on a partnership approach (see Box). Regulation makes a minor contribution to the policies and measures aimed at returning CO_2 emissions to 1990 levels by 2000, but the Programme reflects the Government's belief that it is better to persuade than to regulate. It acknowledges the importance of economic motives and recognises that in the longer term the relative price of energy must rise. The fiscal measures already announced will influence the domestic and transport sectors and are expected to secure 40% of the carbon savings required. The Government will co-operate closely with all sectors to make sure that the UK meets its commitments.

4.6 The Climate Change Programme sets out for the first time the UK's methane programme. The Government has worked closely with industry in formulating the programme. Some measures, including guidance for management of landfill sites, will be implemented shortly. Although

The Government is encouraging the use of methane as a fuel - which recycles carbon and represents no net addition of CO_2 to the atmosphere

estimates are uncertain, the Government expects emissions to fall by 10% between 1990 and 2000, which would more than meet the Convention commitment to return emissions to 1990 levels by 2000.

4.7 The Programme outlines measures to curb emissions of other greenhouse gases. DuPont (UK) Ltd, a major chemical company, is committed to implementing measures which will contribute to a 75% reduction in 1990 nitrous oxide emissions by 2000. Other initiatives include assistance to developing countries, measures to protect and enhance carbon sinks such as forests, and publicity campaigns. A £140 million research programme has made significant progress towards reducing uncertainties in climate change prediction, particularly through the work of the Hadley Centre.

4.8 The Climate Change Programme also considers the options open to the UK to limit emissions after 2000. Any future action by the UK will be linked to agreements under the Convention. The UK is pressing for the rapid and effective implementation of the Convention.

4.9 The UK will continue to provide financial and technical support to the negotiating forum of the Convention, the Inter-Governmental Negotiating Committee for a Framework Convention

on Climate Change (INC), in the run up to the first meeting of the Conference of Parties to the Convention in 1995. The Government intends to hold a conference in July 1994 to follow up the launch of the Climate Change Programme and has established a Forum between Government, motor manufacturers and other interested parties to co-ordinate marketing activities on greener motoring.

THE OZONE LAYER

Science and Research

4.10 The UK has continued to contribute to the scientific study of stratospheric ozone depletion. The European Ozone Research Co-ordinating Unit began a second campaign, the Second European Stratospheric Arctic and Mid-latitude Experiment (SESAME), in winter 1993-94, to investigate chemical ozone loss in both Arctic and mid-northern latitudes.

4.11 While the effects of ozone depletion over the UK on human or animal health or on crop yields should be small, ozone loss is expected to become worse for most of this decade. Record low values of ozone over Europe and other regions were detected during January 1992 and February 1993. Although ozone depletion elsewhere is far less severe than over the Antarctic, the

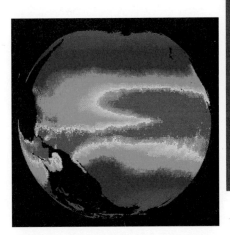

Global warming could produce changes in the heat balance of the world's oceans and may lead to higher global average sea levels

Halon recycling in action

Launch of a sonde to measure ozone at Halley Bay, Antarctica

latest findings confirm the Government's view that further international action is needed.

The Montreal Protocol

4.12 The Montreal Protocol, which provides controls on the production and consumption of ozone depleting substances, was strengthened at the Fourth Meeting of its Parties in Copenhagen in November 1992. Phase-out dates were brought forward for halon by six years to the end of 1993, for CFCs and carbon tetrachloride by four years to the end of 1995, and for methyl chloroform by nine years to the end of 1995. The UK played a major role in the meeting, both as joint chair of the preparatory group and as President of the European Community.

4.13 The Copenhagen amendment to the Protocol also imposes controls on three new groups of ozone depleting substances - HCFCs, HBFCs and methyl bromide. The UK expects to ratify the Copenhagen amendment, with its Community partners, during 1994. An EC Regulation agreed in December 1992 advanced the phase-out date for CFCs and carbon tetrachloride by one year to the end of 1994. Controls will be introduced on HCFCs, HBFCs and methyl bromide under a new EC Regulation, to be agreed during 1994. This is likely to restrict the use of HCFCs and phase out their supply by 2015, while the production and supply of methyl bromide will be frozen at 1991 levels in 1995 and reduced by 25% in 1998.

4.14 Over 130 countries are now party to the Montreal Protocol, which covers almost all global production of ozone depleting substances. An important factor has been the establishment of the Multilateral Fund, which meets the incremental costs incurred by developing countries in fulfilling their obligations under the Protocol.

4.15 The UK contributed $8.5 million to the Fund by the end of 1993. A net replenishment of the fund of $455 million between 1994 and 1996 was agreed in November 1993, of which the UK's share will be $26.2 million.

Recycling and Banking

4.16 The Government aims to ensure that, as the phase-out of production takes effect, more ozone depleting substances are recycled. Arrangements have been made to help recycle halon in fire protection equipment and discussions are under way on similar arrangements for CFCs. Regulations to ban the import and supply of CFC and HCFC refrigerants in disposable containers entered into force early in 1994.

36

REF NO	SUMMARY OF PREVIOUS WHITE PAPER COMMITMENTS	ACTION TO DATE	COMMITMENTS TO FURTHER ACTION
95	Ratify the Framework Convention on Climate Change by end 1993. Press for negotiations to strengthen the Convention (5.16, SYR 68)	UK fulfilled pledge to ratify Convention by end of 1993 along with other major countries and published Climate Change Programme, setting out how UK will meet its Convention commitments UK pressed in March and August 1993 International Negotiating Committee meetings for strengthened financial and reporting arrangements, in preparation for first Conference of Parties to Convention	Present commitments to be reviewed at the first meeting of the Conference of Parties in 1995, and again in 1998
96	Return CO_2 emissions to 1990 levels by 2000. Monitor and inform public of results (5.20, SYR 69)	Climate Change Programme included programme of measures to return CO_2 emissions to 1990 levels by 2000 Carried out public consultation, including discussion document, workshops, and conference for leaders of business, industry, consumer and environmental groups System established in EC for monitoring progress in meeting CO_2 commitments	Implement and monitor measures on CO_2 in Climate Change Programme
97	Take forward work on Commission's proposal for carbon/energy tax (SYR 69)	Concluded that carbon/energy tax proposal neither appropriate nor necessary for UK at this stage. Proposed more flexible approach to EC taxation	
98	Draw up by end 1993 national programme to meet Convention commitments (SYR 69)	Climate Change Programme, published on 25 January 1994, sets out how UK will meet its commitments under Convention. Includes measures aimed at returning greenhouse gas emissions to 1990 levels by 2000, inventories of emissions and measures on overseas aid, carbon sinks, education and research	
99	Help developing countries combat global warming and implement their Convention commitments by providing financial and technical support, including through the GEF (4.7, SYR 70)	Committed £40.3 million to GEF's pilot phase and contribution for second phase when GEF restructured Pressed in negotiations for major restructuring and replenishment of GEF £784 million contribution in 1992-93 to multilateral aid programmes includes substantial number of projects related to climate change, such as forestry conservation Funded participation of developing countries in meetings of Inter-Governmental Panel on Climate Change and Inter-Governmental Negotiating Committee on Climate Change	

REF NO	SUMMARY OF PREVIOUS WHITE PAPER COMMITMENTS	ACTION TO DATE	COMMITMENTS TO FURTHER ACTION
100	Develop energy efficiency aid incentives (4.17, SYR 70-71) (ODA)	£670 million bilateral aid programme includes projects on energy efficiency, including £86 million electricity project in Western and Southern India and major energy project in China	
101	Work with the EC to reach agreement on measures to improve the fuel consumption of vehicles (5.49, SYR 72) (DOT)	Fuel consumption measuring Directive amended to include CO_2 and new test cycle. Two reports submitted to EC on measures to encourage better fuel economy	
102	Consider further changes in the taxation of fuel and vehicles to encourage greater fuel economy. Monitor changes in fuel economy (5.51, SYR 73) (HMT)	Road fuel duties increased by 10% in March 1993 Budget and by 8-10% in November Budget	Road fuel duties to be increased by at least 5% on average above rate of inflation in future Budgets
103	Explore scope for a code of practice on vehicle advertising (5.52, SYR 74) (DOT)	Pressed Advertising Standards Authority about importance of effective monitoring. Independent Television Commission issued new guidance prohibiting references to top speed capabilities	
104	Improve and extend guidance on fuel economy and publicise links between fuel saving and the environment (5.45, SYR 75) (DOT)	New leaflet, *Motoring and the Environment*, published July 1993. Average new car fuel consumption included in *Transport Statistics GB* for first time in 1993	Set up a forum with motor manufacturers and others to co-ordinate action on greener motoring. Extend DOE/EEO 'Making a Corporate Commitment' campaign to fuel efficiency in company cars
105	Improve enforcement and monitoring of speed limits (5.49, SYR 76) (DOT)	Road Traffic Act 1991 introduced new measures for enforcement, including speed cameras. DOT authorised nearly seventy 20mph zones and launched speed policy paper	
106	Promote effective means to encourage bus travel. Issue new advice on bus priority measures and promote bus use through Ministerially chaired group. Consider other measures under deregulation, including new guidelines for passenger information (5.59, SYR 77) (DOT)	£20m allocated over two years to local authority bus priority schemes. Guidance to local authorities published and research into alternative fuels for urban buses initiated	Issue guidelines on passenger information when research completed in 1994
107	Continue to support high levels of investment by British Rail and London Transport. Privatise BR and provide a right of access to the rail network for new operators (5.57, SYR 78) (DOT)	Railways Bill received Royal Assent in November 1993, enabling Government to make necessary changes to take BR into private sector New access and charging arrangements put in place and Railtrack, new body responsible for track and infrastructure, established April 1994	

REF NO	SUMMARY OF PREVIOUS WHITE PAPER COMMITMENTS	ACTION TO DATE	COMMITMENTS TO FURTHER ACTION
108	Draw up by end 1993 a programme on methane emissions under Framework Convention (SYR 79)	Methane programme set out in Climate Change Programme, which provides for a 10% reduction between 1990 and 2000 Programme includes inventory of methane emissions and working estimate of possible future trends	
109			Implement and monitor measures in Climate Change Programme on methane, nitrous oxide and other greenhouse gases. Carry out research to improve inventory of methane emissions and estimates
110	Consider guidance to landfill operators and licensing authorities on the need to control methane emissions (SYR 79)	Methane programme includes a new waste management system to promote landfill gas collection	Publish guidance to landfill operators to encourage landfill gas collection
111	Continue discussions with British Coal and British Gas on options for limiting methane emissions (SYR 79) (DTI)	Methane programme includes requirements for coal operators to publish statements on methane emissions and a study into options for reducing emissions. British Gas implementing leakage control strategy to reduce emissions	
112	Continue discussions with oil and gas production industry on options to limit methane emissions. Continue to restrict consents for flaring and venting of gases from operations to the minimum necessary (5.71, SYR 79) (DTI)	Methane programme includes study into options for reducing emissions from oil and gas production and commitment to produce guidance, which should cover flaring and venting of gases	
113	Continue to encourage the management of existing woodlands and tree planting schemes (5.67, SYR 80) (FC)	Sustainable Forestry Programme sets out how UK is protecting existing forests and steadily expanding tree cover, including through incentive schemes. Inventory of UK carbon sinks, including forests, compiled	Fund research to improve UK inventory of carbon sinks
114	Maintain Britain's contribution to international work on climate change. Seek to ensure Inter-Governmental Panel on Climate Change (IPCC) begins work on its Second Assessment Report (17.7, SYR 58)	Government-funded Hadley Research Centre provided national focus for incorporating UK results into international programmes. Funded £140m Climate Change Programme, including work on data acquisition, climate modelling and prediction, impacts and adaptation and response strategies. Work on IPCC Second Assessment Report started in 1993, with UK chairing science working group and supporting its secretariat	
115	Fund research to improve prediction of ozone depletion, including development of three-dimensional model (4.45, SYR 81)	Six research projects funded in 1992-93. Fifth report of UK Stratospheric Ozone Review Group published	

REF NO	SUMMARY OF PREVIOUS WHITE PAPER COMMITMENTS	ACTION TO DATE	COMMITMENTS TO FURTHER ACTION
116	Work for earliest practicable phase-out of ozone depleting substances during 1992 Montreal Protocol negotiations (4.46, SYR 82)	Protocol tightened at Fourth Meeting of Parties in November 1992. Funding provided for further reviews of controls on HCFCs and methyl bromide and consideration of possible exemptions. 1992 EC Regulation brought forward controls beyond those required by Protocol. Funding provided for studies on effects of controls on HCFCs and earlier phase-out dates for CFCs in solvents and refrigeration. New controls on HCFCs and methyl bromide agreed within EC in December 1993	
117			In light of current assessments, negotiate appropriate controls on HCFCs and methyl bromide at 1994 and 1995 Meetings of the Parties to the Montreal Protocol
118	Phase out supply of CFCs by end 1995 or earlier and consumption in Britain by 2000 (4.44, SYR 83,84)	EC phase-out of CFCs by end 1994 agreed under UK Presidency	
119	Contribute £9.4m over three years to assist developing countries comply with Montreal Protocol. Agree increase when India becomes Party. Help develop CFC substitution (4.44, SYR 85)	Promissory note deposited with Fund, from which £4.8m has been drawn so far	Deposit further note following replenishment agreement at Fifth Meeting of Parties
120	Assist developing countries to carry out country studies under Montreal Protocol (SYR 85)	Assisted Algeria with preparations for country study	
121	Provide bilateral assistance to India for plans on phasing out CFCs (SYR 86)	Discussions with India about possible assistance have taken place	

5 ENERGY AND THE ENVIRONMENT

5.1 In December 1993 the UK ratified the UN Framework Convention on Climate Change and the Government announced the completion of the programme of measures to meet the Convention commitment to reduce carbon dioxide and other greenhouse gas emissions. The UK Climate Change Programme, published on 25 January 1994, is based on a partnership approach between the Government and non-governmental organisations. The main elements of the Programme include the use of the Energy Saving Trust to promote energy efficiency, the phased introduction of VAT on domestic fuel and power, strengthening the energy conservation requirements of the Building Regulations, and increasing resources devoted to providing information and advice to households and business. The targets for installed capacity of Combined Heat and Power and the figure for new renewables generating capacity have also been increased.

ENERGY EFFICIENCY

5.2 The Government's commitment to energy efficiency remains strong. Expenditure on the Energy Efficiency Office's (EEO) programmes in 1993-94 will be around £70 million, some 75% higher than in 1991-92. For 1994-95, the budget will be increased further to over £100 million.

5.3 The Best Practice Programme continues to promote improvements in energy efficiency by providing authoritative and independent advice on energy efficiency in industrial processes, building design and management techniques. The target for energy savings has progressively been increased from £500 million to £800 million per year by 2000. Resources for the Programme in 1994-95 will be increased to over £17 million.

5.4 The Programme includes the promotion of Combined Heat and Power (CHP). The target for installed CHP capacity in the UK by 2000 has been increased from 4000 MW to 5000 MW as part of the Climate Change Programme.

5.5 Other initiatives in industry and commerce include the 'Making a Corporate Commitment' campaign, which seeks top management commitment to good energy management. Organisations that join are invited to develop or reassess their energy efficiency strategy, to set performance improvement targets and to ensure that plans are considered regularly at Board level. Over 1600 organisations have rallied to the campaign banner so far. Contact with them shows the campaign is helping to raise the profile of energy management and provides a focus for action. The Energy Management Assistance Scheme encourages smaller companies to obtain consultancy advice on the design and implementation of energy efficiency projects. Over 1200 applications were dealt with in the first year of the Scheme and, after 8 months of the second year, a further 2700 applicants had been accepted and nearly £1 million paid in grants.

Energy efficiency in the home

5.6 The domestic sector accounts for about a third of energy consumption in the UK and the promotion of energy efficiency in this sector is an important part of the Climate Change Programme.

5.7 The Home Energy Efficiency Scheme, which provides low income households with advice and grants for insulation and draught-proofing, has provided insulation in over 500,000 homes since the scheme began. In 1994-95, provision for the scheme is to be almost doubled and the scheme extended to pensioners and disabled people. The client contribution has also been abolished.

5.8 The 'Helping the Earth Begins at Home' campaign continues to convey the message that householders can help combat global warming - and save money on their fuel bills - by improving the energy efficiency of their homes. The EEO, with regional electricity companies, has organised a voluntary scheme for the labelling of domestic electrical appliances ahead of EC legislation. The first EC Directive, on refrigerators and freezers, is expected to come into effect in the UK in 1994.

5.9 The EEO and the Building Research Establishment have published the Standard Assessment Procedure (SAP) as the basis for home energy rating of domestic properties. The EEO has begun discussions with lending institutions about the scope for providing energy ratings as part of a valuation survey and additional funding to cover the cost of energy efficiency measures, perhaps linked to grants from the Energy Saving Trust.

5.10 In the March 1993 Budget, the Chancellor announced that VAT would be charged on domestic fuel and power at 8% from April 1994 and 17.5% from April 1995. It is estimated that this will help reduce CO_2 emissions by 1.5MtC a year by 2000, by encouraging energy efficiency.

Building Regulations

5.11 The UK is currently consulting on proposals for further amendments to the Building Regulations, which include the provision of double glazing, improved insulation, better heating controls and the incorporation of a SAP home energy rating. The Building Regulations also include provisions for improving energy efficiency when an alteration or conversion of an existing building takes place. These should lead to an improvement in energy efficiency of 25-35% compared with current Regulations.

Public sector campaign and Supplementary Credit Approvals

5.12 The Government continues to work towards its target of a 15% reduction in energy consumption on its own property over five years to March 1996. The progress of individual Departments towards the 15% target is shown in Tables 1-3. Further targets for the Government estate will be set to take consumption well below 80% of 1990 levels by 2000. The Government expects other public sector bodies to adopt similar targets. Local Authority Associations have encouraged their members to reduce energy consumption in their non-housing buildings by 15% over a similar period. The Department of the Environment has made Supplementary Credit Approvals of up to £3 million available in 1993-94 for energy efficiency in local authority administrative buildings in England to help achieve this target.

Contract Energy Management

5.13 The EEO works to promote the wider application of Contract Energy Management (CEM), particularly in the public sector. Following the Chancellor of the Exchequer's 1992 Autumn Statement, the procedures to be followed before employing CEM in the public sector were simplified and new guidelines were published in February 1993. In particular, the investment in capital equipment which the private sector makes will no longer lead to offsetting reductions in Departments' budgets.

The Best Practice Programme includes the promotion of Combined Heat and Power engines

The Government has increased resources devoted to providing information to households

5.14 Even though some Departments show a regress for 1992-93 over the base year, there has been an improvement in the overall position for 1992-93 over 1991-92 and CO_2 emissions per square metre have been reduced by 6% since 1990-91. The benefits of the substantial investment made by Departments should become apparent in the remaining years of the campaign.

European Community

5.15 The Government has continued to work within the European Community to encourage further improvements in energy efficiency through a series of Directives under the SAVE programme.

5.16 A Directive on efficiency standards for new hot water boilers took effect from 1 January 1994. Discussions are continuing on minimum energy efficiency standards for refrigerators and freezers, with a view to their introduction in two stages, the first in 1997. A Directive on appliance labelling will introduce labelling for refrigerators, freezers and fridge-freezers by the end of 1994. Further Directives on dishwashers, tumble dryers and washing machines will follow.

5.17 A new Directive which sets out guidelines in a number of areas relating to non-traded goods, including energy labelling of buildings and energy metering, was adopted in September 1993. The Government believes that current and planned UK activities will meet the requirements of the Directive, which must be implemented by the end of 1994.

NON-NUCLEAR ENERGY

5.18 Government policy is to stimulate the development of new and renewable energy sources wherever they have prospects of being economically attractive and environmentally acceptable, in order to contribute to: diverse, secure and sustainable energy supplies; a reduction in the emission of pollutants; and the encouragement of internationally competitive industries. The Government will be working towards the figure of 1500 MW of new electricity generating capacity from renewable sources for the UK by 2000.

5.19 One element of the Government's strategy is the Department of Trade and Industry's (DTI) programme of research, development, demonstration and dissemination on new and renewable energy. The Government's policy is to concentrate resources on key technologies such as biofuels, wind, hydro, solar and fuel cells and remove inappropriate market barriers. The emphasis on technology transfer will continue in line with the 1993 White Paper on Science, Engineering and Technology. The Government's geothermal research and development programme will be closed when current commitments end and the tidal programme is completed. A fuller strategy document is expected to be published this year.

5.20 Arrangements for a third Non-Fossil Fuel Obligation Renewables Order for England and Wales, and plans for the first Orders for Scotland and Northern Ireland, were announced in July 1993.

Oil and gas licensing

5.21 Licences for exploration and extraction of oil and gas from the UK continental shelf were awarded following the 14th Offshore Licensing Round in 1993. Full account was taken of environmental concerns at every stage of the Round and a number of blocks in sensitive areas were not offered for licensing. Applicants were required to submit a statement of their environmental policy and the quality of environmental awareness was taken into account when considering awards in these areas. Stringent conditions have been applied to blocks awarded in areas of environmental sensitivity.

Coal use

5.22 The Government announced in the Coal Review that it intends to provide an additional £4 million a year for three years to support the DTI clean coal technology programme. The main future use of coal is likely to remain within the field of power generation. Most of the additional funding committed to the programme will be devoted to the development of the key components of clean coal technologies, which offer high environmental performance at greater efficiency than is achievable with conventional pulverised fuel technologies.

Government policy is to stimulate the development of new and renewable energy sources wherever possible

Table 1: Departmental Expenditure, Investment and % Progress on the Standard Performance Indicator (£/m²) relative to 1990-91

Department	Energy Expenditure 1992-93 (£m)	Own Investment in Energy Efficiency 1992-93 (£k)	% Progress on £/m² Relative to 1990-91	
			1991-92	1992-93
MAFF - Main Estate	3.9	417	(4)	(6)
- Buffer Depots	0.1	0	0	21
Cabinet Office	0.5	40	(18)	(4)
Customs	3.6	650	2	13
Defence - Civil	28.7	N/A	N/A	N/A
- Royal Navy	36.1	2800	(2)	(2)
- Army	90.5	N/A	(10)	3
- RAF	74.1	2300	1	2
- Total	229.4	N/A	N/A	N/A
Education	0.5	N/A	(21)	(83)
Employment	9.8	1175	(7)	(1)
Environment	2.0	208	2	5
FCO	1.0	165	(3)	7
Health	0.8	421	(14)	(1)
Home Office - non-Prisons	2.6	0	(17)	(21)
- Prisons	24.4	1500	(1)	(2)
Inland Revenue	12.7	1631	1	1
Lord Chancellor's	6.4	650	1	3
ODA	0.7	N/A	-	(4)
National Heritage	N/A	N/A	N/A	N/A
National Savings	1.3	84	4	8
N. Ireland Office	10.4	729	5	5
Scottish Office	1.0	416	3	(2)
Scottish Courts	1.0	20	-	4
Scottish Prisons	3.3	N/A	(2)	(5)
Social Security	15.6	843	(6)	0
Trade & Industry	5.5	N/A	1	1
Transport	4.3	368	7	7
Treasury	0.3	4	2	4
Welsh Office	0.6	121	0	2
TOTAL (excl. ODA & Scots Courts)	341.7	14,542	(3.3)	0.9

Table 2: Departmental % Progress on CO_2/m^2 relative to 1990-91

Department	% Progress on CO_2/m^2 Relative to 1990-91	
	1991-92	1992-93
MAFF - Main Estate	(1)	(1)
- Buffer Depots	3	25
Cabinet Office	(8)	1
Customs	1	15
Defence - Civil	N/A	N/A
- Royal Navy	(1)	1
- Army	(12)	7
- RAF	3	8
- Total	N/A	N/A
Education	(16)	(58)
Employment	(6)	3
Environment	7	16
FCO	0	13
Health	(11)	3
Home Office - non-Prisons	(15)	(17)
- Prisons	1	3
Inland Revenue	3	7
Lord Chancellor's	2	8
ODA	-	(2)
National Heritage	N/A	N/A
National Savings	6	13
N. Ireland Office	6	6
Scottish Office	2	6
Scottish Courts	-	6
Scottish Prisons	1	(2)
Social Security	(3)	5
Trade & Industry	5	9
Transport	10	13
Treasury	23	19
Welsh Office	1	7
TOTAL (excl. ODA & Scots Courts)	(3)	6

Table 3: Departmental % Progress on total CO_2 emissions relative to 1990-91

Department	% Progress on CO_2 Relative to 1990-91	
	1991-92	1992-93
MAFF - Main Estate	(1)	(6)
- Buffer Depots	3	24
Cabinet Office	(22)	(13)
Customs	(56)	(38)
Defence - Civil	N/A	N/A
- Royal Navy	(3)	(5)
- Army	(12)	7
- RAF	2	10
- Total	N/A	N/A
Education	(34)	(7)
Employment	(8)	3
Environment	5	20
FCO	(2)	7
Health	(50)	0
Home Office - non-Prisons	(15)	(17)
- Prisons	(5)	(8)
Inland Revenue	0	4
Lord Chancellor's	(12)	(6)
ODA	-	(2)
National Heritage	N/A	N/A
National Savings	6	13
N. Ireland Office	3	1
Scottish Office	(12)	(8)
Scottish Courts	-	(7)
Scottish Prisons	(1)	(2)
Social Security	(3)	(10)
Trade & Industry	7	17
Transport	10	12
Treasury	13	31
Welsh Office	2	17
TOTAL (excl. ODA & Scots Courts)	(5)	3

Notes to Tables

1. Progress under each of the Performance Indicators (PIs) is expressed as a percentage reduction relative to the base year value of the PI in question. 15% improvement on £/m² after five years is the campaign target. Numbers in brackets denote regress rather than progress.

2. The £/m² figure is obtained by weather correcting the energy consumption per unit floor area, and converting to costs using 'standard' fuel prices (6p/kWh for electricity and 1.25p/kWh for all fossil fuels). This conversion to money was done to reflect the relative costs of electricity and fossil fuels, and also their relative environmental impact. Fixed prices eliminate the effects of tariff changes, which distort the comparison of annual bills. Normalising by floor area helps overcome problems of changing estate size.

3. Some Departments have revised earlier years' figures, which explains some differences from last year's published results. Equally, some of this year's figures may be subject to revision.

4. For ODA & Scottish Courts, 1991-92 is the base year; these Departments' contributions have not been included in the 'Progress' totals.

5. Floor area figures are not available for most of the MOD estate. An alternative assessment method to £/m² has been agreed, whereby consumption figures for base and intermediate years are adjusted up or down to allow for the addition or loss of buildings to MOD's estate during the campaign; this also applies to CO_2/m². For total CO_2, since no allowance is made for estate changes to any other Department, unadjusted figures are used for MOD.

6. The progress figures for Customs & Excise partly reflect a widening of the basis for measurement as the Department overcomes problems with collation of data. Operational changes have allowed greater use of buildings where Customs & Excise control the energy use instead of paying an energy-inclusive charge; this process is continuing and may affect future figures.

7. DFE's consumption is dominated by its headquarters building. This changed from a largely naturally ventilated building in the base year to a completely air-conditioned one, with a much smaller floor area, last year. This is the explanation for their large increase in £/m².

8. Investment figures relate only to clearly identifiable energy efficiency measures undertaken by Departments. Energy efficiency is also an integral part of all major construction projects, including building refurbishment and plant replacement carried out by Departments. However, separating out the energy efficiency component is not always meaningful; for example, a well designed energy efficient new building may actually cost the same or less than a conventional one.

REF NO	SUMMARY OF PREVIOUS WHITE PAPER COMMITMENTS	ACTION TO DATE	COMMITMENTS TO FURTHER ACTION
122	Develop Energy Efficiency Office's Best Practice Programme. Increase target energy savings by 2000 from 200 Petajoules (PJ) per year to 250PJ per year - worth £700m per year (5.30, SYR 87)	In 1992-93 over 300 publications produced and over 225 events held under the Programme. Budget increased to £15m in 1993-94. Target energy savings reassessed at £800m per year	Increase Best Practice Programme budget for 1994-95 to £17m
123			Review Best Practice Programme in 1995
124	Promote the use of Combined Heat and Power (CHP). Work to achieve extra 2000MW from CHP by 2000, in conjunction with CHPA (5.30, SYR 88)	14 new publications produced and nine events held under Best Practice Programme, in addition to joint marketing initiative with CHPA. New electricity regulation proposed; work continues to reduce the effects of institutional barriers	Target increased from 4000MW to 5000MW of installed capacity by 2000
125	Encourage use of high efficiency lighting (5.31, SYR 89)	Part of Best Practice Programme and support for industry initiatives	
126	Promote measures which encourage people to use energy more efficiently, or are otherwise worthwhile in their own right (5.24,5.27, SYR 90,92)	Continued with a variety of measures to promote energy efficiency, including the Best Practice Programme, and through publicity campaigns. 'Helping the Earth Begins at Home' campaign continued. A second 'Helping the Earth' week took place in October 1993; and Energy Advice Week and promotion of low cost measures in 1994	
127	Consider further measures in the long term, including increasing the price of energy (5.27, SYR 90)	Chancellor announced in March 1993 Budget the introduction of VAT on domestic energy costs at 8% from April 1994	VAT to be increased to 17.5% from April 1995
128	Establish independent Energy Saving Trust to develop and propose new programmes to encourage the more efficient use of energy (SYR 90)	Established Energy Saving Trust with British Gas and the electricity industry. Trust has so far launched four energy efficiency schemes, including Local Energy Advice Centres sponsored by EEO	
129	Achieve savings from EMAS of £50m per year by 1995 (SYR 90)	EMAS made a slow start in 1992-93, because of the effect of the recession on small businesses. However, in 1993-94, although high number of applications, spend is only what was planned for 1992-93	Achieve savings from EMAS of £20m a year by 1995
130	Complete 240,000 HEES tasks in 1992-93 (SYR 91)	244,000 insulation and draughtproofing jobs completed through the Home Energy Efficiency Scheme in 1992-93. A further 240,000 jobs expected to be completed in 1993-94	
131			Increase budget for Home Energy Efficiency Scheme to complete 440,000 jobs in 1994-95

REF NO	SUMMARY OF PREVIOUS WHITE PAPER COMMITMENTS	ACTION TO DATE	COMMITMENTS TO FURTHER ACTION
132	Help to make buildings more energy efficient by encouraging energy efficient improvements. Consultation on proposals for a further revision of the Building Regulations in 1993-94 to include home energy labelling and common standards (5.31, SYR 93)	Building Regulations proposals have gone out to consultation. Took forward £60m demonstration scheme of energy efficient improvements in local authority housing. Developed a Standard Assessment Procedure for home energy labelling. Produced Best Practice guides and case studies. Held seminars and workshops to encourage improved energy efficiency in building stocks	Aim to lay revised Regulations before Parliament in first half of 1994
133	Adopt EC Application Directive for fridges and freezers; help EC develop further Directives; maintain UK voluntary scheme in interim (SYR 94)	Application Directive on fridges and freezers adopted in December 1993. Further energy labelling Directives under discussion for washing machines, tumble dryers and dishwashers. UK voluntary scheme to label fridges and freezers maintained	Implement Application Directive for fridges and freezers
134	Implement Directive on Boilers. Encourage the EC to bring forward proposals for mandatory minimum standards for electrical appliances, as satisfactory voluntary agreements have not been reached (SYR 95-97)	Boiler Efficiency Regulation 1993 SI No.3083 laid in December 1993 to implement Directive. EC has circulated informal draft proposal for minimum standards for domestic fridges and freezers	Negotiate and adopt minimum standards Directive for fridges and freezers acceptable to the UK
135	Seek savings of 15% in energy consumption for the Government estate over a five year period and monitor success through Green Ministers (SYR 45,46,98)	CO_2 per square metre has been reduced by 6% since 1990-91. Energy efficiency has been a major item on agenda for Green Ministers in 1992-3	Set further targets in due course with the aim of reducing energy use by at least 20% by 2000 compared to 1990 levels
136	Public electricity suppliers to promote efficiency in the use of electricity (5.31, SYR 99)	Electricity supply price control amended to provide regional electricity companies with greater incentives to promote energy efficiency. Director General of Electricity Supply has set standards of performance on energy efficiency	
137	Work with the fuel utilities to promote use of advisory services and monitor the extent of take-up (SYR 99)	Promoted and monitored through 'Helping the Earth' campaign	
138	Keep emergence of competition among electricity generators under review (SYR 100)	Continued to keep development of competition under review. Since 1990, six independent projects with total capacity of 3335 MW have become operational. Another 14 projects with capacity of 10,869 MW are planned to become operational by 1999. Approximately half the capacity is CHP plant	

REF NO	SUMMARY OF PREVIOUS WHITE PAPER COMMITMENTS	ACTION TO DATE	COMMITMENTS TO FURTHER ACTION
139	Carry through research and development of renewable energy sources (3.16, SYR 101) (DTI)	As part of the DTI's programme of research, development, demonstration and dissemination on renewable energy, 349 projects were in progress at 31 March 1993 UK responded to 1993 call for proposals under Altener programme. There were 150 UK participants in proposals for the Joule renewables programme and five renewables projects were successful under the Thermie programme	
140	Publish report by Renewable Energy Advisory Group by end 1992 (SYR 102) (DTI)	Report published in December 1992. Overall strategy review under way	
141	Publish the results of the review of renewable energy strategy in 1993 (SYR 102) (DTI)		Publication expected 1994
142	The Government will work towards a figure of new renewable electricity generation capacity of 1000 MW in 2000 (5.40, SYR 103) (DTI)		Government announced in the Coal Review White Paper its intention to work towards a figure of 1500MW for the UK by 2000
143	Issue final guidance on wind energy by end 1992. Guidance on other forms of renewable energy to be prepared (SYR 104, 105)	Planning Policy Guidance note (PPG22) on renewables and wind energy published in February 1993	
144	Lay further orders under Non-Fossil Fuel Obligation by mid-1990s (SYR 106) (DTI)	Announced intention to make third NFFO Renewables Order in 1994, for 300-400 MW of new renewables capacity. Announced intention to make analogous orders in Scotland and Northern Ireland	Further orders to be laid for England and Wales in 1996 and 1998
145	Amend or repeal anomalous regulations which hinder reductions in greenhouse gas emissions, such as restrictions on cabotage (3.17, SYR 107)	The Government has reaffirmed its intention to make consequential amendments to UK legislation as soon as a suitable opportunity arises	

6 BUSINESS AND INDUSTRY

6.1 Business and industry can play a key role in averting threats to the environment. At the same time, environmental concerns are creating a wide range of business opportunities. Many environmental improvements to products or processes, such as energy efficiency, waste minimisation and recycling, lead to a positive improvement in companies' profit margins. And there are growing opportunities in the rapidly expanding world market for environmental goods and services, which the OECD estimates will be worth $300 billion by 2000.

ACHIEVING ENVIRONMENTAL OBJECTIVES

6.2 It is the Government's responsibility to create a framework of regulations and incentives that enables business to respond positively to the environmental challenge. Companies have to comply with a substantial body of statutory legislation regulating their impact on the environment. Such regulations secure minimum environmental standards, but must not be too prescriptive or impose costs on businesses that are disproportionate to the environmental benefits they are intended to deliver. Voluntary action and economic instruments, separately or in combination, provide alternative means to achieve environmental objectives; they are more flexible and can be more cost effective than regulation. The Government also recognizes the importance of effective dialogue with business, and proposes to review the way in which information is presented to small businesses to ensure that it is easy to comprehend and act on.

RAISING BUSINESS AWARENESS

6.3 The Government wants to encourage businesses to integrate the environment into their management systems and to report openly on environmental performance. Those that do so will be able to gain recognition across the European Community through the EC Eco-Management and Audit Scheme. The Scheme was agreed in March 1993, and is due to begin in early 1995. The Government has asked the National Accreditation Council for Certification Bodies to prepare proposals for accrediting environmental verifiers for the Scheme and to provide accreditation for certifiers to the British Standards Institution's Environmental Management Systems Standard (BS 7750). The competent body to receive registrations under the Scheme will be

EC
ECO MANAGEMENT
AND
AUDIT SCHEME

established in 1994.

6.4 The UK has continued to play a leading role in the development of the EC Ecolabelling Scheme (see also Chapter 17). The label provides encouragement to manufacturers and retailers to design, produce and market genuinely greener products by helping consumers identify products that do least harm to the environment. Achieving agreement across Europe on product criteria has been disappointingly slow, and the Government will continue to press its partners in the Community for faster progress in applying the scheme to additional categories of products. The Scheme is administered in the UK by the UK Ecolabelling Board which keeps manufacturers and other interested parties informed about the development of the Scheme. The Board awarded the first EC ecolabels to washing machines in Hoover's 'New Wave' range in November 1993.

6.5 The Government is also seeking to promote the concept of eco-design - the incorporation of environmental criteria into product development and design. In March 1994, the Government and British Telecom jointly sponsored a workshop organised by the RSA to consider eco-design in the telecommunications industry and draw out messages with a wider application. Around seventy senior executives from the telecommunications industry and research organisations attended this two-day event.

6.6 The Government also has an important role to play in raising business awareness of environmental issues and in providing information to enable companies to improve their environmental performance. The Government is particularly keen to provide help and guidance to small and medium sized firms. The last year has seen the launch of a Promulgation Programme to help small businesses with environmental issues (see Box), and the launch of a pilot network of Business Links, providing a 'one stop shop' for a wide range of advice to business. The Government has also

The first EC Ecolabel was awarded in November 1993 to Hoover's 'New Wave' range of washing machines

PROMOTION OF ENVIRONMENTAL MANAGEMENT TO SMALL FIRMS

The Advisory Committee on Business and the Environment (ACBE) recommended that the Government supports a programme to raise awareness of environmental issues among small and medium sized firms and to help them improve their overall environmental performance. The Secretary of State for the Environment and the President of the Board of Trade accepted this recommendation and agreed jointly to fund ten local initiatives and to work in co-operation with Trade Associations to develop programmes of help and guidance for particular industrial sectors.

Each of the local business-led initiatives will receive Government funding of up to £40,000 per year, matched by private sector funds, for three years, after which time they will need to be self-financing. Eleven initiatives are being supported: in Blackburn, Sheffield, Leeds, Newcastle, Dudley, Plymouth, Amber Valley, Wearside, Hemel Hempstead,

Southampton and Sutton.

The Government plans to work with Trade Associations in the foundries, metal finishers and platers, leather and textile industries to try to develop sectoral projects. These industries have a significant impact on the environment and contain a high proportion of small and medium sized firms. These initiatives will be closely linked to the new Best Practice Programme.

While peer pressure, especially at a local level, and Trade Associations are an effective way of influencing smaller businesses, ACBE also recommended communication of environmental messages through the supply chain, and through lenders and insurers. Material is being tailored for dissemination through the various channels; one example is the ACBE booklet, *The Environment: A Business Guide,* published in September 1993.

established the Joint (DTI/DOE) Environmental Markets Unit (JEMU) to help UK firms take full advantage of the growing international market in environmental goods and services. JEMU has already produced opportunity briefs for major geographical areas and industry is making increasing use of the service it provides.

6.7 In December 1993, the Government announced a new joint DTI/DOE Environmental Technology Best Practice Information Programme to promote the adoption of modern technologies and techniques to improve businesses' environmental performance. The £16 million, five-year Programme will have a strong emphasis on reducing and eliminating waste and pollution at source, and will be directed at priority areas to be selected in consultation with industry and the environmental regulators. By encouraging UK companies to adopt more cost-effective, less polluting equipment and practices, and by encouraging supplier companies to develop such technology, the Programme will help industry to improve its economic as well as its environmental performance.

6.8 The Programme will involve a range of carefully targeted case studies, publications and events to make better environmental technology and techniques more widely known to potential users and suppliers. In particular, it will seek to build on the results of two major demonstration projects in the Mersey Basin and the Aire and Calder Valleys. The 25 companies involved in these projects have found hundreds of ways of reducing waste, which could lead to savings of millions of pounds.

PARTNERSHIP

6.9 The Promulgation Programme and JEMU were established in response to recommendations from the Advisory Committee on Business and the Environment (ACBE). The Committee was appointed in May 1991 for a two-year term by the Secretary of State for the Environment and the President of the Board of Trade following a commitment in *This Common Inheritance* to engage in a closer dialogue with business on environmental issues.

6.10 The Committee provided Ministers with a business view on a wide range of policy issues, both ad hoc and through its five working groups. It produced three action-orientated progress reports, containing over 100 detailed recommendations, to all of which the Government has responded. The Third Report and Government response were published in July 1993.

6.11 Because Ministers found ACBE's work so valuable, they decided to appoint a successor Committee. This is chaired by Derek Wanless, Group Chief Executive of National Westminster Bank. One change from the first Committee is that the agricultural sector is represented among its membership. The new ACBE, which met for the first time in November 1993, has set up working groups to consider waste management and minimisation, transport and the environment, the financial sector, how environmental goals can best be achieved, and the links between agriculture and other industries. The Government looks forward to receiving initial recommendations from the Committee before the end of the year.

REF NO	SUMMARY OF PREVIOUS WHITE PAPER COMMITMENTS	ACTION TO DATE	COMMITMENTS TO FURTHER ACTION
146	Widen support for clean technologies through a joint DOE/DTI grant programme, and make £21m available for projects including clean technology in the 3 years to 1993-94. Continue to promote take-up amongst businesses (14.7, SYR 108) (DOE/DTI)	Grant support of nearly £14m given to complete DOE/DTI Technology Schemes, which have brought forward 77 projects. R&D and demonstration projects funded for: clean technology; recycling; environmental monitoring; industrial waste treatment; and control of emissions to atmosphere	Disseminate results of completed projects, such as through new Environmental Technology Best Practice Information Programme
147	Encourage further cleaner technology projects to come forward and assist Research Councils wherever possible (SYR 109)	Continued to assist SERC/AFRC Clean Technology Unit with development of its programme	
148	Organise workshops with academics and industry on cleaner technology in autumn 1992 (SYR 109)	Workshops held at end 1992 and during 1993	
149	Ensure industry adopts new cleaner cost-effective technologies as they become available; implement IPC across remaining processes and stages to 1995 and continue to update standards (11.15, SYR 110) (DTI/DOE)	Continued introduction of technologies on phased basis. Announced new Environmental Technology Best Practice Information Programme, to include a national clean technology centre to promote the use of clean technology by business	Launch new programme in 1994
150	Work closely with ACBE and continue to respond rapidly and constructively to its recommendations (SYR 111) (DOE/DTI)	ACBE Third Progress Report published July 1993. New ACBE appointed November 1993	
151	Launch a programme to promulgate practical guidance on environmental management, including the recommendations of ACBE, to small and medium sized enterprises (SYR 111) (DOE/DTI)	Programme launched - eleven local initiatives and one sectoral project currently being supported	Launch further sectoral initiative in 1994
152	Reach final accord on EC Eco-Management and Audit Scheme by March 1993 (SYR 111)	EC Eco-Management and Audit Scheme agreed in March 1993 (formally adopted in June). National Accreditation Council for Certification Bodies asked to develop proposals for accreditation of environmental verifiers	
153			Set up arrangements to enable accreditation scheme to come into operation in April-May 1995. Establish competent body to receive registrations by end July 1994 (DOE/DTI)
154	Establish a joint DTI/DOE Environmental Opportunities Unit to collate information on environmental initiatives and spread information to business (SYR 113) (DTI/DOE)	Implemented. Joint Environmental Markets Unit (JEMU) became operational December 1992	

7 LAND USE AND PLANNING

Development Plans - A Good Practice Guide and *Environmental Appraisal of Plans: A Good Practice Guide* published

Development Control - A Charter Guide published jointly with National Planning Forum

New or updated guidance, including *Industrial and Commercial Development and Small Firms, Town Centres and Retailing, Telecommunications* and *Renewable Energy* published

7.1 The town and country planning system plays a key role in making the best use of finite land resources by regulating land use and development. It is a vital instrument for protecting and enhancing the urban and rural environment and for conserving the built and natural heritage, while ensuring that adequate provision is made for new homes and businesses.

DEVELOPMENT PLANS

7.2 Under the Planning and Compensation Act 1991, each District and Borough must produce a local plan for the whole of its area. County-wide structure plans and plans covering waste and minerals must also be prepared. These plans are needed to provide a detailed framework for the control of development and the use of land. The Government expects plan preparation to be substantially complete by 1996, when over 90% of plans will have been prepared.

7.3 To assist local planning authorities draw up their plans, the Government has issued new guidance. Planning Policy Guidance note 12 (PPG12) and its Welsh equivalent on development plans and regional planning guidance were followed in September 1992 by *Development Plans - A Good Practice Guide*. This guide draws on a considerable body of plan-making experience and distils good practice in plan preparation, by focusing on four main areas - plan preparation, content, presentation and implementation. As a follow up to the publication of this guide, the Government organised a series of regional seminars jointly with the Royal Town Planning Institute on good practice in local plan preparation.

7.4 When preparing their plans, local planning authorities are required to take environmental considerations into account.

PPG12 offered preliminary advice on how to meet this requirement through environmental appraisal. In November 1993, the Government published *Environmental Appraisal of Development Plans: A Good Practice Guide*. This guide provides advice on a range of techniques and procedures. It also shows the benefits of environmental appraisal and how this can be easily integrated into each stage of the plan-making process. The Government proposes to undertake new research on how sustainable development can be taken into account in planning policies, with a view to a further good practice guide.

DEVELOPMENT CONTROL

7.5 Plans should improve the consistency of decision-making by local authorities in response to planning applications. They may also ensure faster and better-quality decisions.

7.6 *Development Control - A Charter Guide* was published jointly with the National Planning Forum by the Department of the Environment and the Welsh Office in February 1993. The Welsh Office also published *Development Control - A Guide to Good Practice* in May 1993. The guides provide a model for local planning authorities who wish to explain how planning applications are decided and the particular standards that will apply. The guides represent important initiatives within the principles of the Citizen's Charter.

PLANNING AND POLLUTION CONTROL

7.7 The Government has published a draft Planning Policy Guidance note on planning and pollution controls, to clarify the respective roles of the planning and the pollution control systems and to advise planners on the strengths of environmental protection controls. Publication of the final version of the note in 1994 will take into account the implementation of the EC Waste Framework Directive.

7.8 The research report on ways of locating development to reduce travel distance and increase transport choice, *Reducing Transport Emissions Through Planning,* was published in 1993. Subsequently, the Government issued in April 1993 a consultation draft of a revised Planning Policy Guidance note 13 (PPG13) on planning and transport. Following further research, the Government published the final version of PPG13 in March 1994.

INTEGRATING THE ENVIRONMENT IN PLANNING POLICY

7.9 Work has continued on the comprehensive review of planning guidance. In the past year, as well as the new guidance in PPG13 on transport, the Government has published new or updated guidance on:

- *Industrial and Commercial Development and Small Firms* (PPG4), which provides advice on a range of issues involved in industrial and commercial proposals and on the need to encourage the development of small businesses. It also emphasises the importance of balancing environmental and economic considerations;

- *Simplified Planning Zones* (PPG5), which covers the procedures for preparation of Simplified Planning Zones streamlined by the Planning and Compensation Act 1991 and new regulations;

- *Town Centres and Retail Development* (PPG6), which emphasises the need to sustain or enhance the vitality and viability of town centres which serve the whole community, and ensures the availability of a wide range of shopping opportunities to which people have easy access;

- *Telecommunications* (PPG8), which makes clear that the needs of industry can be met in a way that respects environmental objectives;

- *Tourism* (PPG21), which outlines the economic significance of tourism and its environmental impact and explains how the needs of tourism should be dealt with in the planning system;

- *Renewable Energy* (PPG22), which describes the various forms of renewable energy and gives local planning authorities practical guidance to help them determine applications for development;

- *Regional Planning Guidance for the Northern Region* (RPG7), which provides the framework for the preparation of structure plans;

- *Motorway Service Areas* (Circular 23/92), which advises on the considerations to be addressed in determining planning applications;

The vitality and viability of town centres is the focus of Planning Policy Guidance note 6

• *Development and Flood Risk* (Circular 30/92; MAFF Circular FD1/92; Welsh Office Circular 68/92), which provides guidance on the arrangements for ensuring that planning decisions take account of any risk of flooding, whether inland or from the sea.

7.10 The Government has published Minerals Planning Guidance on the control of noise at surface mineral workings (MPG11), which provides advice on how the planning system can be used to keep noise emissions from surface mineral workings within environmentally acceptable limits without imposing unreasonable burdens on minerals operators (see also Chapter 16). The planning system can also influence the recycling of waste materials (see Chapter 13).

7.11 The Government has also issued draft guidance for public consultation on:

• *Listed Buildings and Conservation Areas,* which sets out Government policy on planning aspects of the conservation of the historic environment and also policies for the listing of historic buildings, for the control of works to listed buildings and for the preservation and enhancement of conservation areas;

• Regional Planning Guidance for the South East, the South West and the East Midlands;

• Guidelines for aggregate provision and on open cast coal mining in England and Wales.

7.12 The Government expects to lay before Parliament in 1994 draft Regulations which will help Britain meet the obligations of the EC Habitats Directive. The Government will publish the new Planning Policy Guidance note on nature conservation after Parliament has considered the draft Regulations. The Government also expects to amend the Town and Country Planning General Development Order to ensure that permitted development rights granted

under the Order do not breach the requirements of the Habitats Directive.

7.13 In July 1993, the Government published a research report, *The Effectiveness of Green Belts,* which concluded that the main Green Belt purposes of preventing urban sprawl and the merging of towns should be maintained. This research has been taken into account in reviewing Planning Policy Guidance note 2 (PPG2) on Green Belts. The Government published a consultation draft on 21 February 1994.

7.14 In November 1992, the Government published *A Farmers Guide to the Planning System,* which explains how the planning system works and gives practical advice about how to present planning applications.

ENVIRONMENTAL IMPACT ASSESSMENT

7.15 Environmental Impact Assessment (EIA) continues to play an important role in the field of planning and development control. EIA is required for certain categories of development which are likely to have significant effects on the environment. About 180 planning applications are subject to EIA in England and Wales every year. Following the issue of a consultation paper in March 1993, measures will be implemented and guidance provided to apply EIA to projects that would otherwise be permitted. Guidance on the preparation of Environmental Statements will be published in 1994. Research will also be published on evaluating Environmental Statements.

7.16 New guidance on the environmental assessment of new and improved trunk road schemes, including motorways, was issued in 1993 as volume 11 of the *Design Manual for Roads and Bridges.* The guidance in volume 11 will be fully adopted in the preparation and assessment of future road schemes introduced to the National Roads Programme, and will also be applied as appropriate to schemes currently in the Programme.

Movement of aggregrate by rail can offer environmental advantages and for longer distances may be more economic

REF NO	SUMMARY OF PREVIOUS WHITE PAPER COMMITMENTS	ACTION TO DATE	COMMITMENTS TO FURTHER ACTION
155	Substantially complete coverage of district plans under 1991 Planning and Compensation Act expected by end 1996 (6.20-21, SYR 114-5)	Initial results of research into local plan inquiries disseminated November 1993. 25% of local authorities now have district-wide plans	Ensure the continuation of effective strategic planning, following changes to local government structure. Over 90% of plans to be completed by 1996
156			Commission research into enhancing the role of the public in development plan preparation
157	Extend regional guidance to assist new arrangements for development planning; issue guidance on most regions by end 1993 (SYR 116)	Issued guidance for East Anglia and Northern Regions. Issued draft guidance for consultation for South East, South West and East Midlands	Issue final guidance for all regions by end 1994
158	Issue final guidance on development plans, placing greater emphasis on energy conservation. Ensure that environmental policies get built into development plans. Guidance to be updated in 1993 (SYR 117,128,145)	Regional Offices have scrutinised draft plans to ensure that advice in PPGs is being followed. Research into integration of environmental issues into development plans completed. Good practice guide on environmental appraisal of development plans published November 1993	
159			Start new research on planning policies for sustainable development
160	Review the operation of the law for updating mineral workings. Finalise interim development orders (6.33,6.57, SYR 118-9)	Registration of interim development orders largely complete	Publish draft proposals for 1950's, 60's and 70's permissions in early 1994
161	Amend General Development Order. Issue further consultation paper by end 1992 (SYR 118)	Permitted development rights for coal revised in November 1992	
162	Review national minerals planning policy guidance (6.33, SYR 119)	MPG on the control of noise at surface mineral workings published

Research on control of blasting and dust associated with mineral workings under way | Issue MPG6 on aggregates provision in early 1994

Issue consultation papers on peat extraction, provision of silica sand, landslides, stability and quarrying and oil and gas in 1994

Issue draft revised guidance on general considerations and the development plan system, coal and reclamation of mineral workings in 1994 |
| 163 | | | Commission research on environmental costs and benefits of minerals extraction. Research on traffic associated with mineral workings and impacts of extraction on hydrology to commence during 1994 |

REF NO	SUMMARY OF PREVIOUS WHITE PAPER COMMITMENTS	ACTION TO DATE	COMMITMENTS TO FURTHER ACTION
164	Finalise MPG on treatment of old mineshafts and publish in autumn 1992 (SYR 119)		To be published early 1994
165	Establish annual monitoring system on hazardous substances during 1992-93 (SYR 120)	Annual statistical monitoring first published September 1993. Research on controls commenced November 1993	
166	Commission research to monitor new system of controls over new farm and forestry buildings and roads. Any changes to be implemented in 1995 (6.15-16, SYR 121)	Research under way	Research report expected autumn 1994
167	Introduce further controls over telecommunications code operator equipment and issue planning guidance on telecommunications during autumn 1992 (6.14, SYR 123)	Revised PPG on telecommunications issued December 1992. Selective control over telecommunications code operator equipment (radio masts, callboxes and radio equipment housing) brought into force January 1993	
168	Seek to speed up decision taking for the benefit of the environment and the economy (6.12, SYR 124)	Published *Development Control-A Charter Guide* jointly with the National Planning Forum. Information on speed of decisions published in a quarterly information bulletin and checklists of local authority performance against the 8 week target published every six months	
169	Monitor and evaluate operation of provisions of 1991 Planning and Compensation Act (SYR 125)	Monitoring and evaluation systems in place	
170	Consider implications of research into ways of locating development to reduce travel distance and increase transport choice. Update planning policy guidance. Let further research projects where more information is needed (SYR 127)	PPG13 *Transport* consultation paper, containing advice based on research findings, issued April 1993. Research into the economic effects of PPG13 completed. PPG13 Published Ongoing programme of research into wide range of transport issues DOT issued discussion document on its strategy for research	Commission further research on transport planning issues. Issue good practice guidance on transport planning policies
171			Introduce electronic motorway tolling when technology is available, subject to Parliament approving the necessary legislation (DOT)
172	Develop proposals to recreate habitats affected by road schemes, including the involvement of landowners and farmers on a case-by-case basis (7.38, SYR 130,178) (DOT)	Five woodland and habitat recreation schemes carried out	

REF NO	SUMMARY OF PREVIOUS WHITE PAPER COMMITMENTS	ACTION TO DATE	COMMITMENTS TO FURTHER ACTION
173	Revised guidance on environmental assessment of trunk roads to be issued by end 1992. Research planned on monetary evaluation of road traffic noise (SYR 131) (DOT)	*Volume 11 of the Design Manual for Roads and Bridges - Environmental Assessment* published in July 1993	
174	Develop advice on implementation of SACTRA recommendations on environmental assessment of road schemes (SYR 131) (DOT)	Research on evaluation on environmental impacts being undertaken by DOT	
175			Examine the scope for developing the assessment of total and cumulative effects of transport policies and programmes (DOT)
176	Issue guidance on good road design and noise barriers in autumn 1992 (7.38, SYR 132) (DOT)	*Volume 10 of the Design Manual for Roads and Bridges* published January 1993	
177	Produce wild flower handbook in autumn 1992 (SYR 132) (DOT)	Published June 1993	
178	Include provisions for environmental assessment in legislation to establish new approval procedures for railway projects (SYR 133) (DOT)	Application procedure rules made under the Transport and Works Act 1992	
179	Align planning and pollution control mechanisms over special industrial activities. Commission research on possible benefits of further reforming the special industrial classes of Town and Country Planning (use classes) Order 1987 (6.40, SYR 134)	Research not taken forward. Consultation paper on reform of special industrial activities issued December 1993	
180			Consider abolition of special industrial use classes within Town and Country Planning (use classes) Order 1987
181	Issue new Planning Policy Guidance on pollution control and waste management (FYR p108, SYR 135)	Publication held back by need to incorporate EC Waste Framework Directive into British law and provide advice on the planning aspects of its implementation	PPG on Planning and Pollution Control now due mid-1994
182	Review national planning policy guidance. Finalise draft guidance by early 1993 on: industry; commerce and small firms; Simplified Planning Zones; renewable energy; noise; telecommunications; tourism; motorway services; flood risks (6.33, SYR 136,179)	Final guidance issued, except for noise	Finalise draft guidance on noise in early 1994; and on pollution by mid-1994

REF NO	SUMMARY OF PREVIOUS WHITE PAPER COMMITMENTS	ACTION TO DATE	COMMITMENTS TO FURTHER ACTION
183			Report on research on effectiveness of Planning Policy Guidance notes expected autumn 1994
184	Issue final PPG on nature conservation by end 1992 (SYR 129)	Publication held back by need to incorporate EC Habitats Directive into British law and provide advice on its implementation	Issue final PPG when EC Habitats Directive implemented in 1994
185	Issue draft guidance by end 1992 on major retail development and listed buildings and conservation areas (SYR 136,142)	Final guidance issued on town centres and retail development. Draft guidance issued on listed buildings and conservation areas and transport	Finalise guidance in early 1994
186	Review Green Belt effectiveness in light of research (6.33, SYR 136)	Research report published. Draft revised guidance published February 1994	
187	Ratify Helsinki Convention on Environmental Impact Assessment in a Transboundary Context in concert with EC (SYR 137)		Ratification of Convention expected 1994
188	Improve the operation of Environmental Impact Assessments (6.36, SYR 137)	Consultation paper on permitted development and EIA issued in March 1993	Implement measures for applying EIA to permitted development where appropriate and issue guidance in 1994
189	Implement extension of Environmental Impact Assessment to new categories following consultation by end 1992 (SYR 137)		Extend to additional categories of development by early 1994
190	Issue guidance on good practice in preparing Environmental Statements (SYR 137)		Issue by end 1994
191			Publish research on evaluating Environmental Statements in 1994
192	Revise Circular 15/88 on environmental assessment (SYR 137)	Review in progress	Publish consultation draft in 1994
193	Provide funding for land reclamation (6.64-69, SYR 140)	Continued to fund reclamation of derelict and contaminated sites	
194	Discourage dereliction and tackle problems of land contamination through the planning system. Consider response to consultation paper on prevention of dereliction (6.64-69, SYR 140)	Carried out consultation exercise. New derelict land survey under way. Review of contaminated land and liabilities under way (see Chapter 13)	Consider responses and scope for further action, including possible research
195	Further research on urban intensification to be carried out in 1992-93 (SYR 141)	Research under way	
196	Encourage the best use of land in urban areas to keep pressure off other areas of environmental value and to improve local conditions (8.6, SYR 142)	Research on the viability and vitality of town centres being carried out in 1993-94	Publish research and further guidance

REF NO	SUMMARY OF PREVIOUS WHITE PAPER COMMITMENTS	ACTION TO DATE	COMMITMENTS TO FURTHER ACTION
197	Support the use of design guidance and briefs within the planning system and disseminate advice on 'Time for Design' guidance (8.27, SYR 143)	Published further advice on the planning of roads and footpaths in residential areas	
198	Commission research into best practice for design policy in development plans (SYR 142)	Research commissioned	
199	Complete register of sports fields by 1993 and consider scope for extending it to cover other recreational land (8.8, SYR 144)	Register of sports fields and other recreational land in England published in October 1993	

8 COUNTRYSIDE AND WILDLIFE

8.1 The Government issued major policy documents on biodiversity and forestry in January 1994 and published a comprehensive survey of the British countryside in November 1993. It designated a number of Special Protection Areas and Ramsar sites in 1993 and issued a consultation paper on the changes needed to meet the UK's obligations under the Habitats Directive. It launched six new Environmentally Sensitive Areas in England and announced a £31 million package of new agri-environment measures. Work continues under 'Action for the Countryside', which includes measures in England to stimulate the rural economy, conserve and enhance landscapes and wildlife, and promote access to the countryside.

SCIENTIFIC MONITORING AND RESEARCH: COUNTRYSIDE SURVEY 1990

8.2 In November 1993, the Government published the results of *Countryside Survey 1990,* the most comprehensive survey of the British countryside ever undertaken. An innovative combination of satellite mapping of the whole country with detailed field studies provides the ecological equivalent to the population census.

8.3 The Survey provides information on the stock of countryside features and habitats in 1990 and, by reference to previous surveys, details of changes. The results show an increase in the extent of uncultivated land and weedy grassland at the expense of arable and intensively managed grassland. There was a continuing loss of features such as hedgerows and a general reduction of the diversity of plants in the wider countryside. The loss in diversity of lowland grasslands is also of concern.

8.4 The Government is committed to a complete repeat survey for 2000 but, in the meantime, will conduct more selective monitoring on topics of special interest.

8.5 *Countryside Survey* identified a net loss of 85,000 km of hedgerows between 1984 and 1990 and confirmed that inadequate management, rather than deliberate removal, was the main cause. The new Hedgerow Incentive Scheme resulted in 411 restoration agreements, covering 600 km of hedgerow, in its first year. The Government supported a Private Member's Bill on Hedgerows, but this ran out of time at Report Stage. The Government has commissioned further research to establish the causes and rates of loss between 1990 and 1993.

CONSERVING THE DIVERSITY OF BRITAIN'S WILDLIFE AND HABITATS

8.6 *Biodiversity: the UK Action Plan* was published in January 1994 in response to the Convention on Biological Diversity, part of the 1992 Earth Summit. The Plan contains a strategy, programmes and broad targets for conserving and enhancing biodiversity in the UK over the next 10 and 20 years. A Biodiversity Action Plan Steering Group is being set up and will include representatives of central and local

Government, agencies, collections, non-governmental organisations and academic bodies. It will be responsible for overseeing the development of a range of specific costed targets for key species and habitats for 2000 and 2010, which will be published in 1995, European Nature Conservation Year.

8.7 English Nature has extended its Species Recovery Programme to include 20 vulnerable species, and its Wildlife Enhancement Scheme now covers 5000 hectares. The new Reserves Enhancement Scheme helps voluntary conservation organisations with the costs of managing Sites of Special Scientific Interest (SSSIs). Over £1 million will be spent on these schemes in 1993-94.

8.8 The Government has made significant progress on the designation of Special Protection Areas (SPAs) under the EC Birds Directive and Ramsar Convention. In 1993, a further 14 SPAs and 11 Ramsar sites were designated in the UK. In addition, one existing SPA and two Ramsar sites were extended. The UK has now designated 77 SPAs and 70 Ramsar sites - the latter more than any other contracting party to the Convention. The Government is now working on an accelerated designation programme.

8.9 The Government expects to publish a Planning Policy Guidance note (PPG) on nature conservation in 1994, which will describe the main obligations under domestic and international law and how the Government's objectives will be reflected in development plans. In 1993, the Government issued a consultation paper on the changes needed to ensure that the obligations under the Habitats Directive are met. A principal objective of the Directive is the creation of 'Natura 2000', a network of protected sites, to ensure that rare and endangered habitats and species can survive in their natural range.

8.10 The list of species protected under the Wildlife and Countryside Act 1981 was extended in October 1992 to include the Lagoon sea slug, 23 species of moss and 10 lichens. The UK ratified the Agreement on the Conservation of Bats in Europe in

September 1992. The Department of the Environment is providing the Secretariat to the Agreement for the first three years.

8.11 Following recent public interest in the protection of the coast, the Government issued consultation papers to assess arrangements for regulating development and other activities below the low water mark and considered options for coastal management plans. Lundy was designated a Marine Nature Reserve (MNR) and work continues on a number of other MNRs, including the Menai Strait and Bardsey Island.

8.12 The UK played a leading role in negotiations on new EC Regulations to implement the Convention on International Trade in Endangered Species of Wild Fauna and Flora (CITES) (see Chapter 1).

INTEGRATING ENVIRONMENTAL AND ECONOMIC ACTIVITY IN RURAL AREAS

Rural Development

8.13 The Rural Development Commission (RDC) is taking forward a number of schemes to encourage the diversification of the rural economy. The RDC has reviewed its priority Rural Development Areas in the light of new data. The new designations - which cover 7% of the population and around 35% of the land area of England - will enable resources to be focused more

The Government published *Biodiversity: the UK Action Plan* **in 1994**

Revised Rural Development Areas will enable resources to be focused more closely on areas with greatest need

Cockaynes Wood, Essex. Rural Action restoration work in progress

closely on areas with the greatest need. The RDC's Countryside Employment programme, which helps areas vulnerable to changes in agriculture, is now in operation in three pilot areas. The RDC continues to support the Rural Action scheme (see Box). It extended its Redundant Building Grant scheme in February 1993 and also launched a package of measures to help village shops. In February 1994, the Department of the Environment launched Rural Challenge, a new RDC competition designed to stimulate innovative partnerships and approaches to social and economic development in less prosperous rural areas.

8.14 New Government measures have recently been introduced to achieve a more co-ordinated and flexible approach to economic development at a local level throughout England. A Single Regeneration Budget, which came into operation in April 1994, will bring together 20 existing programmes for regeneration and economic development which are currently administered by five Government Departments. At the same time, the existing network of Government Regional Offices will be brought together and will administer the Single Regeneration Budget locally. English Partnerships, the new regeneration agency, will work alongside these programmes to promote the development of vacant, derelict and contaminated land.

8.15 EC Structural Funds are intended to reduce regional disparities in economic prosperity. New regulations, agreed in July 1993, introduced a new Objective 5b, concerning the development of rural areas. The criteria for eligibility as an Objective 5b area include a low GDP, a high share of agricultural employment, peripherality and low population density.

8.16 New Objective 5b areas eligible for assistance were designated by the European Commission in January 1994 on the basis of proposals by the Government of each Member State. The total UK population coverage of 2.84 million represents a slight increase over the original bid. The allocation to these areas for 1994-99 is 817 mecu (£580 million) at 1994 prices.

8.17 Structural Funds may be devoted to environmental projects which contribute to economic development. The revised regulations also provide for a greater level of integration of environmental aspects into Structural Funds procedures. The environmental implications of proposals need to be taken into account at an early stage in the formulation of the relevant rural development plans.

8.18 The Department of Transport's Village Speed Control working group (VISP) is currently monitoring a range of measures on trunk and county roads to reduce speeds. A final report will be published in spring 1994.

Agriculture

8.19 The commitment to pursue

environmental protection as part of the 1992 CAP reform agreement has been followed through in a number of areas. In July 1993, the UK submitted its plans for implementing the Agri-Environment Regulation to the European Commission. Under the plans, expenditure in England will rise to over £70 million per annum. These include proposals to expand the programmes for Environmentally Sensitive Areas (ESAs) and Nitrate Sensitive Areas (NSAs) and new measures, including schemes to:

- protect and enhance the condition of heather and other shrubby moorland;

- promote the creation and improvement of a range of valuable wildlife habitats (eg water fringes);

- encourage farmers to convert to organic production methods;

- increase opportunities for public access to set-aside land and suitable farmland in Environmentally Sensitive Areas.

8.20 In addition, progress has been made in attaching environmental conditions to CAP support schemes. For example, following the introduction of non-rotational set-aside, a range of options with potential benefits for nature conservation is now available to farmers under the Arable Area Payments Scheme. Progress has also been made in the livestock sector, where the UK has secured Community powers which allow Member States to attach appropriate environmental conditions to the suckler cow premium, beef special premium and ewe premium.

8.21 Six new ESAs were launched in 1993 - in the Avon Valley, Exmoor, Lake District, North Kent Marshes, South Wessex Downs and South West Peak - more than doubling the coverage of the scheme to over 800,000 hectares. Revised, up-graded schemes were introduced for the five ESAs originally established in 1988. Preparatory work was undertaken on a further six, which were launched in March 1994, bringing the total area covered by English ESAs to some 10% of agricultural land.

8.22 The success of NSAs in reducing nitrate

leaching was demonstrated in a report, published in December 1993, recording the results of monitoring over the first three years of the scheme. Free advice for farmers continued to be made available on pollution, which now includes the option of a farm waste management plan, and conservation matters. New arrangements were introduced for the provision of advice in the future. A *Code of Good Agricultural Practice for the Protection of Soil* was published in December 1993 to accompany the existing Codes on water and air protection. Assistance to farmers under the Farm and Conservation Grant Scheme continued; by September 1993, some £154 million had been paid to farmers in the UK since the Scheme was introduced in 1989. Regulations were introduced in June 1993 to ban, with limited exemptions, the burning of crop residues on agricultural land in England and Wales, which had been the cause of a significant number of nuisance complaints from the public.

Forestry

8.23 The Government published *Sustainable Forestry: The UK Programme* in January 1994, in response to the Statement of Forest Principles agreed at the Earth Summit in 1992. The publication sets out the Government's forestry policies and the action the Government is taking to meet its aims for the sustainable management of our existing forests, for expanding forest cover in the UK, and for promoting sustainable forestry worldwide.

Set-aside includes a range of options to encourage nature conservation

8.24 In June 1993, at a Ministerial conference in Helsinki on the Protection of European Forests, the Government signed resolutions to promote the sustainable management of European forests and the conservation of their biodiversity. In September 1993, the Forestry Commission announced a multi-disciplinary research programme for improving biodiversity in forests.

8.25 The Government appointed a Forestry Review Group in March 1993, including officials from interested Departments. The Group has been asked to review the effectiveness of the current incentives for forestry investment and options for the ownership and management of Forestry Commission woodlands, and to make proposals for changes to improve the delivery of the Government's forestry policy objectives. The Group will report to Ministers in early 1994.

8.26 The *House of Commons Environment Select Committee Report on Forestry and the Environment* was published in March 1993. The Government published its response in June, outlining action in many areas.

8.27 In furtherance of its policy of encouraging native species, some 15,500 hectares of broadleaves, mainly native species, and over 2500 hectares of native pinewoods, were grant-aided between October 1992 and September 1993.

8.28 The Government is supporting project teams to develop the National Forest in the Midlands, the Central Scotland Woodlands Initiative and the twelve Community Forests in England (see Box). The aim of these forests is to promote:

- the reclamation of damaged areas;
- the improvement of landscape and amenity on the urban fringe;
- the creation of forestry related employment; and
- an alternative use of agricultural land.

8.29 These initiatives all involve a partnership of local interests working through a lead team. In many areas, tree cover is very sparse. Through these projects, tree cover is expected to increase to around 30%, with most of the planting taking place in the next ten years.

8.30 A consultation paper setting out proposals for the new National Forest in the Midlands was launched in October 1993. The Forest covers 500 square kilometres of the East Midlands and will be a catalyst for economic regeneration in the area, as well as providing amenity and recreation benefits. The largest single landowner in the area, British Coal, has agreed to restore its redundant sites to forestry-related use. The Forestry Commission's Forest Enterprise has acquired land for planting within the area of the new National Forest and for the Central Scotland Woodland Initiative, which provides similar benefits in Scotland.

Forest initiatives

COMMUNITY WOODLANDS

Trees, forests and woodlands are a key part of Britain's rural heritage. To encourage the planting of new woodlands near urban centres, the Government has introduced a Community Woodland Supplement as an element of the Woodland Grant Scheme. This provides additional incentives to landowners to plant woods with opportunities for public access, to help cater for the demand for recreation from those living in towns and cities.

Since the introduction of Community Woodland Supplement in April 1992, some 1900 hectares of new woodlands in over 250 schemes have been approved for planting in Great Britain. This provides for new woodland in a third of the local authority areas in England. In Scotland, 90% of the population lives in an area where a strategic plan for creating woodlands has been agreed.

In England, the business plans for three Community Forests - the Great North Forest (Tyneside), the Forest of Mercia (South Staffordshire) and Thames Chase (East London) - have already been approved. Nine more forests are under development.

8.31 In October 1993, the National Parks and the Forestry Commission signed an agreement to conserve and extend native woodlands in National Parks, and to sponsor a conference in 1994 to review developments and promote new interest. Conservation initiatives for Caledonian pinewoods and birch are also under way in the Scottish Highlands.

8.32 The 17th national Forest Park at Gwydyr, North Wales, was opened in May 1993. Recreational use will be one of the principal management objectives of the 13,500 hectares of woodland which make up the Forest Park.

8.33 The Farm Woodland Premium Scheme was launched in April 1992. By the end of December 1993, some 2000 farmers had received approval under the scheme to plant over 13,000 hectares of woodland in the UK. Three-quarters of this area is to be planted with broadleaved trees. The scheme forms a key component of the UK national programme submitted to the EC Commission in July in accordance with Council Regulation 2080/92 on forestry measures in agriculture.

FLOOD AND COASTAL DEFENCE

8.34 The Ministry of Agriculture/Welsh Office Strategy for Flood and Coastal Defence was published in October 1993. This provides a policy framework for Government and the operating authorities and emphasises that environmental considerations should be central to decision making. In addition, further guidance for operating authorities was produced during the year to encourage the proper consideration of environmental issues during the planning, design and implementation of flood and coastal defence schemes.

CONSERVING AND IMPROVING THE LANDSCAPE AND ENCOURAGING OPPORTUNITIES FOR RECREATION

8.35 The Countryside Stewardship scheme, which offers incentives to protect English landscapes and habitats and to improve opportunities for public enjoyment of the countryside, has continued to expand. Agreements for the first three years now cover over 85,000 hectares.

8.36 The Government provided £900,000 for the first year of the Countryside Commission's new Parish Paths Partnership initiative to stimulate improvement through Parish Councils and other local groups. Sixteen local authorities had signed up to the scheme by the end of 1993. Interest from Parishes has exceeded the capacity of the scheme.

8.37 The Ministry of Defence has continued to conserve its large and varied landholding. In July 1993, it signed a joint Declaration of Intent with Scottish Natural Heritage to protect sensitive areas under its ownership in Scotland. It will shortly begin negotiations with the Countryside Council for Wales. It is currently commissioning Environmental Impact Assessments to assess the potential effects of changes in deployment on major training areas. Public access to MOD land, within the constraints of security and safety, continues to be given a high priority.

8.38 The Government completed its consultation exercise on the future of the New Forest in February 1993. It hopes to announce its proposals shortly.

8.39 Although no place was found in the Government's legislative programme to establish independent authorities to administer the National Parks, Lord Norrie has introduced a Private Peer's Bill for this purpose.

8.40 The designation of the Nidderdale Moors Area of Outstanding Natural Beauty was confirmed in January 1994. A proposal for the Tamar and Tavy Valleys, the last in the Countryside Commission's designation programme, is also expected in 1994.

REF NO	SUMMARY OF PREVIOUS WHITE PAPER COMMITMENTS	ACTION TO DATE	COMMITMENTS TO FURTHER ACTION
200	Launch Rural Action scheme in autumn 1992 and continue to develop and support the initiatives in 'Action for the Countryside' (SYR 146)	Scheme launched December 1992	
201	Continue support for Countryside Commission (7.40, SYR 147)	£45.5m provided for Countryside Commission in 1993-94	
202	Continue to monitor and develop Countryside Stewardship (SYR 147)	Countryside Stewardship scheme extended with £9.3m in 1993-94	Provide funding of £31.4m over 3 years to 1995-96
203			Establish a Biodiversity Action Plan Steering Group to oversee the development of a range of targets for biodiversity, so that they can be adopted in 1995
204	Monitor impact of Hedgerow Incentive Scheme and provide continued funding (SYR 148)	Providing funding of £5.3m over 3 years to 1995-96	
205	Give guidance to local authorities and others if Hedgerow Protection Bill approved (SYR 148)	Bill failed at Report stage May 1993	Legislate when Parliamentary time permits
206	Endorse the Countryside Commission's target to bring all public footpaths and bridleways into good order by the end of the century. Extend scheme to 25 highway authorities by 1995 (7.43, SYR 149)	16 local authorities signed up to Parish Paths Partnership scheme by end 1993. Interest from Parishes has exceeded capacity of scheme	Finance provided to allow expansion of scheme to 25 highway authorities within 3 years
207			Results of follow-up survey of condition of network in England to be available by mid-1994
208	Continue to support National Parks. Give statutory status to New Forest; establish independent National Park Authorities and introduce legislation as soon as Parliamentary timetable permits (SYR 150)	Preparatory work for legislation completed. Awaiting place in Parliamentary timetable	
209	Increase resources from the Countryside Commission to AONB management (SYR 151)	Resources directed to AONB work increased from £1.0m for 1992-93 to £1.5m for 1993-94	
210	Look at designation orders for Nidderdale Moors and Tamar and Tavy Valleys when received from the Commission (SYR 151)	Nidderdale Moors AONB confirmed early 1994	Tamar and Tavy AONB Designation Order expected 1994
211	Work towards better arrangements for common land management and access and legislate when Parliamentary time allows (7.59, SYR 152)	Informal consultations begun on management and registration issues	

REF NO	SUMMARY OF PREVIOUS WHITE PAPER COMMITMENTS	ACTION TO DATE	COMMITMENTS TO FURTHER ACTION
212	Support reorganised nature conservation agencies in all their nature conservation functions (7.63, SYR 153)	Total funding in 1993-4 of £93.8m, comprising £37.9m for English Nature, £36.1m for Scottish Natural Heritage and £19.8m for Countryside Council for Wales	
213	Ensure that UK meets deadline to have in place provisions necessary for implementation of EC Habitats Directive (SYR 154)	Consultation paper on implementation proposals issued October 1993	Transposition Regulation to be in place by June 1994
214	Develop criteria for site selection under EC Habitats Directive; submit UK's national list to European Commission by June 1995 (SYR 154)	Consultations in progress with Joint Nature Conservation Committee over elaboration of site selection criteria	Commence consultation on national list sites by June 1995
215	Work towards designating more Marine Nature Reserves (7.69, SYR 158)	Second round of consultations on proposed Menai Straits MNR completed	Prepare management plan for Lundy MNR. Proceed with work on proposed Lleyn Peninsula MNR
216	Consider whether to extend Marine Consultation Area scheme concept to all British waters as well as Scotland (7.69, SYR 157)	Proposals withdrawn due to improvements in arrangements for protection and management	
217	Provide special protection for threatened species (7.70, SYR 155)	A further 78 species of plants and 13 animals given statutory protection in October 1992 UK ratified Agreement on the Conservation of Bats in Europe in September 1992 and provided interim Secretariat	Provide Secretariat from when Agreement came into force in January 1994 and convene first conference of the Parties in 1995
218	Continue to Support EN's Species Recovery Scheme. 3rd quinquennial review to be held in 1996 (SYR 155)	Species Recovery Scheme budget in 1993-4 is £250,000 and supports projects for 20 species. A small grants programme supports other species work	
219	Support Heritage Coast initiatives. Promote management plans for reclamation and conservation. Review powers to regulate activities below low water mark. Develop a national strategy for flood and coastal defences (SYR 156)	Discussion papers issued in October 1993 on regulating activities below low water mark and scope and form of coastal management plans. Strategy for flood and coastal defence in England and Wales published October 1993	Publish response to discussion papers during 1994
220	Continue to work through the Rural Development Commission to promote enterprise and economic activity in the countryside (7.33, SYR 160)	RDC's revised priority areas map approved. Areas eligible for Redundant Building Grant extended. New package of assistance launched for village shops. Rural Challenge initiative launched	
221	Village Speed Control working group to report on study on reducing speeds in villages early 1993 (SYR 192) (DOT)	Village Speed Control working group monitoring range of measures installed on trunk roads and county roads	Results to be given in final report in spring 1994

REF NO	SUMMARY OF PREVIOUS WHITE PAPER COMMITMENTS	ACTION TO DATE	COMMITMENTS TO FURTHER ACTION
222			Follow-up schemes to Village Speed Control study to be undertaken in 1994 on a number of trunk roads (DOT)
223	Develop a new strategy with countryside agencies through Environmental Action Fund (SYR 161)	£4m offered to national voluntary organisations under Environmental Action Fund	
224	Seek further integration of environmental considerations into agricultural measures in reform of CAP. Press European Commission for proposals which reflect Council of Agriculture Ministers' agreement (7.20, SYR 162-3,168) (MAFF)	At UK insistence, EC has committed itself to pursuing requirements of environmental protection as part of CAP. Beef regime reformed to include stocking density limits and a payment to reward extensive beef production. Specific UK pressure secured EC provisions which allow Member States to attach environmental conditions to the suckler cow premium, beef special premium and ewe premium	Press the European Commission to reflect EC commitment in future proposals. Consult interested parties on appropriate environmental conditions to be attached to suckler cow premium, beef special premium and ewe premium
225	Consult on implementation in UK of Agri-Environment action plan (7.20, SYR 162) (MAFF)	UK Agri-Environment Programme submitted to EC for approval July 1993	Introduce Agri-Environment Programme through 1994
226	Introduce a new arable support system in autumn 1992 with management conditions for set-aside which have regard to environmental concerns (SYR 166) (MAFF)	New system introduced autumn 1992 with non-rotational option added autumn 1993, offering wide range of options designed to maximise environmental benefits	
227	Evaluate pilot Extensification Schemes for Beef and Sheep and consider wider application in the context of Common Agricultural Policy reform (7.14, SYR 164) (MAFF)	Experience of pilot Scheme fed into development of Moorland Scheme as part of Agri-Environment Programme	Introduce Moorland Scheme in 1994
228	Continue to encourage organic farming and consult on a grant scheme to assist conversion to organic farming under EC Extensification Schemes (7.21, SYR 165) (MAFF)	Agri-Environment Programme includes proposal for an Organic Aid Scheme	Launch Organic Aid Scheme
229	Review the operation of Environmentally Sensitive Areas. Follow up second round consultation and launch 6 more ESAs (7.57, SYR 167) (MAFF)	Revised second round ESAs, and six new ESAs (third round) launched January 1993. A further six ESAs (fourth round) launched in March 1994	
230	Monitor and evaluate data from Nitrate Sensitive Areas to guide decisions on the implementation of EC Nitrate Directive. Final report on NSA scheme to be produced in 1996. Socio-economic monitoring to be carried out in 1994 (7.15, SYR 169) (MAFF)	Monitoring carried out in winter 1992-93. Report published. Socio-economic evaluation begun. Consultation meetings held for new round of NSAs in England	Socio-economic evaluation to be completed in 1994. Designate new Nitrate Sensitive Areas covering some 35,000 ha in 1994

REF NO	SUMMARY OF PREVIOUS WHITE PAPER COMMITMENTS	ACTION TO DATE	COMMITMENTS TO FURTHER ACTION
231	Continue to help farmers tackle pollution and conserve the countryside. through Farm and Conservation Grant Scheme (7.16, SYR 170) (MAFF)	Grants totalling £154m paid under Scheme, mainly to reduce pollution risks	
232	Continue to provide assistance to farmers for diversification through Agricultural Development and Advisory Service (7.34, SYR 171) (MAFF)	Scheme achieved objectives with over 40% of farmers now engaged in diversified activities. Free advice withdrawn April 1993. Grant aid withdrawn early 1993	
233	Review the provision of conservation advice and regularly revise guide on conservation and diversification grants (7.22, SYR 172) (MAFF)	Research commissioned into provision of conservation advice. Report published October 1993 New contractual arrangements with ADAS and FWAG introduced for the delivery from 1992-93 of free conservation advice Guide revised and reprinted as *Conservation Grants for Farmers* in March 1993	Consider report on conservation advice and implemention of main recommendations Guide to be updated in 1994
234	Publish *Code of Good Agricultural Practice on Soil* following public consultation (SYR 172) (MAFF)	Code on soil protection published December 1993, complementing codes on air and water protection published in previous two years	
235	Keep the special problems of the urban fringe under review (7.58, SYR 173) (MAFF)	Funding provided to Groundwork Trust for first two years of three-year £170,000 pilot Farmlink scheme, aimed at establishing beneficial links between farmers and local urban communities	
236	Continue to promote environmentally sensitive forestry practice (SYR 174) (FC)	Grant-aided some 15,500 hectares of broadleaved planting and 9800 hectares of conifer planting, including 2500 hectares of native pine woods Guidance on growing broadleaves for timber published March 1993 Biodiversity initiative announced and *Biodiversity in Britain's Forests* published September 1993 *Sustainable Forestry: the UK Programme* published January 1994	
237	Review current incentives for forestry investment (SYR 174) (FC)	Forestry Review Group established to review effectiveness of incentives for forestry investment	

REF NO	SUMMARY OF PREVIOUS WHITE PAPER COMMITMENTS	ACTION TO DATE	COMMITMENTS TO FURTHER ACTION
238	Publish guidelines for woodland recreation and for semi-natural woodland by end 1992 (SYR 174) (FC)	Forest recreation guidelines published September 1992. *Forests and Water Guidelines (3rd Edition)* published November 1993	
239			Publish guidance on forestry and archaeology (FC)
240	Encourage positive management of woodlands through Woodland Grant Scheme (7.29, SYR 175) (FC)	Grant aid approved for management of over 90,000 hectares of woodlands Simpler application and grant claim forms and public registers of applications for Woodland Grant Scheme introduced May 1993	
241	Support the development of new forestry initiatives, as in Central Scotland, Community Forests and National Forest (7.30, SYR 176) (FC)	259 grant aid applications approved for planting community woodlands covering 1900 hectares Conference to promote woodlands in and around towns in England and Wales held August 1993 Agreement signed in October 1993 to conserve and extend native woodlands in National Parks 17th national Forest Park created in Gwydyr Forest, North Wales, June 1993 Initiatives to regenerate native pinewoods and birchwoods launched October 1993 Guidance on creating new native woodlands published January 1994	Publish guidance for managing all types of semi-natural woodlands in 1994
242			Publish national guidelines on sustainable forestry in 1994 (FC)
243			Hold conference to promote management and extension of native woodlands in National Parks in autumn 1994 (FC)
244			Hold conference on the marketing of hardwood timber in spring 1994 (FC)
245			Prepare guidance on forest road design in 1994 (FC)
246			Implement forest design plans in Forestry Commission forests (FC)

REF NO	SUMMARY OF PREVIOUS WHITE PAPER COMMITMENTS	ACTION TO DATE	COMMITMENTS TO FURTHER ACTION
247	Consider proposals by project teams for establishment of National and Community forests (SYR 176) (FC)	Consultation launched on proposed land use strategy for area within new National Forest October 1993. Business plans for three Community Forests launched August 1993	Agree business plan for National Forest. Consider business plans for a further 9 Community Forests
248	Issue guidance on indicative forestry strategies to LAs and National Park Authorities in England and Wales (SYR 176) (FC)	*Guidance on Indicative Forestry Strategies for England and Wales* published December 1992	
249	Set up advisory panel for native woodlands in Scottish Highlands in autumn 1992 (SYR 176) (FC)	Advisory Panel established October 1992	
250	Monitor operation of environmental safeguards and review position each year to ensure Farm Woodland Premium Scheme continues to operate in an environmentally beneficial way (7.28, SYR 177) (MAFF)	By December 1993, some 2000 applications to plant over 13,000 hectares (75% broadleaves) had been approved in UK. Scheme continues to operate in an environmentally beneficial way	

8. COUNTRYSIDE AND WILDLIFE

75

9 TOWNS AND CITIES

HIGHLIGHTS

Unified approach to regeneration through new single budget

New regeneration body, English Partnerships, launched

Twelfth Urban Development Corporation created

New 'package approach' to urban transport funding

Over 1100 hectares of derelict land treated by Groundwork Trusts

9.1 Over the last year, the Government has continued to develop its strategy for improving the urban environment as part of its wider objective of improving all aspects of urban living. The Government announced the Single Regeneration Budget, which came into operation in April 1994, to help bring government programmes and services together at a local level. English Partnerships, a new sponsored body, was launched in November 1993 and began operating from April 1994. The European Regional Development Fund remains a significant source of funding for environmental improvement. The voluntary sector also continues to play a key part in improving urban areas. Under the new 'package approach', local authorities are drawing up integrated transport strategies, which focus on managing the demand for car travel in urban areas and promoting alternative methods of transport.

IMPROVING THE URBAN ENVIRONMENT

9.2 The Government announced on 4 November 1993 that, from April 1994, it would bring together into a Single Regeneration Budget 20 existing programmes for regeneration and economic development in England currently managed by the Departments of Environment, Employment, Trade and Industry, the Department for Education and the Home Office. At the same time, the existing network of Government Regional Offices would be brought together to administer the existing range of main housing, transport, enterprise and training programmes and the new budget locally. This will give local communities power over decisions on local regeneration and development measures. It will also help to provide flexible support for regeneration and development in a way that meets local needs and priorities, and should ensure that full account is taken of local environmental concerns in formulating regeneration strategies.

English Partnerships

9.3 English Partnerships, set up in statute as the Urban Regeneration Agency, is a key new body in the Government's regeneration strategy. It will promote the development of vacant, derelict and contaminated land throughout England, bring land and buildings back into productive use, stimulate local enterprise, create job opportunities and improve the environment. It will act primarily as an enabler, working in partnership with the public, private and voluntary sectors. On its launch in November 1993, English Partnerships took over City Grant; it will incorporate Derelict Land Grant and English Estates in spring 1994, when it will be brought into full operation.

9.4 There have been 380 City Grant projects since its inception in 1988, of which 290 have either been completed or are under construction. A recent evaluation of City Grant by external consultants concluded that the programme generated significant environmental benefits, with all projects contributing to improvements on their respective sites and areas.

9.5 Since 1991, Derelict Land Grant (DLG) has continued to be used for development. However, since 1991, it has been increasingly used to reclaim land which is either unsightly, or poses a threat to public health and safety or to the environment. In 1992-93, 77% of land reclaimed was for 'soft end' use, such as woodland, compared with 54% in 1987-88.

City Challenge

9.6 The 31 City Challenge partnerships, which involve co-operation between local authorities, the private sector and local communities, continue co-ordinated programmes to tackle comprehensively the environmental, economic and social problems of local areas. The Government provided £232.5 million funding for City Challenge in 1993-94.

Urban Development Corporations

9.7 A twelfth Urban Development Corporation (UDC), Plymouth, was set up in 1993. All twelve UDCs are pursuing programmes of land reclamation as part of their wider aims of regenerating their designated areas. By March 1993, they had restored over 2150 hectares and the reclamation of a further 235 hectares is planned for 1993-94.

Reclaiming derelict and contaminated land, a key role for English Partnerships

Lavender Pond, London Docklands. An ecological park providing an educational facility for local children

9.8 Many UDCs promote environmental improvements such as cleaning docks and canals and opening up riverside walkways. Programmes include the Tees Barrage, which will help clean up the River Tees, and tree planting initiatives. London Docklands alone has planted around 100,000 trees during its lifetime, and Sheffield is a partner in setting up the South Yorkshire Community Forest.

Housing and the Environment

9.9 The Government's Estate Action and Housing Action Trust programmes are being brought together with other programmes under the new Single Regeneration Budget from April 1994.

9.10 The Government continues to provide extra funding for local authorities to restore run-down housing estates through Estate Action. Estate Action schemes provide physical, environmental, management, social and economic improvements. In 1992-93, environmental improvements accounted for 20% of the total budget.

9.11 One of the objectives of the five Housing Action Trusts (HATs) currently established in Hull, Waltham Forest, Liverpool, Birmingham and Tower Hamlets is the improvement of the general environment of the areas in which they operate. All HATs attach great importance to energy efficiency initiatives.

77

The Clarences, Stockton-on-Tees. Housing improvements supported by Teesside Development Corporation and the Department of Environment's Estate Action Programme.

Fly tipping on the urban fringe, one of the problems being tackled by the Groundwork Trusts.

9.12 Under the new system of grants to renovate run-down private housing introduced in 1990, over 90% of expenditure now goes on mandatory grants to deal with unfit housing. Responding to the pressures of a demand-led system for grant assistance is placing increasing financial pressures on local authorities. The Government is currently reviewing the system. So far, 50 Renewal Areas have been declared by 33 local authorities.

European Community funding for environmental measures

9.13 The European Regional Development Fund (ERDF) jointly funds measures which include environmental improvement schemes. ERDF assistance comes within the framework of the EC's economic programmes. New EC Regulations agreed in 1993 require proposals to be assessed according to sustainable development principles. Total ERDF funding for England is expected to be in the region of £300 million in 1994, rising to £500 million in 1999.

Voluntary sector

9.14 Voluntary effort plays a key part in work to improve urban areas. In 1992-93, the Groundwork Trusts treated over 1100 hectares of derelict land and more than 33,000 volunteers and 77,000 children worked on 4400 environmental projects in England.

9.15 In 1993, Groundwork started work in London by establishing Trusts in Camden and Hackney. A Trust was also approved for Birmingham. This brought the number of operational Trusts to a total of 32 in England and Wales.

9.16 The Royal Society for Nature Conservation, supported by the Department of the Environment, is continuing work on the Environment City programme. Four cities, Leeds, Leicester, Middlesbrough and Peterborough, have now been selected to test theories of sustainability and their experiences will be shared with other towns and cities. A review of the programme was published in 1993.

Trees in towns

9.17 The Government continues to promote the planting and management of trees through grants for urban regeneration and support for voluntary organisations. Two major research reports, *Action for London's Trees* and *Trees in Towns*, were published in October and November 1993, and provide information about the stock and condition of trees in English towns. These were followed up by regional seminars with local authorities and voluntary groups on the reports' findings, as a prelude to developing amenity tree policy in 1994. The London Tree Forum was inaugurated in February 1994 to share experience of managing London's trees among its Boroughs.

TRANSPORT IN URBAN AREAS

9.18 The Government has changed the way in which it funds transport spending by local authorities in urban areas. Under the new 'package approach', authorities bidding for Government funds submit strategic programmes which cover all forms of transport, including walking and cycling. These programmes should encourage people to use alternatives to the car by improving public transport facilities and by restricting parking and car access to sensitive areas.

ENVIRONMENTAL ASSESSMENT OF BUILDINGS

In 1990, the first version of the Building Research Establishment Environmental Assessment Method for Buildings (BREEAM) was introduced to cover new offices. Over 1.2 million square metres of office space has since been assessed under this voluntary scheme. Coverage was extended in 1991 to include homes and superstores. In April 1993, the Secretary of State for the Environment launched a new version for existing office buildings.

BREEAM provides a cost-effective way for organisations to reduce the impact of their buildings on the environment and can help fulfil an environmental policy or improve the marketability of a building. Typically, a BREEAM assessment will happen during design, alterations, refits and refurbishment and indicate to the developer, landlord or occupant where improvements can be made.

Organisations can apply for a BREEAM assessment, which provides an authoritive record of a building's environmental performance. A BREEAM certificate covers:

Global issues, including CO_2 emissions, energy policies and use of timber from sustainable sources;

Local issues, including water conservation, access to public transport and noise emissions;

Indoor issues, including lighting, air quality and radon.

As around half UK CO_2 emissions are caused by the energy used in providing heat, light, hot water and other services to buildings, BREEAM assessments are a practical step to encourage lower energy use and reduce CO_2 levels.

9.19 There are a number of other transport initiatives:

- the Department of Transport will continue to encourage local authorities to make appropriate provisions for cycling and to assist them with technical guidance. Research into the Cycle Routes programme was published in September 1993;

- the Department of Transport has introduced Traffic Calming Regulations. These enable a wider range of physical measures to help reduce vehicle speeds and improve drivers' behaviour in sensitive locations, such as residential areas or near schools;

- the Traffic Director for London is developing a network of priority (red) routes in London designed to assist the movement of traffic (particularly buses), reduce congestion and improve the environment;

- the Department of Transport's Bypass Demonstration Project is entering its third year. Schemes have been implemented in three of the six project towns and work is in progress in the others. The final report containing guidance material derived from the Project will be issued in 1995.

9.20 City congestion charging - a charge to drive in congested urban areas otherwise known as urban road pricing - is potentially another important instrument open to local authorities. Legislation would be needed to introduce it. There remains, however, a great deal of work to be done before the feasibility and impact of schemes can be established. The Government is continuing its research into congestion charging in London. This programme is due to be completed by the end of 1994. Local authorities have also been studying the possibilities of city congestion charging in Bristol, Cambridge and Edinburgh.

The Government is reviewing with local authorities the scope for congestion charging

REF NO	SUMMARY OF PREVIOUS WHITE PAPER COMMITMENTS	ACTION TO DATE	COMMITMENTS TO FURTHER ACTION
251	Co-ordinate City Grant and Derelict Land Grant programmes prior to establishment of Urban Regeneration Agency in second half of 1993, subject to passage of legislation (SYR 181)	Urban Regeneration Agency launched under the name of English Partnerships to promote regeneration through the reclamation, development or redevelopment of derelict or vacant land and buildings	EP will come into full operation from April 1994, bringing together City Grant and Derelict Land Grant with English Estates from DTI
252	Continue to monitor and support funding for environmental improvement in urban areas (SYR 182)	In 1992-93, forecast spend on environmental improvements under Urban Programme is £65.6m. From May 1988 to October 1993, 790 hectares regenerated under City Grant. 1522 hectares reclaimed in 1992-93 by Derelict Land Grant. Results of Derelict Land Survey to be published mid-1994	
253	UDCs to reclaim a further 235 hectares in 1992-93 (SYR 182)	Twelfth UDC – Plymouth – set up in 1993 to regenerate its area. By March 1993, UDCs had reclaimed over 2150 hectares. UDCs to reclaim a further 235 hectares in 1993-94	
254	Continue to develop City Challenge initiative (8.37, SYR 183)	All 31 City Challenge partnerships have started work on 5-year programmes in accordance with approved action plans. All plans contain specific environmental improvement measures as part of their wider regeneration strategies	
255			Single Regeneration Budget to take over 20 programmes from 5 Government Departments from April 1994. Priorities, set at local level, will reflect environmental concerns where appropriate
256	Support other specific steps to improve urban areas, including help for the expansion of the Groundwork Trust movement in England and Wales (8.45, SYR 184)	In 1993-94, establishment of 2 further Trusts approved. Groundwork allocated £6m in 1994-95	
257	Avoid creating new road capacity simply to facilitate car commuting into congested areas. Seek ways of tackling urban congestion (8.11, SYR 185) (DOT)	Research into congestion charging in London under way. Reviewing, with local authorities, the scope for congestion charging in other cities, including Bristol, Cambridge and Edinburgh	
258			Report on congestion charging in London to be completed by end 1994 (DOT)
259	Issue guidance to the London Boroughs and apply the new parking restrictions in London (FYR p123, SYR 186) (DOT)	First Orders made in summer 1993, introducing new local authority parking enforcement arrangements in specified Boroughs	All London authorities to be operating new arrangements in respect of enforcement of controls at designated parking places from July 1994. DOT to make Orders as necessary

REF NO	SUMMARY OF PREVIOUS WHITE PAPER COMMITMENTS	ACTION TO DATE	COMMITMENTS TO FURTHER ACTION
260	Issue guidance on control of pavement parking and voucher parking schemes (8.12, SYR 186) (DOT)	Advice to local authorities on voucher parking, best practice and experience to date issued in February 1993. Guidance on pavement parking issued December 1993	
261	Continue to support public transport investment and examine the case for funding light rail schemes (8.19, 5.59, SYR 187-8) (DOT)	DOT investing £2.3bn in public transport in 1993-94. Supported investment in Manchester Metrolink, South Yorkshire Supertram and Leicester–Derbyshire Ivanhoe line	
262	Continue to assist the development of safe and convenient cycling networks and publish results of cycle route research (8.16, SYR 189) (DOT)	Final results of Cycles Routes Programme published in September 1993	
263	Develop a 'Red Route' network in London (8.14, SYR 190) (DOT)	Funding has been given to London Boroughs to develop a complementary network of bus priority measures	Local plans of priority (red) route measures for each part of the network to be ready by June 1994
264	Continue examination of transport and land use interactions to help identify network improvements which can increase choice and reduce congestion (5.61, SYR 191) (DOT)		Surveys of trip attraction rates at different land use sites to be completed by 1996
265	Set up database, using data from 1991 London Area Transport Survey, by mid-1993 (SYR 191) (DOT)	Time series database combining 1971 and 1981 surveys completed	
266	Clarify regulations relating to highway authorities' powers to install traffic calming measures (SYR 192) (DOT)	Traffic Calming Regulations came into effect in August 1993	
267	Provide for more effective direction signs (SYR 192) (DOT)		Revised Traffic Signs Regulations to be published 1994, subject to approval of Parliament
268	Provide bypasses where appropriate to relieve towns of through traffic (8.18, SYR 194) (DOT)	9 new bypasses completed in 1993 and 14 started	Further 5 bypasses due for completion in 1994
269	Disseminate results of Bypass Demonstration Project (8.18, SYR 194) (DOT)	Schemes implemented in three of six project towns. Two interim reports published	Project due to be completed in 1994. Final report in 1995

9. TOWNS AND CITIES

10 HERITAGE

HIGHLIGHTS

Major statement on DNH policy for the heritage

National Lottery etc Act: 20% of money for good causes to help preserve the national heritage

Royal Parks Agency established

Wide consultation on planning controls in conservation areas and Planning Policy Guidance for historic buildings

10.1 The aims of the new Department of National Heritage (DNH) were set out by Peter Brooke, the Secretary of State, in his speech, 'Shaping our Heritage', at the Royal Fine Art Commission on 3 December 1992:

"The Department of National Heritage aims to conserve, nurture, enhance and make more widely accessible the rich and varied cultural heritage of the countries of the United Kingdom."

10.2 The Department seeks to create the conditions which will preserve ancient sites, monuments and historic buildings, and improve their accessibility for study and enjoyment.

PROPERTIES CARED FOR BY THE GOVERNMENT

10.3 Twenty-six Government Departments and agencies are already implementing the Plan of Action for the care of the Government's historic estate developed by DOE's Conservation Unit. Their annual reports have, for the first time, provided an overview of the Government's historic buildings and this was submitted to the Secretary of State for the Environment in December 1993. The current Efficiency Scrutiny of the management of the Government civil estate examines specifically how management can most effectively secure the protection of its historic buildings, and whether present disposal arrangements are effective in securing the long-term future of historic buildings which are surplus to Government requirements.

10.4 The Historic Royal Palaces Agency opened the Tudor rooms at Hampton Court Palace in July 1993 and the new display of the Crown Jewels at the Tower of London in March 1994. Much of the Royal Armouries collection will move to a new museum now being constructed in Leeds, due to open in 1996.

10.5 A conference was held in 1993 to discuss the findings of the review of St James's, Green and Regent's Parks. The Government will use this to frame new policy objectives for these parks.

The Tudor rooms at Hampton Court Palace opened in July 1993

PROMOTING ENJOYMENT AND UNDERSTANDING OF THE HERITAGE

10.6 In 1993, for the first time, DNH sponsored European Heritage Days in conjunction with the Civic Trust and local amenity societies. European Heritage Days highlight the European architectural heritage by providing access to historic buildings not normally open to the public. The pilot scheme enabled 10,000 visitors to enjoy the event on 11 and 12 September.

10.7 DNH's Access Initiative was launched in June 1993 to widen access to all areas of heritage, sport, art and cultural activity. A series of conferences is being held to assess regional views on access and how this might be improved.

10.8 In 1992-93, English Heritage (EH) published 99 bulletins, leaflets, magazines, guidebooks and educational and general history publications. Its 'Framing Opinions' campaign drew attention to the need for sympathetic treatment of traditional doors and windows when historic houses are repaired. EH's Education Service completed a series of teacher-training videos which promoted the effective use of the historic environment in National Curriculum subjects. The Fort Brockhurst Training Centre, run in conjunction with the University of Bournemouth, was opened in June 1993 to provide courses on practical conservation for those in the building industry, conservationists and EH's own staff. As part of its response to Industrial Heritage Year, EH is producing a report on grant aid and assistance to industrial monuments and buildings, with illustrated case histories.

TOURISM AND THE ENVIRONMENT

10.9 During the UK Presidency of the EC at the end of 1992, DNH staged an international conference - 'Tourism and the Environment: Challenges and Choices for the 90s' - reflecting the UK's leadership in sustainable tourism policies and practices. The Department has continued to encourage and, through the English Tourist Board, support the spread of sustainable tourism. This has included setting up local visitor management initiatives, such as the Peak Tourism Partnership, and supporting other industry-led measures like the British Home and Holiday Parks Association's Environmental Code.

ENCOURAGING PRIVATE SECTOR EFFORTS AND PROVIDING FINANCIAL ASSISTANCE

10.10 In October 1992, English Heritage announced its Forward Strategy for the 1990s. The Strategy includes plans to concentrate resources where most needed and to raise private sector funds to widen support for key projects. The message was one of partnership between Government, local authorities and communities, and the private sector.

10.11 Partnership is also central to the National Lottery. The National Heritage Memorial Fund, which received a £12 million Government grant in 1993-94, will also distribute 20% of the Lottery funds available for good causes to help the acquisition or preservation of the best of the national heritage.

IDENTIFYING AND RECORDING THE HERITAGE

10.12 During 1992-93, DNH, on English Heritage's advice, added 1762 entries to the list of buildings of special architectural or

Trainees at work on the Fort Brockhurst 'ruinette'

Buxton Crescent was saved from decay through the joint efforts of central and local government with English Heritage and the NHMF

The Alexandra Road Estate, LB Camden, listed grade II* in August 1993

historic interest. Full geographic reviews of existing statutory lists are no longer planned, as initial results have demonstrated that a thematic programme may be more effective. In the Monuments Protection Programme, 655 entries were added to the schedule in 1992-93. The Buildings at Risk survey continues and by March 1993, 123,000 buildings had been surveyed.

10.13 In September 1993, a major DNH-led programme for the computerisation of the statutory lists was announced. This will cost £3 million over 3 years and will greatly improve access to the information contained in the lists.

10.14 The Royal Commission on the Historical Monuments of England established its new National Monuments Record database (MONARCH) in April 1993, at a cost of some £250,000. MONARCH brings together information on 200,000 archaeological sites and historic buildings, for use by professional and private researchers.

ADVICE AND REGULATION

10.15 Draft Planning Policy Guidance, setting out national policy for historic buildings and conservation areas, was published by DOE in July 1993. The PPG will be published later this year. Consultation also took place on the case for stronger controls over minor development in conservation areas.

THE INTERNATIONAL CONTEXT

10.16 DNH continues to play a full role in the work of the Council of Europe, including offering technical assistance on the preservation of the heritage to the countries of Eastern Europe. In April 1993, DNH organised a workshop in Budapest on the conservation of historic buildings under the 'Know How Fund' arrangements.

REF NO	SUMMARY OF PREVIOUS WHITE PAPER COMMITMENTS	ACTION TO DATE	COMMITMENTS TO FURTHER ACTION
270	Government to ensure the properties it manages are kept in good condition and open to visitors. DNH to fund a building programme for national museums and galleries (9.8, SYR 195)	26 Departments and agencies now signed up to Plan of Action for Care of Government Historic Buildings and have produced first annual reports. Over 1500 listed buildings on Government estate so far identified	Publish annual Conservation Report for the Government's Historic Estate. Complete implementation of Efficiency Scrutiny of the Management of the Government Civil Estate, with special reference to historic building issues
271	DNH to work to improve the environment in the Royal Parks (9.8, SYR 195)	Royal Parks Agency established April 1993	Frame new policy objectives for St James's, Green and Regent's Parks. Develop plans for improvement of area in front of Buckingham Palace
272	Promote the educational value of sites (9.13, SYR 196)	Supported English Heritage in promoting the educational value of sites, including completion of Fort Brockhurst training centre in June 1993	Through English Heritage publishing and training, promote the greater historic environment in curriculum studies in further and higher education
273	Develop proposals for improved presentation of treasures in the Tower of London (9.13, SYR 196)	Historic Royal Palaces Agency opened new display of Crown Jewels in Tower of London March 1994	
274	Following creation of DNH, make statement on Government policy for the heritage (SYR 197)	Secretary of State made policy statement in December 1992	
275	Ask the Archaeological Diving Unit (ADU) to identify more wreck sites for protection (9.36, SYR 198)	ADU investigating more historic wreck sites	
276	Take initiatives to raise awareness about the importance of historic wreck sites (SYR 198)	Over 1000 guidance notes issued explaining wreck laws	Implement programme of interpretive panels near protected sites; 6 to be installed by summer 1994
277	Stage international conference on 'Tourism and the Environment' during UK Presidency of EC to exchange information and disseminate good practice (SYR 179,199)	International conference held in late 1992	
278	Continue tax relief and grants to support the heritage (9.20, 9.22, SYR 200) (HMT/DNH)	National Lottery etc Act passed to provide for additional funding for the heritage	Work with National Heritage Memorial Fund to establish systems for distribution of Lottery funds, and with English Heritage on examination of fiscal mechanisms to help the heritage
279	Make grants available to help cathedrals; ask English Heritage to target grant programmes on defined areas of need (9.23, SYR 201)	Grants offered through English Heritage of at least £4m a year under the cathedral repairs grant scheme	
280	Complete review of the early resurvey results on historic buildings by 1992 (9.32, SYR 202)	Listing policy re-examined in light of initial results of review	Develop listing policy for historic buildings on basis of current thematic research

REF NO	SUMMARY OF PREVIOUS WHITE PAPER COMMITMENTS	ACTION TO DATE	COMMITMENTS TO FURTHER ACTION
281	Commission a register of battlefield sites to inform planning decisions; ask English Heritage to develop a register of historic landscapes (9.13, SYR 203)	English Heritage have consulted on proposals for battlefields and historic landscapes registers	English Heritage to produce framework for action during 1994
282	Support introduction of computer software for sites and monuments records (9.30-31, SYR 204)	New National Monuments Record database (MONARCH) operational April 1993. Report published by Royal Commission on Historical Monuments of England on effectiveness and future role of national and local sites and monuments records	
283	Support completion of initial record of underwater sites by 1995 (SYR 204)	Underwater record on target	
284	Publish for consultation new guidance on historic buildings and conservation areas (9.34-35, SYR 205)	Draft PPG published July 1993. Major consultation on planning controls in conservation areas	Final PPG to be published 1994
285	Review ecclesiastical exemption (SYR 205)	Ecclesiastical exemption reviewed and to be withdrawn for denominations which have no adequate internal arrangements for protection of historic buildings	Order effecting partial withdrawal of ecclesiastical exemption to be laid spring 1994
286	Legislate, as Parliamentary time permits, to implement proposals for new controls for archaeological sites (9.37, SYR 206)		

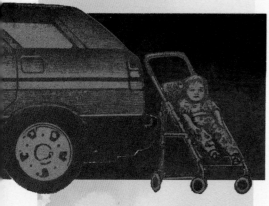

11 AIR QUALITY

HIGHLIGHTS

New reduction targets for sulphur dioxide emissions

National strategy published to reduce volatile organic compounds

Authorisations from local authorities and HMIP now control air emissions from over 9000 industrial sources

66% of public places now have a policy on smoking

11.1 During 1993, almost all indicators of air quality, including measurements from the Government's expanding air quality networks, showed improvement over 1990. Surveys of UK tree health and surface water acidification pointed to only minimal improvement, but these are also influenced by a range of other factors. However, concern increased during the year over air pollution as one of the factors affecting human health and the general quality of urban life. Of particular concern was the possible scale of effects of traffic-related pollutants, particularly on asthmatics and others with respiratory illness, who form an important target group in assessing the priorities for improved air quality.

THE EFFECTS BASED POLICY

11.2 The 1990 White Paper recognised that as our knowledge of air pollution improved it was right to move away from a philosophy based mainly on technology control towards a more targeted policy based on effects on health and the natural environment. This approach not only enables better assessment of priorities, but also encourages innovative approaches aimed at less burdensome means of regulatory control.

11.3 As a preliminary step, the 1990 White Paper set a target for the attainment of the existing air quality standards throughout the UK by 1993. That target has been reached. Its attainment marks the conquest of the classic air quality problems of the 1950s and 1960s, sulphur dioxide and smoke. The Clean Air Acts provided the necessary powers to identify areas at risk and apply appropriate local action. The required smokeless zones are now in place throughout the UK, and derogations from the maximum permissible SO_2 and smoke concentrations under the relevant EC Directive have been withdrawn. Annual average concentrations of smoke and SO_2 are steadily declining and have fallen by a

further 5% since 1991-92. Further regulation, such as control of the sale of unauthorised fuel in smokeless areas and control of the sulphur content of domestic fuel, therefore appears unnecessary at present, but the Government will review the need for further controls in the event of any future risk to the air quality standards.

CRITICAL LOADS

11.4 A major step towards an effects based air quality policy has been the development of the 'Critical Loads' approach to the assessment of environmental effects. The UK has played a leading part in the development of this approach, which has informed the negotiations for a second Sulphur Protocol under the UNECE Long Range Transboundary Air Pollution Convention, designed to tackle the problem of Acid Rain. The approach, which will be developed further, has provided the basis for a strategy to reduce future damage by focusing on the areas of Europe which are most sensitive to acid deposition. The Protocol is expected to be agreed and opened for signature by June 1994. This approach will now be used to inform work on further Protocols, first on emissions of oxides of nitrogen (NOx), and then on other transboundary pollutants.

11.5 The first Sulphur Protocol in 1985 required a uniform 30% cut in 1980 emissions by 1993. Although the UK, among others, did not sign the Protocol, it is among the countries which expects to meet that target. In the course of the negotiation of the new Protocol, the UK has indicated its willingness to reduce sulphur emissions further, by 70% by 2005, and agreed in principle an 80% target for 2010 against the same baseline. The UK expects to sign the new Protocol on this basis. These are challenging targets and represent a substantial advance on UK expectations in *This Common Inheritance*. Based on current estimates of critical loads, this should enable the UK to reach the goal of substantial protection for most of the sensitive areas in the UK over the timetable of the Sustainable Development Strategy. The Government believes that these new commitments constitute a challenging timetable for the UK, but one that meets justifiable environmental goals in a cost-effective way.

New air quality standards

11.6 A further element of an effects based approach is assessment of the critical levels of air pollutants at which health effects emerge and which therefore provide a basis for setting standards. In line with the White Paper commitment, the Government's priority is to establish a full set of air quality standards for pollutants with significant health related effects. The Expert Panel on Air Quality Standards has now produced recommendations on the first two of a series of health based air quality standards as the next step towards an effects based approach. The Panel has recommended figures that should be attained now and also recommended longer term targets. The Government welcomes this approach. It believes that the UK should already accept air quality standards that protect against significant health effects. However, the more ambitious goals for air quality proposed by the Panel will assist the assessment of relative priorities between

different pollutants, allow costs and benefits to be compared and provide a more effective basis for managing air quality.

11.7 The EC is shortly to bring forward its proposals for an Air Quality Framework Directive. Provided that the principles of subsidiarity and cost-benefit analysis are fully recognised, the UK will welcome the proposals as the basis for a rational approach to air quality management in Europe.

NATIONAL AIR QUALITY STRATEGIES

11.8 Air quality management strategies have long been a part of UK environment policy. The 1956 and 1968 Clean Air Acts have provided local authorities with the powers to designate smoke control zones and control emissions of smoke and fumes from industrial premises. Since the 1990 White Paper, a number of national strategies have been developed to target action on certain pollutants.

11.9 The first was developed in 1990 to implement the EC's Large Combustion Plant Directive, dealing with emissions of SO_2 and NOx. During 1993, the Government developed a strategy with industry to reduce emissions of volatile organic compounds (VOCs), the precursors of ground level ozone. Based on existing and planned actions, the Government will

The Government believes the attainment of the existing air quality standards marks the conquest of the classic problems of the 1950s and 1960s, sulphur dioxide and smoke

The Government spent nearly £10 million in 1993-94 on research on the incidence and effects of air pollution

Photochemical smog over London. The Government intends to establish 24 enhanced monitoring sites in urban areas by 1997

meet, and indeed is likely to exceed, the target set out in the UNECE VOC Protocol of 30% reductions by 1999 on 1988 levels. This strategy was the first to consider all sources of a pollutant. It provides a possible model for the future development of UK sulphur and NOx abatement strategies, on which the Government will be consulting in due course.

11.10 A particular advantage of targeted strategies of this kind is that they provide a framework within which we can seek to improve the cost-effectiveness of regulatory control. For example, the Government believes that it should be possible within the strategy for sulphur emissions to redistribute the annual sulphur emission quotas between relevant undertakings, provided that the UK fulfils its international obligations. The Government will be working with industry covered by the Large Combustion Plant Directive to establish whether a suitable scheme can be drawn up to allow this, taking into account experience elsewhere in the industrialised world.

LOCAL AIR QUALITY MANAGEMENT SCHEMES

11.11 National strategies, combined with international co-operation where necessary, are most appropriate to pollution that can be transported far from its source. As best available techniques not entailing excessive cost are applied to industrial sources and

vehicle emissions, significant air quality problems should be confined to progressively more limited areas in the UK. The most cost-effective solution to such problems will depend on the particular mix of local circumstances and it may involve selective application of a wider range of tools than have previously been employed together. This suggests an important role for local air quality management plans.

11.12 The Government recognises that local air quality management plans must be tailored to the local mix of problems. They should not be constrained by a single national prescription. Nor should they be constrained by administrative boundaries. Air quality plans could involve a number of local authorities and various local authority functions, from pollution control to planning and transport. HMIP, industry and local residents would need to be involved.

11.13 As a first stage, the Government will look to the possibilities of voluntary approaches using existing powers. Many local authorities are already developing responses appropriate to their local circumstances. The Department of the Environment will be discussing with them ways in which innovation and co-operative ventures can be encouraged. To this end, it proposes, later in 1994, to identify for support on a competitive basis experimental projects which would test ways in which tools already to hand can be brought together to improve local air quality.

BRINGING IN CLEANER TECHNOLOGY

11.14 The main instrument available for implementing national strategies and for advancing local air quality management is the introduction of new plant meeting current state-of-the-art standards. Such standards have now been agreed for the processes used by over 13,000 firms under the regulatory control regimes, IPC and LAAPC, introduced by Part I of the Environmental Protection Act 1990 and regulated by HMIP and local authorities respectively. The priority now is for firms to agree with the regulators their emission

REDUCING THE REGULATORY BURDEN: LOCAL AUTHORITY AIR POLLUTION CONTROL (LAAPC)

The Government's aim in LAAPC is to improve air quality whilst minimising the regulatory burden on industry.

The objective is to provide systems which are simple and clear and to this end, LAAPC uses a prior approval system to give industry greater certainty when planning ahead. Guidance has been issued to local authorities and business, which will be revised at least every four years. Reviews will also be undertaken from time to time to check local authority performance in implementing LAAPC. A new forum for joint DOE and industry discussion of LAAPC met for the first time in November 1993.

The regulations to determine the scope of LAAPC are currently being reviewed. The Government is considering banding the charges payable to local authorities under the Act, and a review is in hand to clarify the monitoring specifications in the guidance notes.

More generally, the Government is considering how the aims can be achieved more effectively and the regulatory burden reduced further, by the application of market-based instruments or by the encouragement of innovation.

The Secretary of State for the Environment checking car exhausts as part of the Westminster Initiative

reduction plans in accordance with established criteria, including the principle that excessive cost should not be entailed.

11.15 Further EC agreements have advanced the standards for new vehicles. By the end of 1994, all light vans, off-road vehicles and cars will need to meet emission standards securing 75% reductions on 1980s levels. In line with its commitment to public access to environmental information, the Government will be discussing with the automotive industry whether test emission figures of all new models released into the UK market can be publicly released. However, vehicle projections suggest that in some localities, pollutant concentrations will begin to increase in the future as traffic growth continues. Projections of national particulate emissions, primarily from diesels, show smaller reductions than do those of the gaseous pollutants arising from both petrol and diesel vehicles. The Government will continue to work with the industry to develop the possibilities for future clean diesel technology.

11.16 Since new vehicles still represent only a small fraction of the vehicle fleet, it is important to ensure that existing vehicles make their contribution to improving air quality and that expensive action on new vehicles does not inadvertently protract the life of existing polluting vehicles. Since a

disproportionate amount of urban air pollution comes from a small proportion of vehicles, the Government will also give priority to the further development of policies on vehicle testing and in-service checks.

INDOOR AIR QUALITY

11.17 As most people spend most of their time indoors, the quality of the indoor environment is crucial to health and well being. Babies, children, the elderly and sick are particularly vulnerable. The Department of the Environment is continuing its programme of research and monitoring of the sources and levels of air pollutants in homes. The main pollutants of concern are carbon monoxide, radon, tobacco smoke, nitrogen dioxide and allergens such as house dust mites and mould spores. The significance of the results for the health and well being of people is uncertain and will be assessed by the newly created MRC Institute for Environment and Health at Leicester University.

11.18 The Government will take appropriate action, based on this advice, to achieve a reduction in levels of pollutants in homes, for example by setting emission standards for construction and consumer products and publishing advisory guidelines for indoor air quality.

'House Dust Mites - A Step-By-Step Guide to Controlling Your Allergy' will be published by the Department of the Environment in 1994

11.19 Smoking is a significant health threat to the smoker and also to others exposed to the smoke, and is a major source of air pollution in the home and in public places. The Government's aim is that 80% of public places should be covered by effective policies on smoking by 1994. Guidance is set out in a Code of Practice on Smoking in Public Places. While the voluntary approach has many advantages, the Government will, if necessary, consider statutory measures to protect non-smoking members of the public.

11.20 In October 1993, the Government published the results of market research on smoking in public places. The research showed that 66% of places surveyed had a policy on smoking, and the number is increasing, and that four out of five people are in favour of either banning or restricting smoking in public places.

11.21 The Government has since mounted a campaign to urge managers of pubs, restaurants and cafés to introduce suitable policies on smoking. Further market research is planned for early 1994.

AIR QUALITY AND CLEANER CITIES

Rapid traffic growth, combined with domestic and industrial emissions, creates localised air pollution hotspots in urban areas throughout the world. The problems of British cities are far from the most severe, but new and imaginative approaches will be needed if health is to be protected and the quality of life in urban areas is to be improved.

The Government will set out the national strategy. But, as particular problems vary from one area to another, the Government cannot prescribe a single solution. However, it can help local authorities promote innovative air quality management programmes. Since many of the relevant powers already rest with local authorities, they are well placed to give a lead. Local policies and management plans might, for instance, include monitoring, emission inventories, experiments in traffic management and traffic calming, or voluntary campaigns to draw drivers' attention to smoky vehicles.

The Government believes that much can be achieved quickly and cheaply with local initiative and the imaginative and co-ordinated use of existing local regulatory powers, rather than large scale capital investment. In 1994, the Government will encourage a number of experimental local initiatives, which it will use to review the need for a wider range of measures for tackling air pollution at a local level.

REF NO	SUMMARY OF PREVIOUS WHITE PAPER COMMITMENTS	ACTION TO DATE	COMMITMENTS TO FURTHER ACTION
287	Issue consultation paper on integrating DOE and local authority monitoring systems in 1993 (SYR 207)	Consultation paper issued	Begin development of integrated national system
288	Continue expansion of urban network to all major cities by 1997 (SYR 56,207)	12 enhanced urban monitoring sites now established	Aim for a further 12 enhanced urban sites by 1997
289			Extend air quality bulletins to hourly update, and forecasts to take in more pollutants
290	Issue consultation document on scope of local authority air pollution control by end 1992 (SYR 208)	Consultation paper issued March 1993. Further consultation on draft Amending Regulations issued November 1993	
291			Regulations on local authority air pollution control to be made May 1994
292	Issue discussion paper on bringing pollution levels down where needed to achieve new air quality targets or guidelines in 1993 (SYR 209)	Paper issued March 1994	
293			Prepare new policy framework for local management of air quality and establish pilot programmes by autumn 1994
294	Continue substantial funding for air quality research. Manage programme to monitor and improve understanding of air pollution incidence and effects, and support policy development (FYR p132, SYR 210)	£9.9m programme in 1993-94	Mid-term independent review of programme by spring 1994
295			Set up national archive of UK air quality and emissions allowing improved free access to data from monitoring network by 1995
296	Set new standards for ground level ozone, benzene and carbon monoxide in 1993; and for sulphur dioxide, and 1,3- butadiene in 1994 (SYR 211)	Reports on benzene and ozone standards issued May 1994	Issue reports on carbon monoxide, 1,3-butadiene and sulphur dioxide by end 1994. Consider standards for nitrogen dioxide and particulates by end 1995
297			Negotiate EC Air Quality Framework Directive compatible with UK policies on air quality standards by end 1994
298			Issue consultation document on progress towards the achievement of Expert Panel on Air Quality Standards (EPAQS) targets for ozone, benzene and CO by end 1994

REF NO	SUMMARY OF PREVIOUS WHITE PAPER COMMITMENTS	ACTION TO DATE	COMMITMENTS TO FURTHER ACTION
299	Advise public on concentration and medical effects of widening range of air pollutants and identify areas for further research (SYR 212)	Committee on Medical Effects of Air Pollution reported on SO_2 in 1992 and NOx in 1993	Committee to study mixtures and report in 1994 DOE to assess personal exposure to air pollutants which affect human health; first pollutants (CO and NO_2) by end 1994
300	Support research on SO_2, NOx and CO_2 as part of Coal Research Programme (FYR p133, SYR 214) (DTI)	Programme is supporting 17 projects on SO_2 emissions from coal combustion and gasification technologies; 11 projects addressing formation mechanisms and control strategies for NOx emissions; and a project on CO_2 emissions from coal-fired plant	
301	Publish a response to the Coal Task Force report (SYR 214) (DTI)	Strategy proposed by Coal Task Force being implemented as funds permit. Coal R&D programme worth £170m now under way, with DTI contribution of £35m	Strategy Paper to be published in 1994
302	Ensure that the remaining handful of areas comply with EC smoke Directive standards by the April 1993 deadline (SYR 215)	All areas complied with smoke standard by deadline. One area exceeded sulphur dioxide standard in 1992-93	
303	Regulations to control the sale of unauthorised fuels in smoke control areas to be made by autumn 1992; and to limit the sulphur content of solid fuels for domestic use by end 1992 (11.23, SYR 216,227)	In view of decline in smoke and SO_2 levels and in emissions from domestic sources since regulations were first proposed, the need to implement further controls over such fuels will be reviewed in the event of any significant risk to the air quality standards	
304	Implement new EC controls over car emissions at end of 1992 and over heavy diesel vehicles in two stages by 1996 (FYR p43, SYR 193) (DOT)	Controls implemented 1992	Additional new limits for vans to be implemented October 1994
305	Seek early agreement to tighter EC vehicle emissions standards for implementation from 1996 (SYR 217,220) (DOT)	New controls for cars and heavy diesels in force. New limits for light commercial vehicles also adopted and implemented	Prepare UK position for next round of EC vehicle emission negotiations
306	Strengthen hydrocarbon and carbon monoxide emissions standards in line with EC legislation (5.49, SYR 218) (DOT)	Revised test procedure for emissions from light diesel engines introduced February 1994	

REF NO	SUMMARY OF PREVIOUS WHITE PAPER COMMITMENTS	ACTION TO DATE	COMMITMENTS TO FURTHER ACTION
307	Continue to help develop less polluting vehicle technology. Support collaborative research into more efficient and less polluting engine design (5.49, SYR 219) (DOT)	Continued support for research on means to retain emissions performance and advancement of engine and fuel technologies Currently examining the feasibility of conducting a series of field trials of alternative fuels for road vehicles Offered support of up to £100,000 for conversion of buses to alternative fuels Completing reviews on alternative engines and alternative fuels and fuel life cycle emissions	
308	Press EC for tougher standards for emissions from lorries and buses, increase roadside spot checks and place emphasis on emissions standards in granting goods vehicle operator licenses (11.18, SYR 221) (DOT)	EC Directive on heavy diesel emissions implemented October 1993 Published telephone contacts for public to report excessively smoking vehicles to the vehicle licensing authority	
309	Monitor implementation of smoke checks and consider increasing the stringency of the tests (SYR 221) (DOT)		Promote EC review aimed at increasing both stringency and effectiveness of new vehicle and in-use vehicle smoke tests
310	Introduce stricter roadworthiness testing standards in line with EC legislation (SYR 222) (DOT)		New standards to be introduced in 1994
311	Press EC to improve the quality of fuels and develop Government control over diesel fuel quality (11.20, SYR 223) (DOT)	Participating in EC development programme on improved fuels	
312	Ensure that power stations and other large combustion plants meet stringent EC requirements for reduced emission of pollutants which cause acid rain (11.36, SYR 224)	HMIP continuing to secure compliance with national targets of 60% SO_2 reductions by 2003, 30% NOx reductions by 1998	Begin consideration of new LCP NOx targets beyond 1998 and revised SO_2 targets
313	Prepare maps for nitrogen and ground level ozone (SYR 225)		Nitrogen report due 1994. Ozone maps due November 1994
314	Secure Sulphur Protocol acceptable to UK by 1993 (SYR 226)	Negotiations on new Protocol completed. Research continuing on timing and scale of SO_2 (and other acidifying compounds) reduction in context of ecosystem recovery	Finalise Protocol. Begin consideration of revised national strategy to 2010 following UNECE second Sulphur Protocol
315			Begin review of NOx Protocol in 1994. Ensure future emissions do not rise above 1987 level

REF NO	SUMMARY OF PREVIOUS WHITE PAPER COMMITMENTS	ACTION TO DATE	COMMITMENTS TO FURTHER ACTION
316			Agree timetable for achievement of critical loads for acidity within UNECE by 1996
317			Secure agreement to incorporate Photochemical Ozone Creating Potential (POCP) approach in renegotiation of VOC Protocol by mid 1996
318			Reduce acid emissions to a rate which is sustainable by the UK's natural environment
319	Publish strategy to control ground level ozone and volatile organic compounds for implementation autumn 1992 (SYR 228)	Consultation draft published autumn 1992. National strategy published autumn 1993	
320			Establish method for assessing compliance with UNECE VOC Protocol and national strategy
321	Work for early EC agreement on control over fuel evaporation throughout the fuel chain (SYR 229)	Agreement expected by June 1994 on EC Directive on petrol vapour recovery between refineries and petrol stations (Stage 1)	Prepare regulations to implement the Directive in UK within 12 months of adoption. Negotiate Stage 2 Directive acceptable to UK
322	Press for tough but realistic EC controls on VOC emissions from solvent using industries (SYR 230) (DOT)	UK actively participating in discussions leading towards EC Directive and pressing for controls which will encourage development and use of low-solvent products	Ensure Directive reflects subsidiarity, cost-effectiveness and other UK interests
323	Secure reduction in permitted summer-time volatility of petrol in 1994 (SYR 231) (DOT)		Aiming to implement for summer 1995; draft Regulations to be issued for consultation
324	Introduce ban on burning of crop residues in England and Wales by 1993 (SYR 232,292)	Regulations banning the burning of crop residues, with limited exemptions, introduced June 1993	
325	Market research to monitor success of *Code of Practice on Smoking in Public Places* to be undertaken in autumn 1992. Aim to ensure that at least 80% of public places are covered by effective policies by 1994 (SYR 232-3)	Results of market research published October 1993. Targeted campaign conducted early November 1993 on pubs, clubs, etc	
326			New market research planned for early 1994 to establish progress towards target
327	Keep Building Regulations under review and extend the area under which guidance on radon protection applies in the light of recommendations from National Radiological Protection Board (11.69, SYR 234)	Areas have been extended as recommended and publicity campaigns mounted	

REF NO	SUMMARY OF PREVIOUS WHITE PAPER COMMITMENTS	ACTION TO DATE	COMMITMENTS TO FURTHER ACTION
328	Apply EC Construction Products Directive and help develop supporting standards. Begin work on measuring emissions and developing standards for a priority list of building products in 1993 (SYR 235)	Development of EC standards progressing. Emissions of 6 types of products measured using the environmental chamber at BRE	
329			Work in European Standards Organisation (CEN) for emission standard for formaldehyde from particle board to be agreed at the technical level in 1994
330	Issue a series of booklets for householders on indoor pollution problems, the first on house dust mites by end 1993 (SYR 236)		House dust mites booklet to be published in 1994
331	Continue research and monitoring for indoor air quality. Carry out detailed assessment of combustion products and indoor air quality to determine adequacy of current controls of sources of indoor pollution and set guidance values where feasible (11.92, SYR 237)	Analysis of levels of indoor pollutants in Bristol area almost complete. Feasibility of setting guideline values for pollutants in homes under discussion	Publish results of Bristol study and hold seminar on findings. Publish first guidelines for indoor air quality
332	Introduce regulations requiring registration of wet cooling towers and evaporative condensers (SYR 238) (HSE)	Regulations came into force in November 1992. Revised guidance (HS(G)70) published early 1993	
333	HSE/DH working group to issue first report on longer term control of legionellosis (SYR 238) (HSE/DH)	Recommendations of report being pursued	

97

12 WATER

HIGHLIGHTS

Guided regulators on drinking water and water environment improvements relevant to water charge limits

Made new river classification regulations

Published draft policy statement on water resource development

Published report on drinking water quality in 1993

12.1 The Government's objective remains to promote the provision of sufficient water resources and to protect and improve water quality, including groundwater, taking into account the economic and other implications and priorities for the use of resources in environmental improvement generally. Capital investment by the water industry during 1992-93 of £3 billion was in line with the programmes anticipated at privatisation, with increases where necessary to take account of new obligations. The Government has also taken steps to assess the cost of environmental improvements in relation to the benefits they bring, providing guidance to the Director General of Water Services in respect of water companies' obligations. It is actively participating in the EC's review of the Drinking Water Directive and clarifying with the Commission the obligations of the Urban Waste Water Treatment Directive in the light of emerging information about costs. The Government has also reviewed water legislation and controls and proposed a number of deregulatory measures. It has published proposals for water resources policy and is contributing to the Commission's review of the Bathing Waters, Groundwater and Dangerous Substances Directives. Following consultation, River Ecosystem classification regulations have been made. Progress continues on phasing out disposal of waste to sea and preparations for the 1995 North Sea Conference are under way. Work is continuing on consultation proposals on water pollution charging and incentive charging for abstraction.

INVESTMENT

12.2 The water industry in England and Wales will invest about £30 billion between 1989 and 2000 to improve the quality of drinking water, rivers, canals, estuaries and coastal waters. This includes additional resources to improve the quality of bathing waters and £2 billion to ensure that public water supplies comply with the EC Drinking Water Directive. Substantial investment is also being undertaken by farmers and manufacturing industries to reduce water pollution.

12.3 Since the privatisation of the water

industry, a number of additional obligations for environmental improvements have arisen. In July 1993, the Office of Water Services (OFWAT) published *Paying for Quality*, which examines the framework for ensuring that the water undertakers can provide sufficient finance to discharge their functions. The Government set out its position on these commitments in a memorandum to the Director General for Water Services, *Water Charges: The Quality Framework*, which was published in October 1993. The Director General will take this into account in setting revised price limits for water companies in 1995.

CONSERVATION AND PROTECTION OF RESOURCES

12.4 The National Rivers Authority (NRA), which is responsible for safeguarding and improving the water environment and overseeing the use of water resources, will, following consultation with the statutory water undertakers and other interests, publish a *Water Resources Development Strategy* in spring 1994. As a counterpart, the Government will also publish in spring 1994 a statement setting out how the various agencies involved in water resource development should work together (see Box).

12.5 The effects of the drought in Southern and Eastern England disappeared during winter 1992-93, although some local groundwater levels remained very low. The NRA published its *Policy and Practice for the Protection of Groundwater* in December 1992 for its own internal guidance. The protection of groundwater will be the subject of considerable research and policy development over the next few decades.

12.6 The NRA is continuing to develop plans to reduce low flow problems in a number of rivers in England and Wales. Details of these and of some of the solutions proposed are contained in *Low Flows and Water Resources,* published by the NRA in March 1993.

DRINKING WATER QUALITY

12.7 The third annual report of the Drinking Water Inspectorate (DWI), published in July 1993, confirmed that the quality of drinking water in England and Wales remains high. Rigorous quality standards have been set which incorporate, and in some cases exceed, those in the EC Drinking Water Directive. Of 3.75 million tests in 1992, 98.7% complied with the regulatory standards. Where standards are not met, water companies have programmes in place to meet these standards, most of which should be completed by 1995. In October 1993, the Government announced that it would give the DWI more formal independence by transferring some powers from the

Secretaries of State for the Environment and Wales to the Chief Inspector. Legislation will be introduced in due course to make the necessary changes.

12.8 The Government has been having discussions with the European Commission about the review of the Drinking Water Directive and will play an active part in negotiations once the Commission's proposals are published, probably later in 1994.

INLAND AND COASTAL WATER QUALITY

12.9 The Government has strengthened the NRA's ability to carry out its tasks by enabling it to increase its budget for pollution control by around 40% between 1990-91 and 1993-94. The NRA continues to bring significant numbers of prosecutions for water pollution offences. Over the past year, the NRA has published reports covering pollution incidents, groundwater protection and bathing waters. It has also reviewed data on water pollution from contaminated land and abandoned mines, and will publish reports on both these topics early in 1994. The Department of the Environment is reviewing the legal framework for discharges from abandoned mines.

12.10 The Government will gradually replace informal river quality objectives (RQOs) with statutory water quality

The water industry will increase investment to improve the quality of drinking water, rivers, canals, estuaries and coastal waters.

Bathing water improvement scheme nearing completion

80% of bathing waters now meet the mandatory coliform standards of the EC

objectives (SWQOs). It has now completed consultations on draft Fisheries Ecosystem river classification regulations, the core element of the classification system, and plans to lay them shortly. This will open the way for consultation to start on the first batch of SWQO proposals. The Government will shortly publish its response to a study of freshwater quality by the Royal Commission on Environmental Pollution, which proposed a number of measures for improving monitoring and quality.

12.11 Progress on Regulations to set statutory environmental quality standards (EQSs) for the remaining substances on the 'Red List' of dangerous substances has been slower than expected, but the Government remains committed to making these Regulations. When these have been made, all 'Red List' substances will be covered either by an EC environmental quality objective (EQO) or by a national EQS.

12.12 The Government has consulted on draft Regulations to incorporate the Urban Waste Water Treatment Directive into UK legislation. These Regulations will set standards for collecting systems and sewage treatment of discharges to inland and coastal waters. The Government has been discussing the implementation of this Directive with other Member States and the Commission. Work on implementing the Nitrates Directive, to identify vulnerable zones where agricultural restrictions will apply, is also under way.

12.13 The Government has set SWQOs for 458 bathing waters in accordance with the EC Directive on bathing waters. Water companies are undertaking investment to ensure that virtually all bathing waters will meet the Directive standards by the end of 1995. Monitoring has confirmed the steady improvement in bathing water quality, with 80% meeting the mandatory coliform standards in 1993. The UK pressed the EC Commission to bring forward a proposal to revise the Directive in the light of scientific developments and subsidiarity. The

STATEMENT ON WATER RESOURCE DEVELOPMENT

In September 1993, following the consultation paper *Using Water Wisely*, the Government circulated for comment a draft statement setting out how the various agencies involved in water resource development - the Government, the NRA, OFWAT and the statutory water undertakers (the water companies) should work together. The statement will be published in spring 1994.

To meet the rising demand for water, the Government's strategy will require an integrated approach by regulators, suppliers and Government.

In what is now a private-sector industry, the water companies must determine their own forecasts of demand, and plan and invest accordingly. Because of the importance of water, however, the Government has in the course of the last 18 months assessed with the regulators and the industry whether the system of water regulation will enable the necessary developments to take place in due time.

Nationally, demand for water has been growing up to 1% a year, though there are major regional variations and industrial use has decreased. In the Government's view, major investment in developing new water resources should not be undertaken when wider demand management (such as metering) and day-to-day measures (such as improved leakage control) can make better use of existing resources. Its strategy is therefore one of balancing new investment, demand management and day-to-day management against assessments of demand.

Demand assessment must underpin investment by water companies and other major users, as well as the NRA's management of catchments and monitoring of proposals. Whereas all parties have a role in demand management, day-to-day management and, in England and Wales, supply-side investment are clearly the duty of the water companies.

Commission agreed their proposals in February 1994. The Government announced the publication of the results of a four-year programme of research into the effects of sea bathing on health in January 1994.

12.14 Following the Commission's report on subsidiarity at the December 1993 European Council, the Government is discussing with the Commission its work to draw up a Framework Directive on freshwater management and groundwater protection.

12.15 Work is under way on Regulations setting minimum construction standards for industrial fuel oil and chemical stores. The Government intends to consult on the industrial fuel oil Regulations in 1994.

12.16 A pilot study is currently being undertaken to encourage farmers to spread manure and organic wastes in the most economical and environmentally friendly way. In the first phase, 76% of farmers in four pilot areas took part. The Government is targeting further river catchments to encourage more farmers to draw up plans. The National Farm Waste Forum continues to provide a forum for the Government, the NRA and major farming bodies to exchange information and ideas. Farmers have responded well to the Government's package of measures and there has recently been a significant decline in the number of major agricultural pollution incidents (from 239 in 1990 to 67 in 1992).

THE QUALITY OF OUR SEAS

12.17 An international task force has completed work on a comprehensive quality assessment of the North Sea. *The Quality Status Report* was reviewed by Ministers of all the North Sea states in Copenhagen in December 1993, and the implications of the report (which shows that, although there are certain specific or localised problems, the North Sea is generally not subject to major problems) will be considered further in the run up to the next North Sea Conference, to be held in 1995. The UK will be publishing, alongside *The Quality Status Report,* those of

the supporting sub-regional reports on parts of the North Sea and of the English Channel, where it has taken the lead because of their importance to the UK.

12.18 Progress has been made towards achieving North Sea Conference deadlines for phasing out disposal at sea of certain categories of waste. Disposal at sea of liquid industrial waste and of power station fly ash was brought to an end in December 1992. Two of the nine water companies involved in disposing of sewage sludge at sea have already stopped, six years ahead of the target date of 1998.

12.19 The Ministry of Defence ended the dumping of redundant munitions at sea at the end of 1992. MOD ships now meet the standards set for oil discharges and comply with sewage disposal regulations. Further improvements are being made to garbage-handling equipment on warships.

12.20 Following the Shetland tanker accident in January 1993 (see Chapter 19), the Government introduced a voluntary code for ships operating around the UK coast. The code was subsequently endorsed by the International Maritime Organisation. In July 1993, higher standards were introduced for oil discharges, and statutory requirements were introduced for tankers to have oil pollution emergency plans and double hulls or their equivalent.

12.21 Integrated pollution control will play a major part in securing the required reductions of inputs of 'Red List' substances

The Government is discussing with the Commission work on drawing up a Framework Directive on freshwater management and groundwater protection

Farmers have responded well to the Government's package of measures to reduce pollution from agriculture

101

Integrated pollution control will help secure reductions of input of dangerous substances into the North Sea

by the target date of 1995 agreed under the Third North Sea Conference. Trials are taking place on alternatives for dichlorvos and approvals for the non-agricultural use of atrazine and simazine were revoked at the end of August 1993. The Government has issued a consultation paper on proposals for a UK Action Plan to phase out and destroy remaining polychlorinated biphenyls (PCBs) by 1999 (see Box). A draft Waste Management paper on the safe

handling and disposal of PCBs was issued at the same time.

12.22 The UK continues to take an active part in programmes of assessment and action for protection of the North East Atlantic as a whole. The UK is closely involved in international working groups taking forward a wide range of issues under the Action Plan of the new North East Atlantic Convention.

POLYCHLORINATED BIPHENYLS (PCBs)

PCBs are chemicals which were once widely used in industry and commercial and domestic products. They are, however, toxic, persistent and accumulate in the fatty tissues of animals at the top of the food chain. The manufacture and sale of PCBs were banned in the EC in 1986. Some exemptions were made, for instance in electrical transformers and capacitors in use before July 1986.

These measures have contributed to falling levels of PCBs in the UK environment.

Because of continuing concern about the effects of PCBs, the UK and other North Sea states agreed in 1990 to destroy all remaining PCBs by the end of 1999. In 1993, the Government published proposals for a national action plan to meet this commitment and revised draft guidance on the safe disposal of PCBs. Owners of equipment containing PCBs would have to register them and agree a date for their destruction. Monitoring by the regulatory authorities will be increased to ensure that PCBs are disposed of safely.

REF NO	SUMMARY OF PREVIOUS WHITE PAPER COMMITMENTS	ACTION TO DATE	COMMITMENTS TO FURTHER ACTION
334	Bring drinking water up to standard by the mid-1990s and monitor the implementation of programmes (SYR 239,241)	Improvement programmes reviewed and implementation on schedule Third annual DWI report published, confirming the high quality of drinking water in Great Britain	
335	Seek to reduce pesticide use in water catchment areas where concentrations exceed drinking water standards (13.29, SYR 317)	Ban on non-agricultural use of atrazine and simazine came into effect 31 August 1993. Guidance on safe and minimum use of herbicides for non-agricultural purposes published December 1992	
336	Bring bathing water up to EC Directive standard by the mid-1990s. Monitor the implementation of water and sewage improvement proposals and of bathing water and sewage treatment programmes (SYR 240)	Third NRA report on *Bathing Water Quality* published, confirming sustained improvement in water quality. Number of bathing waters meeting EC Directive standards in 1993 increased to 80%	Complete bathing water improvement programme
337	Private water companies to invest £13.7bn to improve sewerage works (including £3.6bn for estuarial and coastal discharges) and bathing waters (12.12, SYR 242)	Proceeding on schedule	
338	Establish statutory water quality objectives on the basis of advice from the National Rivers Authority and introduce from 1993 (12.6, SYR 243) (NRA)	Government consultation paper on SWQOs published December 1992. River Ecosystem classification regulations made in April 1994	Regulations to be made in spring 1994. Introduce SWQOs gradually, taking into account the relevant costs and benefits
339	Continue monitoring of river quality and regular publication of results (SYR 244)		Further river quality surveys to be carried out in 1995
340			Publish statement in spring 1994 setting out how agencies involved in water resource development should work together
341	Keep under review the effectiveness of the water bodies' statutory responsibilities for conservation and recreation (12.27, SYR 245)	First report of Government Standing Committee on Conservation, Access and Recreation in the Water Industry published July 1993	
342	Consult on proposals to set minimum construction standards for industrial fuel oil and chemical stores by end 1992 (SYR 246)	Developing proposals on industrial oil storage. No action on chemical storage pending further work	
343	Ensure regular reports on all types of water pollution, including those from farm waste, are published (12.16, SYR 247)	Report on pollution incidents in 1992, including those involving farms, published by NRA October 1993	

103

REF NO	SUMMARY OF PREVIOUS WHITE PAPER COMMITMENTS	ACTION TO DATE	COMMITMENTS TO FURTHER ACTION
344	Continue to provide 50% grants towards improving or providing facilities for storage, treatment and disposal of agricultural wastes and silage effluent (12.16, SYR 248) (MAFF)	£119m paid in grants to end September 1993 for these facilities under the Farm and Conservation Grant scheme. In England alone, 9000 farmers have received assistance, which has led to a steep drop in the number of major agricultural pollution incidents. Grant rate was reduced to 25% in December 1993	
345	Keep under review the need for more controls over livestock waste (12.16, SYR 249) (MAFF)	First phase of pilot farm waste plans study completed and further river catchments for 1993 farm waste campaign targeted. Scope of free pollution advisory service widened to include plans as well as general advice	Target further selected river catchments for campaigns during 1994
346	Use National Farm Waste Forum to keep risks from farm wastes under review and develop policies (SYR 249) (MAFF)	Forum continues to meet on a regular basis	
347	Implement the Urban Waste Water Treatment Directive (SYR 250)	Second consultation paper on identifying sensitive areas issued March 1993 Draft implementing Regulations and guidance issued April 1993	
348	Monitor the 10 pilot Nitrate Sensitive Areas and 9 Advisory Areas (12.21, SYR 251) (MAFF)	Monitoring reports published by MAFF	Monitor nitrate levels in pilot NSAs in 1994-95
349	Implement EC Nitrate Directive by December 1993. Issue consultation documents on designating nitrate vulnerable zones. Designate zones and establish action programmes (SYR 251)	Consultation document on the methodology for designating NVZs issued in March 1993	Measures to be established by end 1995 and implemented 1995-99
350	Press for consistent and compatible Community-wide arrangements for monitoring and reporting water quality standards through the European Environment Agency (3.21, SYR 252)	EEA Management Board held its first meeting in December 1993	
351	Stop sea dumping of liquid industrial wastes and flyash by 1993, of stone waste from mining by 1997, and dumping on beaches by 1995 (12.35, SYR 254)	Ended all disposal at sea of liquid industrial waste and of power station flyash in December 1992. Most minestone dumping has ceased because of mine closures	
352	Terminate first licences for sewage sludge by 1993 and the remainder by 1998 (SYR 254) (MAFF)	Ended the first disposal licence for sewage sludge – 6 years ahead of target	
353	Take further action to prevent pollution from ships and oil rigs, and to control illegal discharges. Seek higher standards on chemical discharges (12.37, SYR 255) (DOT)	Amended oil pollution regulations to introduce stricter discharge limits, mandatory oil pollution emergency plans, regular programme of inspection of ships in ports, and phased withdrawal from service of single-hulled tankers	

REF NO	SUMMARY OF PREVIOUS WHITE PAPER COMMITMENTS	ACTION TO DATE	COMMITMENTS TO FURTHER ACTION
354	Amend UK shipping legislation on control of oil pollution and garbage from ships (SYR 255) (DOT)	Amended garbage pollution legislation to include new Special Areas, including Antarctica	
355	Continue to improve the notification and testing and other aspects of approvals scheme for use and discharge of chemicals on offshore platforms. Develop a database on discharges from offshore installations (12.37-39, SYR 256) (DTI)	Discussions are continuing with industry over an interim Offshore Chemicals Notification Scheme, to be introduced on a voluntary basis. UK hosted a Paris Commission workshop to discuss a hazard and risk management programme	
356	Promote development of new annex to MARPOL, dealing with atmospheric pollution from ships (SYR 255) (DOT)	IMO discussions proceeding successfully; agreement may be reached in 1994	
357			Complete consultations to enable UK to ratify MARPOL Annex IV (Sewage) (DOT)
358	Apply new standard for oil-based muds for exploration and appraisal wells by December 1993, and for development wells from end 1996 (SYR 255) (DTI)	Standard for exploration and appraisal wells applied	
359	Phase out anti-fouling paints containing tributyltin (TBT) on Royal Navy vessels (SYR 255) (MOD)	Anti-fouling paints containing TBT compounds no longer used on vessels with docking cycles which match currently established performance of replacement products	
360	End sea dumping of redundant munitions by 1992 (SYR 255) (MOD)	Ended late 1992	
361			Discuss with interested parties further anti-pollution measures, including anti-fouling coatings and oily water separators (DOT)
362	Work towards meeting objectives in North East Atlantic Convention Action Plan (SYR 256)	New North East Atlantic Convention signed 31 November 1992. 1993 OSPAR Commission meeting reviewed Action Plan progress and adjusted priorities accordingly	
363	Set targets for the reduction of the inputs of 'Red List' substances by 50% between 1985-1995 and halve inputs from atmosphere of 17 harmful substances to sea by 1999 (12.33-4, SYR 257,259)	Progress continues to be made in achieving reductions	
364	Phase out the use of polychlorinated biphenyls (PCBs) by 1999. Issue consultation paper in 1993 (12.34, SYR 258,293)	Issued consultation papers on UK Action Plan and draft waste management guidance	Issue final version of waste management paper by end 1994
365	Support the introduction of pollution control charges and consider greater use of economic mechanisms to discourage pollution. Publish consultation papers on options for incentive charging (12.25, SYR 260)	*Making Markets Work for the Environment* published November 1993	

13 WASTE, RECYCLING, CONTAMINATED LAND AND LITTER

HIGHLIGHTS

Initiative on producer responsibility for wastes announced

Agreement reached on EC Packaging Directive

Waste management licensing due to be introduced 1 May 1994

Instruments laid for ratification of Basel Convention on control of waste movements

Review of contaminated land and liabilities under way and response to EC Green Paper on Remedying Environmental Damage published

13.1 During 1993, the Government continued to make progress in encouraging - where the best practicable environmental option - waste reduction, re-use and recovery (including recycling), and the safe disposal of remaining wastes. It is looking increasingly to producers of waste to take responsibility for its consequences. In July, it announced a major initiative on producer responsibility for wastes. Also during the year, the EC made substantial progress on a Packaging Directive with similar objectives. Waste management licensing was due to be introduced on 1 May 1994. The UK has become a Party to the Basel Convention on the control of transboundary movements of wastes. The Government is conducting a wide-ranging review of the arrangements for dealing with contaminated land and the related liabilities. The Government addressed the issue of liability for environmental damage in the UK response to the European Commission's Green Paper on Remedying Environmental Damage.

13.2 The Government has set out its approach to the management and disposal of waste in its Sustainable Development Strategy (Chapter 23). It is based on a hierarchy of waste management options from waste reduction at the top, through re-use, materials recycling and energy recovery, to final disposal at the bottom. The Government's aim is to move more of the UK's waste management up this hierarchy, and to this end it is developing a more strategic approach to the development of waste management policy.

WASTE REDUCTION

13.3 The Government believes that industry should seek to reduce waste at source in order to reduce pollution; and both the integrated pollution control and local authority air pollution control regimes established under Part I of the Environmental Protection Act 1990 require the use of best available techniques not entailing excessive cost (BATNEEC) to

prevent or minimise releases of specified polluting substances. By putting the emphasis on cleaner technology and production methods rather than end-of-pipe abatement solutions, many companies have found that waste reduction can save money. The Government is currently supporting two pilot projects, in the Mersey Basin and Yorkshire, the results of which will be made public this year. The Government plans to encourage the development of further projects. The new Environmental Technology Best Practice Information Programme, with a budget of £16 million over a five-year period, aims to reduce waste at source. It will seek to encourage the adoption of existing best practice by industry, largely through the provision of information in selected priority areas.

13.4 Industry has made significant progress in recent years in reducing the amount of waste arising from its products. One notable area is in packaging, where there have been significant savings as a result of

Table 1: Number of Recycling Collection Points

	1990	1992	1993
Glass [1]	5800	7500+	10600+
Save-a-Can [2]	200	700+	1100
Aluminium Cans [3]			
Recycling Centres	330	333	655
Recycling Points	660	1100	1457
Newspapers and Magazines	N/A	3770	6000+
Plastics [4]			
Bottles	120	567	900+
Carrier Bags	250	316	300
Textiles [5]	N/A	2500	2500+
Vending Cups [6]	63	250+	1050+

[1] Source: British Glass

[2] Source: Steel Can Recycling Information Bureau (Save-a-Can accepts both steel and aluminium cans)

[3] Source: Aluminium Can Recycling Association

[4] Source: British Plastics Federation

[5] Figs include banks supplied by Recyclatex, Salvation Army, Oxfam and Spastics Society, but do not include independent schemes run by local authorities or charity shops/schemes which collect textiles for recycling

[6] Source: Save-a-Cup Ltd

techniques such as 'lightweighting', 'thinwalling' and material substitution. For example, raw material use in some glass bottles has been reduced by about 30% since 1980 and the weight of cardboard packaging has been reduced by about 25% since 1978. The Government believes that further progress is possible in this area and that its producer responsibility initiative will provide an additional incentive to industry to reduce waste at source.

RECYCLING, RE-USE AND RECOVERY

Materials Recycling

Action by Individuals

13.5 The number of recycling collection points in the UK has increased during 1993 (see Table 1). Save-a-Can reached its target of 1000 can banks, a year ahead of schedule. British Glass reached its target of 10,000 glass banks, two years ahead of schedule, and has set a new target to recycle 55% of glass containers by 1999.

13.6 The Government co-ordinated 'Watch Your Waste Week' in March 1993, to raise public awareness of the benefits of waste reduction, re-use and recycling, and to encourage people to buy recycled goods.

Action by Local Authorities

13.7 The Government promised Supplementary Credit Approvals worth £15 million in 1993-94 to develop some 300 recycling projects in 161 local authority areas in England. Projects range from large-scale reclamation works to household composting schemes. The Government has announced that £15 million will be available in 1994-95. Grants to voluntary organisations for recycling are available through the Environmental Action Fund.

Action by Business

13.8 The Government believes that producers of waste should take some responsibility for the waste they produce. Ministers have invited businesses in key waste streams to take responsibility for their waste by developing and implementing voluntary plans to increase significantly the proportions recovered for beneficial use. The packaging industries were asked to prepare a plan by Christmas 1993 to recover between 50% and 75% of packaging waste by 2000. The plan was presented to Ministers on 7 February. It commits the packaging industry to recovery of 58% of packaging waste by the end of the decade. Among the key actions for 1994-95, the plan envisages a doubling of the collection of plastic bottles for recycling and a 50%

Adding kitchen waste to a 3-bin compost heap, Cotswolds

Rotary screen for sorting refuse. The Byker reclamation plant, Newcastle

increase in throughput for aluminium can recovery. By 1996, 15% of UK households will be covered by high density bring and kerbside collection schemes.

13.9 In addition, newspaper publishers were asked to report back on the steps which they intend to take to increase the proportion of waste paper in newsprint to 40% by 2000. Responses from both industries are being considered by Ministers. The Government also invited an industry group to produce a plan to reduce the environmental impact of 'end of life' vehicles. The plan has been agreed with Ministers and is now being implemented. The plan aims to increase vehicle recycling and recovery from 75% to 95% by 2015. Ministers have also held meetings with manufacturers from these and other waste streams such as electronic equipment, tyres and batteries and plans for these waste streams are being developed.

13.10 The Government has continued to provide support and encouragement for the development of recycling initiatives. This includes a survey of best practice in recycling plans. A review of the recycling credits scheme, where savings in collection and disposal costs are passed on to recyclers, was completed in April 1994. The Government is part-funding a number of recycling projects through its Environmental Technology Innovation Scheme (ETIS), the Department of Trade and Industry's Environmental Management Options Scheme (DEMOS), and the EUROENVIRON programme. Projects include schemes to investigate recycling mixed plastics and to develop technologies to recycle plastics and rubber together, and a plant for co-composting domestic waste and sewage sludge.

Recovering Energy from Waste

13.11 The Royal Commission on Environmental Pollution, in its study of waste incineration published in May 1993, concluded that incineration of waste with energy recovery would provide an environmentally acceptable option to the disposal of municipal waste in the future. The Government will be responding to the report's recommendations in due course. During 1993, the Government published two

reports which explored the potential for using economic instruments to encourage the development of incineration with energy recovery, which may be a more environmentally sustainable option than landfill. Extensive consultation took place and comments are now being considered ahead of a decision on whether to introduce a landfill levy.

13.12 Under the Government's Non-Fossil Fuel Obligation (NFFO) on public electricity suppliers, 15 'waste-to-energy' schemes have been contracted to generate electricity. These schemes have a capacity of 4.3 million tonnes of waste per year. Seven schemes are likely to be in operation by 1995. In July 1993, the Government made further proposals aiming to stimulate a market in this sector.

Keeping, Treating and Disposing of Waste Safely

13.13 The Government's commitment to higher standards for the storage, treatment and disposal of waste is being implemented through the enhanced waste management licensing system established by the Environmental Protection Act 1990, which was due to come into force on 1 May 1994. In framing the new system, the Government has had to take account of European Community measures on waste (Framework Directive on Waste, 91/156/EEC).

13.14 The new system places tougher requirements on licensees, who will retain responsibility for disused sites while they remain a hazard to health or the environment. A charging scheme for licences is also being introduced.

Environment Agency

13.15 The Government is committed to establishing an Environment Agency for England and Wales, which will include waste regulation amongst its functions (see Chapter 3).

INTERNATIONAL DEVELOPMENTS

13.16 The Waste Shipments Regulation, which was due to come into force on 6 May

1994, will implement EC obligations under the UN Environment Programme Basel Convention on the Control of Transboundary Movements of Hazardous Wastes and their Disposal. The Regulation incorporates the principle of self-sufficiency, reflecting the Government's policy that developed countries should become self-sufficient in the final disposal of waste. The Regulation prohibits exports of waste for final disposal, except to EFTA countries which are Parties to the Convention. The Government welcomes the decision at the second meeting of the Parties to the Convention that, from 1998 onwards, there will be a ban on all movements of hazardous wastes for recycling or recovery from OECD to non-OECD States. Until the end of 1997, exports of waste for recycling or recovery to non-OECD countries can continue provided that the countries agree to receive the waste and have provided relevant information to the Basel Secretariat.

13.17 The UK ratified the Convention on 7 February 1994 and was due to become a Party on 8 May. The UK is an active participant in meetings under the Convention, to which it has been making voluntary financial contributions on an annual basis, starting in 1990. As a Party, the UK will make mandatory contributions for the operation of the Convention.

EC INITIATIVES

13.18 During the past year, agreement was reached on the European Waste Catalogue, an illustrative list of wastes under the Framework Directive. There has also been consultation on the provisions of the Batteries Directive. The EC has a continuing programme of initiatives. These will require active consideration by the UK over the coming year. These initiatives are:

- **Directive on Packaging and Packaging Waste**
  A common position was agreed by Council in December 1993. The agreed position sets banded targets for the recovery (50%-65%) and recycling (25%-45%) of packaging waste, with a minimum requirement of 15% recycling

for each packaging material. The Government believes this agreement provides a sound basis for harmonising Member States' approaches to packaging and the environment. The UK will work to ensure that a harmonising Directive is adopted as soon as possible.

- **Landfill Directive**
  Negotiations began during 1993 on the European Commission's proposal for a Directive on the Landfill of Waste. The Directive is intended to ensure that landfill waste disposal operations in the Community are carried out without endangering the environment. Landfill to high environmental standards is an important part of the UK's waste management strategy, and the UK is playing an active part in negotiations. Negotiations are continuing under the present Greek Presidency of the Community.

- **Hazardous Waste Directive**
  Implementation of this Directive has been deferred by Council, probably until spring 1995, in order to allow more time to produce a list of hazardous wastes. The Government will continue to consult on the list and will also consult further on proposed changes to the Special Waste Regulations which will implement the Directive in the UK.

- **Directive on PCBs and PCTs**
  Negotiations will continue on a proposed Directive. The Government will wish to ensure that this accords with North Sea Conference commitments, including the phase-out of these wastes by 1999.

- **Priority Waste Streams**
  The UK has led the Community's priority waste stream group which has looked at healthcare waste. The group's conclusions will be sent to the European Commission shortly. The UK is also participating in the work of the groups which have been looking at used tyres, chlorinated solvents, end-of-life vehicles, demolition waste and electronic waste.

Lord Strathclyde and stars of Coronation Street help the Tidy Britain Group's campaign 'Getting a Grip on Litter'

Beach cleaning machine, which collects litter each evening, Margate

'Scooping the Poop'

CONTAMINATED LAND

13.19 The Government is developing guidance for the public and private sectors on the assessment and treatment of contaminated land. Annual expenditure on the current research programme is £1.5 million. Other research on contaminated land, funded jointly by the Department of the Environment and industry, is also being carried out.

13.20 Proposals to register sites subject to contaminative uses have been withdrawn following public consultation. A review of the arrangements for dealing with contaminated land and the associated liabilities is under way. The review will consider whether there is a need for amending legislation in this area.

13.21 The Government concentrates its support on problems which cannot be addressed by the market. Derelict Land Grant is available to schemes in the public and private sectors involving the treatment of contamination. Supplementary Credit Approvals are also provided to local authorities to investigate possible threats, and to treat their own sites and those where it is impracticable to recover costs from those responsible. Approvals totalled about £10 million in 1992-93. The provision of £12 million for 1993-94 was fully taken up, and bids were invited for a further £12 million in 1994-95.

LIABILITY FOR ENVIRONMENTAL IMPAIRMENT

13.22 In May 1993, the European Commission issued its consultative Green Paper on Remedying Environmental

Damage. This considers the use of civil liability and joint compensation schemes to encourage the remediation of environmental damage. The UK responded to the Green Paper in October, arguing that there was no case for general, Community-level action, since these matters could be better handled at Member State level. That debate will continue during 1994. In June 1993 at Lugano, the Council of Europe opened for signature its Convention on Civil Liability for damage resulting from activities dangerous to the environment - the UK decided not to sign that particular convention.

LITTER

13.23 Last year's report described the considerable progress made in improving the cleanliness of streets, parks and other open spaces. Surveys by the Tidy Britain Group show that progress was maintained in 1993. London came out cleanest overall, when comparing equivalent central areas of nine European Capital Cities. Nevertheless, litter remains a problem in many areas.

13.24 The Department of the Environment has formed an advisory group to examine how well the litter provisions of the Environmental Protection Act 1990 are working and to make recommendations for further improvements. The group will report in spring 1994.

13.25 Cleanliness is one of the areas featured in two initiatives which the Department of the Environment is currently piloting. One is to encourage volunteers to improve their local environment, acting as the eyes and ears of the community and as a catalyst to get improvements under way; the other is to enable local people to help keep clean designated stretches of road and verge.

DOGS

13.26 The Government launched a 'Scoop The Poop' campaign in May 1993, which was supported by local publicity initiatives. The DOE has produced two further leaflets on responsible dog ownership.

REF NO	SUMMARY OF PREVIOUS WHITE PAPER COMMITMENTS	ACTION TO DATE	COMMITMENTS TO FURTHER ACTION
366	Aim to meet a target of recycling half of recyclable household waste by 2000 (14.23, SYR 261)	£15m borrowing approvals promised to local authorities for 1993-94 to invest in recycling equipment. £25m issued for 1991-92 and 1992-93 Packaging industry invited to produce a plan for recovering between 50% and 75% of packaging waste by 2000. Plan presented to Ministers on 7 February 1994 Other waste streams invited to develop producer responsibility plans	A further £15m committed for 1994-95
367			Secure implementation of packaging waste plan and plans for other waste streams
368	Consider use of further economic instruments to help achieve target. Announce conclusions early in 1993 (SYR 261,265)	3 studies on the introduction of economic instruments published 1993. Interested parties invited to comment and help form decision	
369			Commission study of environmental externalities of recycling
370	Act on the recommendations of ACBE on further measures to promote recycling. Publish regular reports of progress on the recommendations (SYR 261)	Final report and Government response published July 1993	
371	Change basis of recycling credits to long-run marginal costs by 1 April 1994 (SYR 262)	Announcement about revised basis for calculating recycling credits made in November 1993 New regulations introduced 1 April 1994	
372	Require local authorities to prepare and publish draft recycling plans by August 1992 (14.29, SYR 263)	Recycling plans from all English waste collection authorities, 85% of Scottish authorities and 95% of Welsh authorities produced	
373	Scrutinise draft recycling plans by 31 December 1992. Monitor implementation of recycling plans (SYR 263)	95% of English plans, 70% of Scottish plans and 86% of Welsh plans approved Recycling plans survey published	
374	Encourage recycling facilities at new shopping developments (14.29, SYR 263)	Now standard practice for recycling facilities to be located at new shopping developments	
375	Substantially complete coverage of waste development plans expected by end 1996 (SYR 264)	Advice on content of waste local plans will be included in forthcoming Planning Policy Guidance note on planning and pollution controls	

REF NO	SUMMARY OF PREVIOUS WHITE PAPER COMMITMENTS	ACTION TO DATE	COMMITMENTS TO FURTHER ACTION
376	Take further action if voluntary recycling provisions prove inadequate (FYR p56, SYR 265)	Not necessary at present	
377	Support pilot projects to test separate collection and sorting techniques, and report in 1993. Publish annual monitoring reports and hold seminars to promote best practice in recycling (14.26, SYR 266)	Over £11m of borrowing approvals allocated to pilot projects over past 3 years. 5 detailed reports on collection and sorting systems produced. Overview report published in February 1993. Conference held to disseminate results of monitoring work in February 1993	
378	PPG on planning and pollution controls to be issued in 1992 (14.50, SYR 274)		Publish shortly
379	Draw up proposals for a new waste disposal planning system under the Environment Agency (SYR 270)	Discussions held with interested organisations	Announce proposals
380	Separate local authorities' waste regulation and disposal functions. Approve schemes for all affected authorities by October 1992 (14.45, SYR 271)	Schemes approved in 29 authorities in England and 36 in Wales	Complete approval for all affected authorities by June 1994
381	Establish local authority waste disposal companies by summer 1993 (SYR 271)	20 waste disposal companies established	Establish all waste disposal companies by summer 1994
382	Review provisions for separation of regulation and disposal functions in the light of proposals for an Environment Agency and local government reorganisation (SYR 271)	Need for separation of powers will be removed when Environment Agency established. Paving Bill due to be introduced in 1993-94 Parliamentary session	
383	Implement new licensing regime under EPA 1990 by April 1993 (14.45, SYR 274)	Regulations due to come into force on 1 May 1994	
384	Issue six Waste Management Papers by April 1993 (14.52, SYR 273)	Issued consultation drafts on clinical wastes, PCBs and waste disposal plans. Two further papers on waste management licensing and landfill published	Publish papers
385			Publish a further three papers covering landfilling
386	Continue to work on the improvement of data on municipal waste. Develop a research programme to identify ways of collecting information about wastes. Continue work on the development of a site record system (14.69, SYR 275)	National Household Waste Analysis programme established and is yielding useful results. Site record system close to completion	Complete site record system by mid-1994 and commence programme of work to expand its database to cover England and Wales by end 1996

REF NO	SUMMARY OF PREVIOUS WHITE PAPER COMMITMENTS	ACTION TO DATE	COMMITMENTS TO FURTHER ACTION
387			Publish research report on potential markets for household waste derived compost. Extend work to cover co-composting with other waste
388			Continue development of a strategy to assess the risks posed by various waste management activities to the environment and human health
389	Publish and complete follow-up study on specification of building materials by end 1992. Study of recycling of demolition and construction wastes to be carried out in 1993 (SYR 276)	Research on aggregates specifications published by BRE in spring 1993 EC Priority Wastes Streams Initiative working towards firm strategy on recycling of demolition and construction wastes	Publish research into accommodating waste and recycled materials in construction specifications, and into recycling demolition wastes in spring 1994
390	Ensure that international trade agreements respect the international environment and take account of the dangers associated with shipments of hazardous wastes. Work for EC ratification of the Basel Convention to limit the export of hazardous waste (4.53, SYR 277-81)	Basel Convention ratified in February 1994. EC Waste Shipments Regulation, fulfilling Basel obligations, due to apply from 6 May 1994	
391			Assist UN to develop new guidelines on transboundary movements of wastes for recovery
392			Publish supplementary legislation and guidance for implementing the EC Waste Shipments Regulation
393	Earmark funds to tackle problems on old landfill sites and collect methane where possible (5.70,14.59, SYR 267-8)	£12m allocated in 1993-94 for Supplementary Credit Approvals to enable local authorities to take action on contaminated land, including old landfill sites	A further £12m to be made available in 1994-95 for local authorities to deal with contaminated land
394	Require District Councils to prepare registers of land which may be contaminated (SYR 139)	Proposals for registers withdrawn in the light of responses to two rounds of consultation. Review begun of machinery for dealing with contaminated land and related issues	Announce and implement conclusions of review
395	Develop new standards for assessment of contamination (SYR 139)	Research projects under way as part of programme to develop assessment procedures and guidelines	Publish guidance
396	Ensure hazardous waste incineration Directive sets exacting but practical standards (SYR 279)		

REF NO	SUMMARY OF PREVIOUS WHITE PAPER COMMITMENTS	ACTION TO DATE	COMMITMENTS TO FURTHER ACTION
397	Monitor the effects of the litter measures (14.72, SYR 282)	Regular surveys of principal litter authorities undertaken by Tidy Britain Group. Annual cleanliness surveys of sample local authorities undertaken	
398			Tidy Britain Group to publish league table of cleanliness of cities
399	Maximum fine for leaving litter to be increased to £2500 from October 1992 and review fixed penalty amount (SYR 283)	Maximum fine increased to £2500 in October 1992	Litter Advisory Group to report on fixed penalty in spring 1994
400	Review Code of Practice on litter in 1993 (SYR 284)	Litter Advisory Group convened mid-1993 to review effectiveness of litter legislation	Litter Advisory Group to report spring 1994
401	Inform people about 1991 litter legislation and their rights, such as the inclusion of litter regulations in the Environment Charter (14.74, SYR 285)	Reprint of leaflets publicising duty made available by major supermarket chains. Tidy Britain Group continues to draw attention to legislation during campaigns	
402	Continue to support the anti-litter work of voluntary bodies (14.76, SYR 286)	£2.9m allocated to Tidy Britain Group in 1993-94	

14 HAZARDOUS SUBSTANCES AND GENETICALLY MODIFIED ORGANISMS

HIGHLIGHTS

Institute for Environment and Health established

Statutory requirements for testing and assessing new and existing chemicals now in place

Principle of prior informed consent introduced for the most dangerous chemicals

Regulations implementing EC Directives on GMOs came into force; 30 day 'fast track' for consent to release GMOs introduced January 1994

Advisory Committee on Pesticides considered 21 new and existing pesticides

14.1 The Government's main aim on hazardous substances and genetically modified organisms (GMOs) is to ensure that UK legislation protects human health and safety and also protects the environment from emissions and general release of harmful products. This requires adequate, cost-effective protection with the minimum administrative friction and the maximum opportunity to deliver the environmental objectives through innovative approaches. Assessment of the risks to human health and the environment is of key importance in the control of hazardous substances and GMOs.

14.2 The Government funds research and monitoring aimed at developing and evaluating policies. The results are published in Government reports, in reports of international agencies and others, and researchers are encouraged to publish in the open scientific literature.

INSTITUTE FOR ENVIRONMENT AND HEALTH

14.3 The Medical Research Council established the Institute for Environment and Health (IEH) at Leicester University in July 1993 to act as a focal point on research into the links between environmental quality and health. It is supported by the Department of the Environment and the Department of Health and will assist in co-ordination of research activities. The IEH is helping the Government prepare for the Second WHO European Conference on Environment and Health, which is being convened by the European Regional Office of the World Health Organisation in June 1994. The IEH will be particularly concerned with exposure to chemical hazards through environmental pathways, starting with studies on the possible links between air pollution and asthma and the

development of new techniques such as biological markers for measuring exposure to pollutants.

SMALL AREA HEALTH STATISTICS UNIT

14.4 Government funding for the Small Area Health Statistics Unit (SAHSU) is committed for a further two years. The Unit investigates the local incidence of cancer and other diseases and their possible links to particular local environmental problems.

RISK ASSESSMENT

14.5 A recent review of risk assessment practices within Government Departments has revealed differences in the approaches used. The adoption of a common approach, wherever practicable, is expected to lead to more understandable and balanced decision making. The review seeks to identify good practices within Government and its recommendations will build on these to achieve greater coherence. These will be published in 1994.

INDUSTRIAL CHEMICALS

14.6 Statutory requirements for testing and assessing new and existing chemicals are now in place. The EC Directive on notification of new chemicals was amended in 1992 to introduce uniform principles of risk assessment. Requirements under the Directive for chemicals to be classified and labelled for danger to the environment came into effect in September 1993.

14.7 The EC Regulation on the evaluation and control of the risks of existing substances came into force during 1993, and data on an initial list of chemicals produced in quantities over 1000 tonnes per year will be submitted by June 1994. Data on all other chemicals produced in quantities over 1000 tonnes per year must be provided by June 1995. A priority list will be drawn up and each substance allocated to a Member State for evaluation.

14.8 The EC programme will be co-ordinated with the OECD High Production Volume Chemicals Programme to ensure that the best use is made of international information and expertise. The UK will continue to play its full part in these programmes and has already proposed a list of 33 high-tonnage chemicals for priority assessment.

PESTICIDES

14.9 Ten new agricultural and one new non-agricultural pesticide active ingredients were approved during the year by the Advisory Committee on Pesticides, and seven older agricultural and three older non-agricultural active ingredients were reviewed. The Pesticides Safety Directorate of the Ministry of Agriculture, Fisheries and Food was launched as an executive agency in April 1993 and considerable progress has been made in reducing delays in approval.

14.10 National procedures for the approval of plant protection products will gradually be replaced by the provisions of an EC Directive for approval of active ingredients. A proposal for a similar Directive on biocides was published in September 1993. The Health and Safety Executive will take

the lead in negotiations on this proposal.

14.11 The policy of minimising the use of pesticides set out in *This Common Inheritance* has been pursued through the statutory approvals procedure and by monitoring residues in food and water, guidance to users and by research into more effective pest control. Guidance for the control of weeds on non-agricultural land was published in December 1992.

14.12 The total tonnage of agricultural pesticides used has declined by about 20-25% since the early 1980s. This is partly due to the use, at lower application rates, of more biologically active pesticides, but improvements in agricultural practice, technical developments and economic factors have also been important. It is likely that changes in the Common Agricultural Policy (CAP) will further discourage pesticide use. The UK will work for further reform of the CAP to integrate fully environmental considerations.

INTERNATIONAL PROGRAMMES ON CHEMICALS

14.13 Agenda 21 includes measures to expand and accelerate the international assessment and exchange of information for chemical risks, and to strengthen national capabilities for management of chemicals. Proposals for an Inter-Governmental Forum to consider risk assessment and management of chemicals, developed at the London meeting in December 1991 and endorsed at the Earth Summit, was considered in the International Conference on Chemical Safety (ICCS) held in Stockholm in April 1994.

14.14 The UK, with its EC and OECD partners, is already engaged in major international programmes to assess the risks of chemicals, the results of which will be made widely available through the United Nations International Programme on Chemical Safety.

14.15 International guidelines for the Exchange of Information on Chemicals in International Trade have been agreed by the UN Environment Programme (UNEP)

MAFF's Pesticides Safety Directorate was launched as an executive agency in April 1993

Substances that pollute the aquatic environment will be among the first to feature in risk assessment programmes

117

The fire at Allied Colloids in July 1992 caused a major environmental accident ...

... when fire-fighting water contaminated with chemicals polluted over 50km of the rivers Calder and Aire

and similar principles are included in the Food and Agriculture Organisation (FAO) Code of Conduct on the Distribution and Use of Pesticides. These principles, including the principle of prior informed consent (PIC), have been introduced into an EC Council Regulation concerning the export and import of certain dangerous chemicals.

14.16 The UNCED Conference recommended that consideration should be given to a legally binding international instrument to make application of the PIC procedure contained in the UNEP Guidelines and FAO Code into a legal obligation. An international task force convened by UNEP has begun to consider the elements of a legally binding instrument for the mandatory application of the PIC procedure.

14.17 The Earth Summit also identified the need for technical training and assistance for developing countries on the management of chemicals. The Government supports a wide range of training activities on the safe use of chemicals, especially pesticides, through its bilateral aid programmes and its contributions to international programmes.

MAJOR CHEMICAL ACCIDENTS

14.18 The prevention of major accidents involving dangerous substances at chemical plants and warehouses is covered by the EC 'Seveso' Directive. This Directive also aims

to limit the consequences to man and the environment of any accidents which do occur. This Directive is implemented in Great Britain by the Health and Safety Executive's Control of Industrial Major Accident Hazards (CIMAH) Regulations 1984.

14.19 The EC has carried out a fundamental review of the 'Seveso' Directive and a proposal for a revised Directive is awaited. It is expected to be based on the UK's best practice and will be easier to apply and enforce across Europe. It will also include requirements for land use planning and improved measures for environmental protection. The UK will give this proposal priority when it is published and will strongly support its adoption.

14.20 The Department of the Environment is working to improve protection for the environment from the effects of major accidents. New guidance, based on the results of monitoring after recent accidents, will shortly be published to help prevent future contamination, particularly of water from fire fighting activities.

GENETICALLY MODIFIED ORGANISMS AND BIOTECHNOLOGY

14.21 New regulations to implement EC Directives on the contained use, and deliberate release and marketing of GMOs came into force on 1 February 1993, following consultation with industry and environmental interest groups.

14.22 Under the new regulations, the Advisory Committee on Releases to the Environment (ACRE) was made a statutory body. ACRE has continued to provide Government with valuable advice. Reduced bureaucratic burdens have stemmed from the introduction from January 1994 of 'fast track' procedures for low hazard, or low risk, GMO releases, and for exact repeat applications, in addition to the earlier system of 'standard' and 'streamlined' releases.

14.23 Criteria for new simplified procedures were agreed by the EC in

September 1993. The Government will ask the Commission to apply simplified procedures early in 1994, and aims to encourage acceptance of a risk-based and hierarchical approach to regulation of GMOs throughout the EC.

14.24 In 1994, the Government will launch a new initiative to promote 'green biotechnologies'. These include the use of living organisms as an alternative to chemicals in processes, for example, for cleaning up contaminated land or water.

14.25 The Government will also:

- continue to promote a common approach to risk assessment methods throughout the EC;

- investigate options for policy mechanisms to encourage the application of biotechnology for environmental management and protection;

- through the European Committee for Standardisation (CEN), seek standardisation of methods for the collection of GMO safety data in Europe;

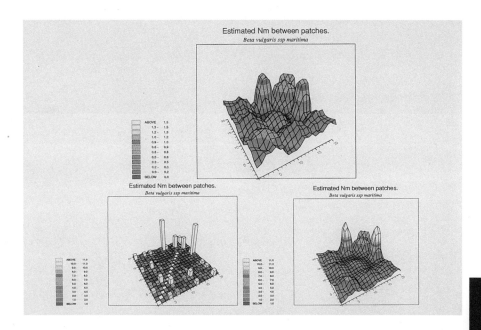

- publish, with ACRE, guidance and a newsletter for informing those wishing to release GMOs; and

- hold further seminars on regulatory policy for biotechnology practitioners.

14.26 The Government will work closely with industry via the Biotechnology Industry Government Regulatory Advisory Group, and with environmental interests via an informal consultation group.

Computer representation of data on beet gene dispersal helped to design risk management safeguards for releases of genetically modified plants

REF NO	SUMMARY OF PREVIOUS WHITE PAPER COMMITMENTS	ACTION TO DATE	COMMITMENTS TO FURTHER ACTION
403	Publish consultation paper on ways to control diffuse sources of the most dangerous chemicals and encourage their substitution with safer ones (FYR p157, SYR 287)	Discussion paper published March 1994	Subject to consultation, develop criteria for selection of priority pollutants
404	Pursue further reductions of lead, cadmium and other dangerous substances. Ban lead solder in water pipes, October 1992. Implement EC Cadmium Directive March 1993 (SYR 288,290-1)	Unleaded petrol now takes 54% of market. HMIP guidance on use of lead, cadmium and mercury in IPC processes published 1993. Regulations controlling use of cadmium introduced July 1993. Ban on lead solder still under consideration	
405			Issue discussion paper on options for reducing exposure to heavy metals, including voluntary agreements
406	Reach a decision on the creation of an Institute for Environment and Health (SYR 289)	Institute established in July 1993 by Medical Research Council	Agree joint DOE/DH/MRC programme of work
407			Participate in Second European Conference on Environment and Health in Helsinki, June 1994. Host working group on air pollution and respiratory disease
408	Take measures to reduce levels of dioxins and other toxic substances in the environment. Implement EC Directive on maximum dioxin limits for pentachloro-phenol (PCP). Continue to monitor toxic micro-pollutants in air (13.10-12, SYR 292,294)	IPC implemented for incineration processes. EC Directive which sets maximum dioxin limits for PCP implemented. Monitoring in progress	
409	Pursue negotiations in Europe to limit asbestos to essential uses only. Reach consensus nationally and in EC on essential uses (SYR 295)	UK proposals to restrict asbestos blocked in EC	Assess options for domestic action to restrict further use of asbestos in UK
410			Review risks to health from asbestos and other fibrous dusts in homes and issue updated guidance by end 1994
411	Scrutinise new chemicals coming on to the market for the first time for risks to human health or the environment (13.14, SYR 296)	Over 500 new chemicals have now been evaluated in EC	
412	Negotiate EC Directive on risk assessment for new chemicals for adoption by April 1993. Implement EC Directive on notification of new chemicals by October 1993 (SYR 297-299)	Notification of New Substances Regulations 1993 came into force on 31 January 1994; Directive on risk assessment agreed and implemented in these Regulations	

REF NO	SUMMARY OF PREVIOUS WHITE PAPER COMMITMENTS	ACTION TO DATE	COMMITMENTS TO FURTHER ACTION
413	Introduce classification and labelling of chemicals for environmental hazard by 1993 (SYR 300)	Regulations requiring environmental labelling introduced September 1993. Classification of 100 chemicals agreed	
414			Further amendments to Regulations for classifying chemicals by 1 January 1995
415	Introduce procedures for obtaining information on chemicals already in use, setting priorities and carrying out risk assessments (13.17-18, SYR 301-4,306)	Eight national environmental assessments of high tonnage chemicals published	Agree priority setting and risk assessment procedures with EC partners by end of 1994. Data on 2000 substances to be submitted by June 1994. Seven more environmental assessments to be published in 1994
416	Adopt EC Regulation on evaluating risks of existing chemicals and prepare UK legislation to implement it (SYR 306)	EC Regulation came into force June 1993	
417	Participate actively in international programmes, including International Programme on Chemical Safety projects and OECD reviews of risks of chemicals produced in high tonnage, and support the creation of inter-governmental mechanism for risk assessment and management (SYR 305-7)	UK has taken lead on nine chemicals as part of the OECD high production volume programme. Contributed to five reviews by IPCS	Complete assessments on seven chemicals as part of OECD programme. Participate in drafting of four chemical status reports. Contribute to a further three IPCS reviews
418			Extend OECD chemicals test guideline programmes to include tests for pesticides, and develop new test methods which require fewer, or no, laboratory animals
419	Host international conference on risk assessment in London in October 1992 (SYR 308)	Successful conference held with participants from 30 countries. Proceedings published in March 1993	
420			Participate in International Conference on Chemical Safety
421			DOE to publish guide to assessment of risks to the environment in 1994
422	Develop rationale for identifying and setting priorities for sources which may become subjects for SAHSU studies (SYR 310)	SAHSU studies into incidence of cancer near municipal incinerators and in South Wales due to be published in mid-1994. Priority setting scheme finalised and agreed by steering committee	Arrange for follow-up resulting from SAHSU investigations as appropriate
423	Treble by 1993 the annual evaluation rate of older pesticides already in use before the statutory approval system was introduced (13.24, SYR 313)	Seven older agricultural and three older non-agricultural active ingredients reviewed EC list of 'top 90' active ingredients agreed and published in Official Journal in December 1992	

REF NO	SUMMARY OF PREVIOUS WHITE PAPER COMMITMENTS	ACTION TO DATE	COMMITMENTS TO FURTHER ACTION
424	Subject pesticides to a rigorous and independent approval system and prepare for the introduction of EC approvals procedures (13.22, SYR 311-4)	Regulations to implement EC plant protection products Directive issued for consultation	
425			UK national programme for reviews of active ingredients to be integrated with EC 10 year review programme. Uniform principles of the Directive, when agreed, to be applied to authorisations
426	Launch Pesticides Safety Division of MAFF as an agency in 1993 (SYR 314) (MAFF)	Pesticides Safety Directorate launched as an executive agency April 1993	
427	Limit pesticide use to the minimum necessary (13.22, SYR 312)	Government is supporting research into minimising pesticide use and its environmental impact. 1992 CAP reform will reduce economic pressures to use pesticides	Amend *Code of Practice on Safe Use of Pesticides on Farms and Holdings,* which will put emphasis on integrated pest management methods and good plant protection product practice
428			Research the practicability of economic instruments to support pesticide minimisation policy
429	Maintain campaign against illegal poisoning (SYR 312)	*1992 Annual Report* of investigations of suspected incidents of animal poisoning published September 1993. Vigorous campaign, in conjunction with countryside and conservation bodies, continued	
430	Seek agreement for EC Directive on biocides by September 1993 (SYR 315)	UK initiative adopted as EC proposal	
431			Consult with UK interests and negotiate a Directive which will protect human health and the environment and secure a single market in biocides, without imposing unnecessary costs on industry
432	Enhance monitoring of pesticide residues in food, water and wildlife and publish results (13.27, SYR 316)	*Third Annual Report of Working Party on Pesticide Residues* published November 1992. *Fourth Annual Report* published January 1994, reporting results for over 3100 samples. Detailed assessment of 1988-90 results published November 1992, reporting results for over 7000 samples totalling over 150,000 pesticide/commodity combinations	Results of the monitoring programmes will continue to be published
433	Consider recommendation of RCEP 16th Report. Publish guidance on use of herbicides for non-agricultural purposes (SYR 312,317)		Government response to be published shortly

REF NO	SUMMARY OF PREVIOUS WHITE PAPER COMMITMENTS	ACTION TO DATE	COMMITMENTS TO FURTHER ACTION
434	Implement international agreements and EC Regulation on the import and export of dangerous chemicals (13.31, SYR 318)	Amended EC Regulation, incorporating the principle of prior informed consent, came into effect in November 1992 and 302 export notifications have been made, including 291 from UK	
435			Strengthen the legal basis of the UNEP and FAO agreements on trade in dangerous chemicals as part of Agenda 21
436	Continue to sponsor training courses for people from developing countries on the assessment and safe use of hazardous chemicals (13.31, SYR 319) (ODA)	ODA, through National Resources Institute, continues to support a range of training activities	
437	Ensure that relevant industrial installations identify the risk of a major accident, demonstrate the safety of their operations and prepare on- and off-site emergency plans (13.38-9, SYR 320-1)	UK strongly supports controls and has continued to press EC to publish proposals for new Directive on control of major accident hazards	
438			Implement revised 'Seveso' Directive, once agreed
439	Existing controls on installations where manufacture, processing or storage of hazardous substances occurs to include consideration of environmental as well as human risks (SYR 321-2)	Research into mitigation and remediation of effects of major accidents on the environment commissioned, and effects on environment of recent accidents monitored, by DOE. Results of studies will be used to prepare new and update existing guidance	
440			Prepare guidance to improve protection of the environment from the effects of major accidents
441			Review HSE risk criteria document for land use planning near major industrial hazards
442	Introduce revised regulations to implement controls on GMO research and release before end 1992. DOE and HSE to establish and operate efficient and effective statutory system to protect human health and ensure environmental safety which does not impose unnecessary burdens on industry (13.50, SYR 323)	Regulations in force from February 1993. New 'streamlined' and 'fast track' clearance procedures introduced for approvals of certain releases to the environment. Criteria for simplified procedures agreed in EC	Amend regulations to implement simplified procedures agreed in EC
443			Extend the scope for 'streamlining' and 'fast tracking' in UK and further develop simplified procedures in EC

REF NO	SUMMARY OF PREVIOUS WHITE PAPER COMMITMENTS	ACTION TO DATE	COMMITMENTS TO FURTHER ACTION
444	Continue to fund extensive research into GMOs, particularly in assessing risks. Produce reports ranking the risks associated with the release of different genetically modified plants and micro-organisms in the waste streams from contained use facilities (13.50, SYR 324)	Risks posed by GMOs likely to be introduced into UK have been evaluated and results have informed decisions on changes to handling regulation of low risk GMOs. Funding continued at same level as 1992	
445	Work within international fora to encourage international guidelines on risk assessment and management of modern biotechnology with a view to an eventual convention. Promote systems for international co-operation on safety, including information on the export of GMOs (13.52, SYR 325)	Significant progress made in OECD on initiating programmes for mutual acceptance of safety data for GMOs used as biopesticides, bioremediation agents and crop plants. Some progress made towards international agreement on safety of modern biotechnology	Agree mutual acceptance of data procedures in OECD. Promote early international agreement on guidelines for safety of modern biotechnology, with view to possible Convention

15 NUCLEAR POWER AND RADIOACTIVE WASTE

15.1 1993 has been dominated by the decision on discharge authorisations for British Nuclear Fuels plc's (BNFL's) Sellafield site, including discharges arising from the operation of the Thermal Oxide Reprocessing Plant (THORP). Following public consultation and the most careful examination of all the issues by the responsible Ministers, authorisations were granted - subject to certain amendments - on 16 December 1993. During 1993, electricity generation from the UK's nuclear stations increased significantly and major progress was made towards the completion of Sizewell B. Preparatory work also began on the nuclear review.

NUCLEAR ENERGY

15.2 In 1992-93, total output from Nuclear Electric and Scottish Nuclear combined was 69 Terawatt-hours (TWH), a 21% increase since 1989-90. If the amount of electricity generated by nuclear power stations had been generated by coal, the UK would have emitted about 17 million tonnes more carbon. If the same amount had been generated by gas, emissions would have increased by around 8 million tonnes. However, although emissions of greenhouse gases from the nuclear fuel cycle are very low - less than 1% of the emissions arising from fossil fuels per unit of electricity generated - nuclear power produces wastes of its own and must remain subject to a very strict control regime.

15.3 The first generation Magnox stations continue to generate electricity reliably. However, some of these are reaching the end of their useful life. During 1993, Nuclear Electric decided on commercial grounds to shut down the Trawsfynydd power station, one of the first generation of Magnox nuclear reactors. Work is in hand to decommission this and the two other commercial reactors which have ceased generation - Berkeley and Hunterston A - so that the sites can eventually be returned to a 'green-field' state.

15.4 Sizewell B, the UK's first Pressurised Water Reactor station, is on target to achieve commercial operation in 1994. Work is now in hand at the station to test the systems and finalise the preparations for fuel loading. Nuclear Electric's application for radioactive waste discharge authorisations in respect of the site are being considered by the authorising Departments. The station can only begin operating if these are granted and the pre-operational regulatory requirements of the Health and Safety Executive's Nuclear Installations Inspectorate have been met. The Government has made it clear that capital expenditure approval for any new station will not be granted pending the outcome of the nuclear review. As part of its preparatory work for the review, the Government is carefully considering representations about the review which it has received from members of the public, the nuclear industry and other interested parties. The Government will announce the precise terms of reference for the review, and how it will be conducted, as soon as possible.

REPROCESSING SPENT FUEL

15.5 BNFL already reprocesses spent fuel from Magnox power stations to separate uranium and plutonium, which can be reused, from high-level wastes. In 1978, BNFL received planning consent to construct THORP to reprocess fuel from Advanced Gas-cooled Reactor stations in the UK and from overseas Light Water Reactors. The plant's construction was completed in 1992. The main issue in 1993 has been the consideration of BNFL's application for discharge authorisations for Sellafield, which would include discharges from THORP.

15.6 In 1992, Her Majesty's Inspectorate of Pollution (HMIP) and the Ministry of Agriculture, Fisheries and Food (MAFF) consulted publicly on their proposed draft authorisations. They concluded that no points of substance had been raised concerning the environmental acceptability of the discharges that would require anything more than minor amendments to the authorisations.

15.7 However, many responses raised questions about the justification for nuclear fuel reprocessing generally and the operation of THORP - in particular, the non-proliferation implications and the security risks of an increasing stockpile of plutonium. The Secretary of State for the Environment and the Minister of Agriculture, Fisheries and Food therefore decided to carry out a further round of consultation in which these questions could be considered.

15.8 On 15 December, the Secretary of State for the Environment announced that, following the consultation, he and the Minister for Agriculture, Fisheries and Food had decided that the authorisations should be granted, subject to a number of amendments. These include a requirement that BNFL should provide HMIP and MAFF with reports each year on the means for further reducing discharges and on its forward research and development programme for krypton abatement technology.

15.9 Only issues relating to the impact of the proposed authorisations on health and the environment were considered relevant to the decision being taken and the Ministers concluded that the discharges permitted by the authorisations would not lead to unacceptable risks to human health or the environment. They therefore decided that the authorisations should be granted. The Ministers also considered the wider matters referred to above, such as the justification for reprocessing, economic issues and concerns about nuclear non-proliferation. They concluded that there was sufficient balance of advantage to justify the operation of THORP, and that had these issues "fallen to be taken into account" in the formal consideration of the authorisations, they were satisfied that they would have reached the same decision.

15.10 Greenpeace and Lancashire County Council challenged the Ministers' decisions in the High Court. After consideration of all the issues, the judgement of the Court was that the Ministers had acted in a proper manner in coming to their decisions. The Court rejected the view put forward by Greenpeace that the second consultation had been inadequate for resolving the issues raised, and also concluded that the Ministers had adequately and properly considered all the matters necessary in order for them to conclude a public inquiry was not necessary. The Court also supported the view of the Ministers that an Environmental Impact Assessment under the appropriate EC Directive was not required because THORP had pre-dated the Directive.

15.11 On the wider issue of justification, the Ministers had taken the view that the question of whether reprocessing was justified was not relevant to their decision, but had nevertheless considered the matter as if it were. The Court ruled that justification was indeed relevant to the Ministers' decision but that the Ministers had in the event properly considered this issue and were therefore entitled to reach the conclusion which they did in respect of the authorisations.

Construction of Sizewell B has now been completed

127

RADIOACTIVE WASTE MANAGEMENT

15.12 UK Nirex Limited, which is responsible for implementing the Government's strategy for the disposal of low- and intermediate-level wastes, is currently carrying out surface-based geological investigations at a site near Sellafield to establish the area's suitability for a deep disposal facility. Nirex proposes to investigate the underlying geology internally by excavating a Rock Characterisation Facility (RCF), or 'rock laboratory', and intends to submit a planning application in 1994. The RCF will help Nirex develop the safety case for the repository itself, for which it expects to submit a planning application in 1998-99. Before a decision is taken to build a deep disposal facility, the Government will hold a full public inquiry into the planning application. Should planning permission be granted, the repository will be subject to licensing under the Nuclear Installations Act 1965 (as amended).

15.13 In November 1993, Contracting Parties to the London Convention - a global agreement on dumping wastes at sea - adopted an indefinite ban on the dumping of radioactive waste. The UK has not dumped such waste at sea since 1982, and is already party to a moratorium until 2008 under the 1992 OSPAR Convention for the Protection of the Marine Environment of the North East Atlantic. But the UK abstained, with some other countries, from voting for the resolution because the scientific evidence confirms that controlled sea dumping

presents no harm to the environment or to human health and so may be the best practical environmental option for certain categories of radioactive waste. A suitable formal declaration needed to be lodged to sustain that objection. Whilst the UK Government continues to believe in the scientific evidence confirming the safety of sea dumping, when carried out under controlled conditions, it has accepted the weight of international opinion on this issue and announced on 17 February 1994 that the UK would accept the ban. The London Convention plans to undertake a scientific re-evaluation after 25 years, and the UK will contribute to that or to any earlier review that might be required by changed international opinion.

HEALTH CONCERNS

15.14 In October 1993, HSE published its study of leukaemia and other cancers in the children of male workers employed at Sellafield. Work has continued on the projects commissioned by the Co-ordinating Committee on Health Aspects of Radiation Research, and jointly funded by HSE and the Department of Health, examining the reported association between paternal exposure to ionising radiation and the incidence of childhood leukaemia. These include a major study linking data on the National Registry of Radiation Workers with information on child cancer databases.

15.15 The more stringent recommendations for radiological protection adopted by the International Commission on Radiological Protection (ICRP) in 1990 have led to proposals for revision of both the International Basic Safety Standards and the Euratom Directive on Basic Safety Standards. The National Radiological Protection Board published its formal advice to the Government on the ICRP's revised recommendations in 1993.

RADIOACTIVE WASTE MANAGEMENT ADVISORY COMMITTEE

15.16 As a result of representations made during consultation on the Sellafield

RIMNET Phase II uses state of the art technology to monitor overseas nuclear emergencies

OVERSEAS NUCLEAR ACCIDENTS

The Chernobyl accident in April 1986 alerted countries worldwide to the need to protect against nuclear accidents on an international scale. The UK Government has taken steps to improve its response to incidents of this kind and tackle the problem at source.

After the Chernobyl accident, the Government reviewed its nuclear emergency contingency planning arrangements. As a result, it decided to set up a new National Response Plan to deal with the consequences of any future overseas nuclear accident. A key feature of the plan was a new nuclear emergency system, RIMNET. Responsibility for installing and operating RIMNET was given to the Department of the Environment.

An interim Phase 1 system, costing over £1 million and providing 46 continuous monitoring stations, has been in operation since 1988. This system automatically raises the alarm if any abnormal increases in radiation are noted at any of the sites.

The installation of the interim system gave time for a larger and more sophisticated Phase 2 system to be designed and procured. This became operational at the end of 1993.

The Phase 2 system uses state-of-the-art technology and is one of the most advanced systems of its kind in the world. It doubles the number of fixed monitoring stations to 92. It also allows approved organisations throughout the UK to enter a wide range of other radiological measurements - of air, food, water and the environment - directly into a national database. Improved communications allow the rapid transfer of data and information between Government Departments, to the relevant local official bodies, and ultimately to the public. Summaries of RIMNET monitoring results will be published regularly. RIMNET will also be used to support the response to any accident at a UK nuclear site.

But it is not enough to be able to take quick and decisive action in response to an overseas nuclear accident; the risk of another Chernobyl-type disaster needs to be reduced. For the countries of Central and Eastern Europe and the former Soviet Union, a multilateral programme of action has been established with a view to helping them in their efforts to improve nuclear safety. This programme includes measures in the areas of operational safety improvements, technical improvements to plants based on safety assessments, and enhancing regulatory regimes. The UK Government, the Nuclear Installations Inspectorate and the UK's nuclear industry are all playing an active part in this effort both bilaterally and in the context of multilateral, including EC, assistance programmes. In furtherance of this, the UK has contributed £8.25 million to the multilateral fund for nuclear safety assistance to the above countries. In the area of radioactive waste management and regulation, the Department of Environment hosted, in November and December 1993, a seminar with senior Russian and Kazakh officials responsible for the countries' nascent regulatory systems. The programme included visits to nuclear sites in the UK and a series of lectures by UK regulators and waste producers.

discharges, the Radioactive Waste Management Advisory Committee (RWMAC) was asked for its views on the usefulness of collective dose assessment. RWMAC considered that it was a useful comparative measure of global radiological impact, but that considerable uncertainties were involved, and Greenpeace's use of it to assert that 600 people would die as a result of the operation of THORP had been misleading.

15.17 In 1993, RWMAC was also asked to provide the Government with further advice on BNFL's proposals for waste substitution, whereby the company would return to the overseas customers with whom it has return of waste contracts an additional amount of high-level waste in place of the intermediate- and low-level wastes arising from reprocessing. RWMAC's views are expected in 1994.

REF NO	SUMMARY OF PREVIOUS WHITE PAPER COMMITMENTS	ACTION TO DATE	COMMITMENTS TO FURTHER ACTION
446	Hold a full scale review of nuclear policy in 1994 (15.38, SYR 326) (DTI)	Work on review brought forward. Preparatory work under way	Precise terms of reference and conduct of the review to be announced as soon as possible
447	Government to publish a strategy for nuclear research and development by early 1993 (15.38, SYR 327) (DTI)	Completed. Information about nuclear R&D programmes set out in DTI's Government Expenditure Plans for 1993-94	
448	Government to ensure that (nuclear) waste arising from post-1976 reprocessing contracts will be returned to overseas customers (15.35, SYR 328)	RWMAC produced first report and is to provide further technical advice on BNFL's proposals for waste substitution	RWMAC's advice awaited. Decide whether BNFL should be allowed to offer substitution to its overseas customers
449	UK Nirex Ltd to speed up investigations into a potential underground (radioactive) waste disposal site. Subject any proposal to a full public inquiry (15.29,15.38, SYR 329,331)	Proposals for a Rock Characterisation Facility (RCF) announced	Nirex to submit planning application for RCF in 1994. Application for repository to be made in 1998-99, leading to a public inquiry
450	Nuclear generating companies to improve the economic efficiency of nuclear stations and complete Sizewell B without compromise to safety standards (15.38, SYR 330)	Nuclear generating companies have continued to achieve record output and reduced costs at existing power stations	Sizewell B is on target to start commercial operation in 1994, subject to the receipt of the necessary regulatory consents
451	Commission further research into the medical aspects of radiation, especially regarding cancers in the children of workers employed in the nuclear industry. Publish results of survey (15.16, SYR 332) (HSE)	Two epidemiology studies currently under way, together with three laboratory studies. One laboratory study finished and due to be published	
452	Continue research into nuclear safety (15.21, SYR 333) (HSE)	HSE co-ordinated programme of some £11m together with a DTI funded programme of some £1.2m in 1993-94	
453	Maintain and enhance emergency arrangements and establish the second phase of the RIMNET overseas emergency monitoring. Extend to 92 sites (15.24, SYR 334)	Second phase of RIMNET installed	
454			Evaluate use of RIMNET for routine radiation monitoring of the UK environment
455	Produce revised regulations in line with EC Directive to implement new standards for radiological protection (15.18, SYR 335)	Regulations introduced in 1993 and January 1994 to implement controls on transfrontier shipments	Reach agreement on revised EC Basic Safety Standards Directive for protection of the health of workers and the general public against the dangers of ionizing radiation
456	Government to keep sea disposal option for large items of radioactive waste arising from decommissioning under review (15.30, SYR 336)	UK has accepted the indefinite total ban on the sea dumping of radioactive wastes agreed by the London Convention in November 1993	

16 NOISE

16.1 The Government has taken action to maximise the effectiveness of environmental noise controls and to extend them where appropriate. Guidance on the control of noise from surface mineral workings was issued in April 1993 and an EC Directive on Aircraft Noise implemented in July. A Private Member's Bill extending local authority powers to control certain types of noise in the street received Royal Assent in November. Consultation has taken place on draft noise insulation regulations for new railways.

HIGHLIGHTS

New legislation to control certain types of noise in the street

Guidance issued on the control of noise from surface mineral workings

Consultation on draft noise insulation regulations for new railways

NOISE AND STATUTORY NUISANCE ACT 1993

16.2 The Noise and Statutory Nuisance Act 1993 received Royal Assent on 5 November 1993. Its provisions closely mirror proposals in a 1992 consultation paper to strengthen the law on noise.

16.3 The Act gives local authorities new powers to investigate and deal with certain types of noise in the street. There are special procedures for serving abatement notices where those responsible for noisy vehicles, machinery or equipment cannot be found, and powers to enable local authorities to take action where the terms of an abatement notice have not been met.

16.4 The Act gives local authorities adoptive powers to give consent to the operation of non-advertising loudspeakers in the street outside the national time band of 8am to 9pm. It also provides adoptive powers to enable local authorities to require burglar alarms to comply with certain technical standards and require those responsible to inform the police of the names and addresses of keyholders. The Act also prescribes a clear basis for the power of entry into premises to de-activate alarms. The Act

also empowers local authorities in England and Wales to put a legal charge on premises to recover expenses incurred in tackling statutory nuisances. With the exception of the audible intruder alarms provisions, the Act came into force on 5 January 1994. The Government has issued a draft circular to local authorities and other bodies providing advice on the use of the new powers. A final circular will be issued as soon as possible.

TRANSPORT

16.5 Draft noise insulation Regulations for new railways were issued for consultation in October 1993. Once the responses to the consultation have been considered, the Government plans to lay Regulations before Parliament in 1994.

16.6 Porous asphalt, which reduces traffic noise, is now being used in noise-sensitive areas where it is justified and trials of quieter concrete road surfaces are under way. Guidance on the design of barriers to contain traffic noise and reduce the visual impact of roads will be issued in mid-1994.

16.7 The UK implemented the EC Directive on Aircraft Noise in July 1993, with the result that older, noisier commercial jet aircraft will be phased out between 1995 and 2002.

16.8 The results of consultation on proposals to change the legislation controlling aircraft noise were announced in March 1993. The main proposal is for a new power of designation for the Secretary of State for Transport. Aerodromes designated under the new power would be required to prepare noise mitigation schemes and agree them locally. Legislation will be introduced when a Parliamentary opportunity arises. In the meantime, the Government will prepare guidance to encourage aerodromes to review their noise measures and disseminate best practice.

MILITARY AIRFIELDS AND RANGES

16.9 The Ministry of Defence (MOD) has recently completed a review of the policy, established in 1985, for noise insulation around military airfields. The review concluded that no major changes were warranted.

16.10 Since 1987, MOD has sponsored research into methods of predicting 'impulsive' noise to minimise nuisance for those who live and work near training and operational areas. An Acoustic Prediction Package, which performs noise calculations and predicts maximum noise levels, will help predict noise pollution more accurately and reduce the nuisance for those near Army and MOD ranges.

16.11 MOD is also involved in NATO studies on helicopter noise. A study on 'startle' noise from low flying military aircraft will begin early in 1994.

PLANNING

16.12 The Government issued Minerals Planning Guidance on the control of noise at surface mineral workings (MPG11), in April 1993. It will shortly issue Planning Policy Guidance describing

how the planning system can minimise the impact of noise. The guidance proposes 'noise exposure categories' to help consideration of applications for residential development which are likely to be affected by transport noise and advises on the use of planning conditions to minimise the effect of noise from development.

NOISE MEDIATION

16.13 The Department of the Environment held a seminar in October 1993 on noise mediation as a means of tackling neighbourhood noise problems and how best to publicise its benefits. The Department will be issuing in spring 1994 an information pack for those interested in setting up noise mediation schemes (see Box).

RESEARCH

16.14 The Government completed its analysis of national noise incidence and noise attitude surveys in 1993. A full review of the content of the noise research programme was also conducted. Research will be commissioned in 1994 into the social aspects of domestic and neighbourhood noise nuisances. The Department of the Environment is also reviewing its neighbourhood noise publicity strategy in the light of research started at the beginning of 1994.

Mediation is a cost-effective and often more appropriate option in responding to domestic noise disputes

The UK implemented the EC Directive on Aircraft Noise in July 1993

Noisy neighbours

An avoidable situation if people reduce the noise they make

16.15 The Government continues to publicise and promote noise awareness; people need to be aware of the noise they make and to minimise it wherever possible. The leaflet *Constant Barking Can Be Avoided* was published in spring 1993. It explains some simple things dog owners can do to prevent dogs disturbing neighbours by constantly barking or whining.

NOISE MEDIATION SCHEMES

Domestic noise, such as music, barking dogs and DIY activities, is the main source of noise complaints to local authorities. Increasingly, local authorities are recognising the value of mediation as a cost-effective and often more appropriate option in responding to domestic noise disputes.

There are over 30 community mediation schemes in the UK and over half the disputes they seek to resolve involve noise. The Government has supported a noise mediation scheme in Bristol, and continues to support one in Southwark, with grants from the Environmental Action Fund.

Mediation aims to help disputing parties resolve conflicts without recourse to litigation. In most cases, contact is through an intermediary, who may counsel the parties individually and agree the terms of a written agreement to resolve the problem. The parties may also choose to meet face to face. Success rates vary but nine out of ten face-to-face mediations end with an agreement.

REF NO	SUMMARY OF PREVIOUS WHITE PAPER COMMITMENTS	ACTION TO DATE	COMMITMENTS TO FURTHER ACTION
457	Monitoring and feedback studies on requirements for sound insulation in Building Regulations to be undertaken (SYR 337)	Study being undertaken to monitor sound insulation between converted flats	
458	New Regulations for the insulation of homes affected by noise from new rail lines to be prepared for consultation by spring 1993 (SYR 338) (DOT)	Draft noise insulation Regulations for new railway lines issued for consultation in October 1993	Lay Regulations before Parliament in 1994, after considering response to consultation
459	Implement EC Directive on Aircraft Noise by mid-1993 (SYR 339) (DOT)	EC Directive implemented July 1993	
460	Implement new noise limit for buses, coaches and heaviest goods vehicles (SYR 339) (DOT)		EC Noise Directive to be implemented by mid-1990s
461	Consider other ways of monitoring and controlling vehicle noise pollution (SYR 340) (DOT)	Preliminary research indicates that, for motor cycles and HGVs, roadside testing is feasible, but further work is needed	Three-year research project to investigate noise measurement methods and limit values to start in 1994
462	Undertake research into nuisance caused by night flying and publish report of main findings in autumn 1992 (16.22, SYR 341) (DOT)	*Report of a Field Study of Aircraft Noise and Sleep Disturbance* published January 1993	
463	Undertake trials for quieter surface textures for concrete roads (SYR 342) (DOT)	Trials begun; porous asphalt being used where justifiable	Consider outcome of trials. Review relationship between skidding resistance of surfaces and noise
464	Update and issue guidance on noise barriers (SYR 342) (DOT)		Design guidance to be issued on reducing the visual impact of roads and noise screening in spring 1994
465			Review construction standards and specification for noise barriers (DOT)
466	Review current arrangements for mitigating noise nuisance at smaller airfields and examine action to limit the temporary use of land for helicopter landing and take off (16.23, 16.27, SYR 343-4) (DOT)	Following consultation, conclusions announced in March 1993	Introduce legislation as Parliamentary time allows. Commission and consult on guidance
467	Qualifying boundary for compensation at each military airfield to be reviewed at 5-yearly intervals or earlier if there is a significant change in the number and/or type of aircraft using the airfield (SYR 345) (MOD)	Compensation schemes have resulted in installation of secondary glazing for more than 15,500 homes. Offers to purchase have been made to about 140 owners of homes subject to particularly intrusive noise levels. Policy review of the criteria for five-yearly reviews of qualifying boundaries and the effect of helicopter noise completed early 1994	
468			Consideration being given to alternative methods of increasing sound attenuation of homes other than by secondary glazing

REF NO	SUMMARY OF PREVIOUS WHITE PAPER COMMITMENTS	ACTION TO DATE	COMMITMENTS TO FURTHER ACTION
469	Issue new guidance on siting developments to avoid noise nuisance (16.26, SYR 346)		PPG *Planning and Noise* to be issued shortly
470	Consider extending the scope of powers to control construction site noise to other similar activities. Issue guidance note by October 1992 (16.36, SYR 347)	MPG11 *Control of Noise at Surface Mineral Workings* issued in April 1993	
471	Make it easier for local authorities to set up Noise Abatement Zones (16.35, SYR 348)	First phase of research completed	Consider effectiveness in the light of findings
472	Introduce mandatory controls over burglar alarms and monitor powers. Act to improve car alarms and encourage development of an EC car alarm standard (16.15, SYR 349)	Noise and Statutory Nuisance Act 1993 includes powers to control noise from burglar and car alarms	
473			Prepare Regulations under UK law to introduce 30 second restriction on car alarms (DOT)
474	Continue to fund noise mediation scheme in Bristol and commence funding noise mediation scheme in Southwark (SYR 350)	Funded schemes in Bristol and Southwark; funding for Southwark scheme continuing. Noise mediation seminar held October 1993	Disseminate good practice and issue information pack
475	Continue to undertake research into reducing and recording noise, including: national noise attitude survey; industrial and low frequency noise; and a model for human response to transport noise (16.46, SYR 351)	Research still in progress on human response to noise from various sources	Let further research projects, including new project to study social aspects of neighbourhood noise
476			Prepare final circular to local authorities on their duties in implementing the provisions of the Noise and Statutory Nuisance Act 1993

17 INVOLVING THE PUBLIC

17.1 Promoting environmental awareness, education and knowledge remains an integral part of the UK's environmental strategy. The Government has strengthened citizens' rights of access to environmental information and has encouraged local authorities to issue charters to inform the public of the environmental services they provide. Government-sponsored publicity campaigns will promote awareness and encourage action across the UK, especially among young people.

HIGHLIGHTS

Improved access to environmental information

Model local environment charter published

'Green Brigade' initiative for young people launched

First Ecolabelled products appear in the shops

ENVIRONMENTAL RIGHTS

Access to Environmental Information

17.2 Regulations to give the public greater access to environmental information came into force on 31 December 1992. The Department of the Environment published guidance in the same month on the implementation of these regulations and has issued a leaflet to explain people's rights. It will produce a booklet in 1994 which will provide advice on how to obtain environmental information using the statutory registers which are open to the public. DOE is also considering the case for an independent tribunal to hear disputes about requests for information.

Citizen's Charter and the Environment

17.3 The Government, with the local authority associations, published a model local environment charter, *Your Council and the Environment,* in November 1993. This provides a model for local authorities to use in drawing up their own charters, which will include declarations of standards and targets for the environmental services they provide locally. The model charter, which sets out citizens' rights to those

services and responsibilities, was developed in consultation with local authorities, business, consumer and environmental groups.

LOCAL ACTION

Encouraging people to act responsibly

17.4 The Government recognises that people can have a significant effect on the environment. For example, the Government-funded campaign 'Helping the Earth begins at Home' is intended to make people aware of the link between energy use and global warming. Other campaigns include advice on protecting the ozone layer, reducing summertime smog, using 'poop scoops' and helping to protect wildlife from illegal poisoning. The Government also supports a number of organisations which provide environmental information and advice.

Ecolabelling

17.5 Individuals can also help protect the environment by taking environmental considerations into account when making purchases. The European Community's Ecolabelling Scheme aims to provide independent and authoritative guidance to consumers by awarding the distinctive ecolabel to products which are less harmful to the environment than the alternatives. By buying ecolabelled goods, consumers can encourage manufacturers and retailers to make and stock greener products.

17.6 The Government has set up the UK Ecolabelling Board to administer and promote the Scheme nationally and in July 1993, the first product criteria, those for washing machines and dishwashers, were adopted and published by the European Commission. The UK is disappointed with the slow progress of the Scheme and is continuing to press the Commission and other Member States for its faster development. The ecolabel should appear on an increasing range of products in the shops during 1994.

Action by Local Government

17.7 Local government has been active in developing policies and programme responses to Agenda 21 and the EC Fifth Environmental Action Programme through its Local Agenda 21 Initiative. The Government has encouraged and supported this initiative and provided practical help by supporting a series of round table meetings to address key environmental issues. The Central and Local Government Environment Forum has continued to meet and has initiated work in a number of areas, including energy efficiency. Guidance to local government on Eco-Management and Audit has also been published. The Government plans to introduce a voluntary local government scheme by 1995, based on the EC Eco-Management and Audit Regulation for the manufacturing industry.

Action by Individuals

17.8 There remains an important role for the individual in the home and at work. Over 70% of people believe that the actions they take in their own lives can make a difference to the environment, but feel that they need more practical advice on what they should do. The Department

of the Environment plans to pilot an initiative in 1994-95 to encourage volunteers to become involved in their local environment. The new Citizens' Environment Initiative mentioned in chapter 3 will also take shape in the coming year. It is designed to give individuals the advice and ideas they are looking for on how to care more for the environment in daily life.

Voluntary sector

17.9 The voluntary sector remains involved in a wide range of activities to influence environmental policy development and tackle practical problems locally, nationally and internationally. The Government is keen to encourage the involvement of as many non-environmental groups as possible. It has decided to review, with representatives of the main environmental groups, whether new initiatives are required to secure greater involvement.

Environmental Action Fund

17.10 The Environmental Action Fund (EAF), launched in 1992, supports voluntary sector environmental projects. In 1993-94, the EAF provided about £4 million to 91 organisations for support in carrying out 104 projects. A Local Projects Fund, set up in 1993, supports local groups.

The Government is keen to encourage the involvement of as many non-environmental groups as possible in tackling environmental problems

The Government, with the Local Authority Associations, published a model local environment charter *Your Council and the Environment* in November 1993

139

In 1993, the Government launched the 'Green Brigade', a programme to encourage young people to put their concerns for the environment into practice

17.11 The LIFE programme is the main source of EC funding for environmental initiatives by local authorities, businesses, voluntary groups and individuals. Fourteen UK organisations were selected by the Commission for funding in 1993. Applications for the 1994 programme are currently being considered.

EDUCATION

Schools

17.12 In England and Wales, environmental issues are taught in a number of National Curriculum subjects, including geography, technology and science. Similar arrangements exist in Northern Ireland. In Scotland, national guidelines on environmental studies are produced for the 5-14 year age group. A number of attainment targets for the over-14 age groups deal specifically with the care of the environment.

Further and Higher Education and Training

17.13 The Expert Committee on Environmental Education within Further and Higher Education reported its findings in February 1993. The Committee's report contained 27 recommendations addressed to all those involved in the provision of further and higher education. A concerted effort by all parties in the system was required to provide the workforce with the knowledge, skills and training it would need to assume a greater environmental responsibility.

THE 'GREEN BRIGADE' INITIATIVE FOR YOUNG PEOPLE

Recent research showed that 8 to 15 year-olds are interested and concerned about the environment and are keen to be involved in local projects. In 1993, the Government launched the 'Green Brigade', a programme to encourage young people to put their concerns for the environment into practice.

After a national competition in which young people were invited to give their views on the environment, the winners attended a Young People's Summit in Manchester in September 1993. They discussed with the Secretary of State for the Environment the issues that concerned them most and chose nine projects to share £100,000 from the Green Brigade.

These projects come from across the UK and cover a wide range of issues. They include a scheme in Birmingham to produce an educational pack on recycling for schools and youth groups across the country, and a project in Sussex to turn a disused signal box into an environmental resource centre for children.

Other projects aim to bring an element of fun into environmental work. A scheme in Cornwall will provide bicycles for use on new cycleways. In West Yorkshire, a series of events will combine environmental projects, such as repairing bridleways, with mountain biking.

All nine projects are well under way. These will be used to show other young people across the country how to become involved in local projects.

The Green Brigade has produced two activity packs, the most recent of which, *Every Home Helps,* encourages energy saving in the home. Another activity pack is planned for launch in summer 1994.

REF NO	SUMMARY OF PREVIOUS WHITE PAPER COMMITMENTS	ACTION TO DATE	COMMITMENTS TO FURTHER ACTION
477	Issue proposals on the arrangements to be made to ensure that environmental information on industrial emissions is widely available (17.27, SYR 354)	EC Directive to provide new rights for public access to information implemented 31 December 1992	
478	Guidance to bodies subject to regulations to be published by December 1992 (SYR 354)	Guidance issued in December 1992	
479			Produce a booklet for use by the public giving details of all registers of environmental information and how to use them
480			Review during 1994 present programmes for encouraging individual commitment to the environment
481	Issue charter for local authority environmental services by early 1993 (SYR 355)	Model local environment charter issued 25 November 1993	
482	EC Ecolabelling Scheme due to come into operation in autumn 1992 and first ecolabels to be awarded by the end of 1992 (SYR 32,112, 356)	UK Ecolabelling Board established as UK competent body in November 1992. Scheme launched July 1993 with adoption of criteria for first product groups	
483	Encourage energy and environmental labelling of building products (17.32, SYR 358)	Pilot studies completed end 1992	
484	Rationalise different forms of financial assistance to voluntary groups to create a combined Environmental Action Fund (SYR 52)	Implemented 1992. £4.2m available in fund for 1993-94	
485			Review whether new initiatives are required to encourage more voluntary groups to become involved with sustainable development
486	Increase the profile of environmental education in the National Curriculum through subjects like science and geography (17.35, SYR 359, 363) (DFE)	Orders published for National Curriculum subjects are being introduced	Monitor the development of environmental education through the National Curriculum
487	Sponsor a database of relevant courses on offer at higher and further education level (17.47, SYR 360)	Supporting continued development of the database	
488	Produce a new leaflet designed to inform school children of job opportunities in environmental subjects, and what further and higher education is needed for each (17.50, SYR 361)	Institution of Environmental Sciences, with DOE support, published a handbook covering these issues in May 1993	

REF NO	SUMMARY OF PREVIOUS WHITE PAPER COMMITMENTS	ACTION TO DATE	COMMITMENTS TO FURTHER ACTION
489	Continue specific grant for local authority in-service training, including work on environmental education. Allocate £46.3m in 1993-94 and devolve a further £77m to schools to spend on training or books for the basic curriculum (17.43, SYR 362) (DFE)	In 1993-94, £45.2m was allocated for basic curriculum in-service training and a further £85m devolved to schools to spend on training or books and equipment for basic curriculum and assessment	Specific grant for basic curriculum INSET will continue in 1994-95
490	Establish an expert committee on environmental education within further and higher education, and follow up its findings as appropriate (17.49, SYR 364) (DFE)	Committee's report published February 1993. Recommendations being followed up	
491	Establish a new unit in the higher and further education sector to improve communications between businesses and those providing environmental education and training (17.57, SYR 365) (DFE)	Expert Committee's report included a recommendation on the new unit. Recommendations being considered	
492	Ensure that vocational standards are in place across all environmental occupations. NVQs at levels 2, 3 and 4 in Environmental Conservation and Field Archaeology will be in place by the end of 1992, followed by further qualifications during 1993 (17.61, SYR 366) (ED)	NVQs at levels 2, 3 and 4 now in place in Environmental Conservation and Ecosystems and in Field Archaeology. Discussions now under way regarding NVQs in Environmental Management	
493	Sponsor a series of conferences to bring industry and course providers together (17.50, SYR 367)	The Council for Environmental Education (CEE), supported by a DOE grant, held a series of seminars during 1993	
494			DOE will provide further support to CEE for the publication and dissemination of reports of the seminars to institutions and course providers
495	Consider legislation, possibly by amending the Trade Descriptions Act, to clarify that environmental claims are covered (17.33, SYR 368) (DTI)		Consider legislating when Parliamentary time permits
496	DTI to assist Regional Technology Centres (RTCs) in examining future networking arrangements to promote more effectively the Department's technology transfer programmes, including those with an environmental emphasis (SYR 369) (DTI)	RTC 'open day' presentation by Directors and Managers held February 1993	

18 THE ENVIRONMENT IN WALES

18.1 The Government's wide-ranging programme to improve the Welsh environment continues to forge ahead. Over the last year, substantial progress has been made in removing dereliction, improving the housing stock and promoting energy efficiency and recycling. A new focus for the roads programme for Wales has also been announced. In all of this, the emphasis is on practical action to benefit the Welsh environment. As a stimulus and guide to further progress, a number of new commitments to additional work are made. The main achievements during 1993-94 are described below.

URBAN RENEWAL

Removal of dereliction

18.2 Through the Welsh Development Agency's (WDA) Landscape Wales programme, 450 hectares of derelict land were reclaimed in 1992-93, 16% of which was hazardous or contaminated land. Another 405 hectares are expected to be reclaimed in 1993-94, including the former North Celynen Colliery site in Gwent, where a major new development is proposed. The Agency estimates that another 5600 hectares in Wales may require significant reclamation and it plans to tackle this by 2000. To this end, another 690 hectares are planned for reclamation in 1994-95. Complementing the Agency's work, the Urban Investment Grant (UIG) scheme is also helping to promote development on derelict sites. UIG-supported projects in 1993-94 will trigger £40 million of private sector investment on such land and provide over 40,000 sq metres of new business and office space. These programmes are making an important contribution to reducing development pressures on greenfield sites, in line with sustainable development principles.

Action in the South Wales Valleys

18.3 The Government's 5-year Programme for the Valleys (PFV) came to an end on 31 March 1993. Its achievements included the improvement of more than 7000 homes and the reclamation of over 1080 hectares of derelict land by the WDA in the largest reclamation programme ever undertaken in Europe. A new PFV was launched on 1 April 1993 to build on the progress of the original Programme. In its first year, the new Programme is expected to see the removal of another 200 hectares of dereliction, the renovation of some 5000 homes and the planting of another 48 hectares of community woodland.

18.4 Building on the success of the Ebbw Vale National Garden Festival, the WDA, Blaenau Gwent Borough Council and Gwent County Council have formed a partnership - the Victoria Partnership - to manage future development of the site. A new 25 hectare park, Festival Park, has already been created; and other plans involve a new urban village - Victoria. Overall, the regeneration programme is aiming to create 1100 new jobs and new homes for 500 families.

Cardiff Bay

18.5 The resources given to the Cardiff Bay Development Corporation have been increased for 1993-94 (to £45 million), in line with the gathering pace of the regeneration and the anticipated start (in spring 1994) of work on the Barrage. During the year, the Corporation's activities were expected to lead to a further 1300 jobs, 120 houses, the redevelopment of 9 hectares and £46 million of private sector investment. A site on the Gwent Levels has been identified for possible use as an area for wintering and breeding waterfowl displaced by the Barrage.

Housing Improvement

18.6 Significant progress continues to be made in upgrading the Welsh housing stock. In 1993-94, £145 million has been made available for mandatory grants and a further £26 million in discretionary awards which should enable local authorities to improve over 8000 homes. In addition, 13 housing renewal areas, containing some 12,000 homes, have been declared. Activity within these areas concentrates not only on housing but also on social, environmental and economic conditions. In 1993-94, some 690 homes are expected to be improved through group and block renovation schemes. Another 170 accommodation units are expected to be made available for rent in the private sector by the conversion of under-used space, providing housing as well as contributing to the regeneration of town centres.

Other Action

18.7 The WDA's Urban Development Programme is promoting economic and environmental regeneration in over 30 urban centres, including Llanelli, Swansea, Merthyr Tydfil, Caernarfon and Holyhead. As well as levering in substantial private investment (over £45 million private sector funds secured in 1992-93), the programme is helping to revitalise towns such as Llanelli, where a major reclamation and coastal protection project will release 64 hectares for high quality housing.

The Brecon Beacons, one of 3 National Parks in Wales

18.8 Environmental improvements will also remain a priority under the new Strategic Development Scheme (SDS), to be introduced from 1994-95, which will bring together the Urban Programme, Rural Initiative, Projects of Regional and National Importance and Special Project schemes. In 1993-94 under the Urban Programme, 127 new factory units were programmed, 367 buildings upgraded in town centres such as Porth and Aberdare, and 68 hectares of industrial land improved or serviced.

ROADS PROGRAMME

18.9 The roads programme makes a vital contribution to Wales's economic infrastructure. At the same time, road building can have important environmental consequences. Acknowledging this, the Secretary of State for Wales announced on 3 March 1994 that the M4, A465 and A55 (including the A5 across Anglesey) corridors are to be regarded as the main strategic east-west routes. Significant increases in traffic capacity would not be made on the mainland A5 and the A40 in mid-Wales, which pass through the Snowdonia and Brecon Beacons National Parks respectively. As a result, several planned improvements on these two routes are being abandoned or deferred.

ENERGY EFFICIENCY AND RECYCLING

18.10 The message that energy efficiency

can save money and at the same time help to safeguard the environment through reduced carbon dioxide emissions continues to be actively promoted in Wales. This work has been given renewed emphasis following the recent publication of *Climate Change: The UK Programme,* in which energy efficiency figures prominently. Recent progress has included:

• Action by Business

- energy reduction measures at Monsanto, Newport, are saving the company £300,000 per annum and the Royal Mint has cut its energy bill by one-third while increasing productivity by 50%;
- over 50 major companies in Wales have joined the 'Making a Corporate Commitment' campaign and membership of the Welsh Energy Managers groups has risen to 1600;

• Action in the Public Sector

- energy efficiency in the NHS has improved by 22% between 1984 and 1992, producing savings of some £12 million which have directly benefited patient care programmes. To take this further, an Energy Roadshow is visiting every NHS Unit and Trust in Wales;
- the Welsh Office has reduced its energy consumption by 2% since 1990-91; and over the last year, has invested nearly £100,000 in further

energy saving measures to help the Department meet a 15% target reduction in energy by 1996;

• Action for All

- the Home Energy Efficiency Scheme (HEES) and Home Energy Rating Scheme are providing practical support to domestic consumers in Wales to save energy - 9900 HEES grants totalling £1.6 million are being processed in 1993-94. Three new local energy advice centres are also being established at Cardiff, Swansea and Newport, Dyfed.

Alternative Energy

18.11 Wales is also playing its part in the provision of new and renewable energy sources, which can provide energy with little or none of the pollution of traditional power sources. Over the last year, 12 wind-power projects have been approved, as well as two new hydro-electric schemes. Further bids are being encouraged across the range of renewable energy sources, including landfill gas and forestry waste.

Recycling and Waste Minimisation

18.12 The sensible re-use or recycling of materials continues to be promoted by the Government where it makes economic and environmental sense. Notable developments over the last year include:

- the preparation of recycling plans for their areas for virtually all Welsh local authorities, in line with the Government's target for 25% of household waste to be recycled by 2000. The number of recycling facilities is being increased, including in the more rural areas; and many authorities are investigating alternative methods, including composting household waste;

- the introduction by the Welsh Office of paper and can recycling schemes at its headquarters building in Cardiff. Since the end of 1992, these schemes have

Lady Windsor Colliery, before and after reclamation by the WDA. Part of the largest such programme ever undertaken in Europe

collected 45 tons of paper and 24,000 cans for recycling. Other related measures are being taken within the Department's Green Housekeeping policy, published in March 1993.

PROTECTED AREAS

18.13 During 1993, further sites in Wales have been given protective status:

- two more sites have been added to the List of Internationally Important Wetlands under the Ramsar Convention, bringing the total in Wales to seven;

- the number of Sites of Special Scientific Interest (SSSI) has increased from 841 to 870;

- four new Environmentally Sensitive Areas have been designated (Ynys Môn, Radnor, Preseli and Clwydian Range), taking the total in Wales to seven.

18.14 To aid the positive environmental management of protected sites, the Countryside Council for Wales negotiated 175 new or renewal agreements, covering some 20,000 hectares of SSSI land, in 1992-93.

BUILT HERITAGE

18.15 Significant developments in 1993 to achieve enhanced protection for the built heritage in Wales include 500 more buildings and ancient monuments afforded statutory protection; £2.5 million allocated in support of conservation projects by private individuals and local authorities; and additional support for the Architectural Heritage Fund (over £100,000 in 1993-94). Cadw (Welsh Historic Monuments) has also published a new Heritage Charter under the Citizen's Charter Initiative.

IMPROVEMENT IN RURAL AREAS

18.16 Attention has also been given to the sensitive improvement of rural areas. For example, over the last year, 58 projects in

towns and villages in rural Wales were supported under the Rural Initiative grants scheme. The WDA is also supporting rural environmental improvements: over 100 projects in 1993-94, including a new pedestrian link at Pwllheli.

Support for Agriculture

18.17 Continued emphasis is being given to supporting farmers in their role as custodians of the Welsh countryside. Of particular significance is the new Agri-Environment Programme for Wales announced in March 1993. As well as an expansion of the Environmentally Sensitive Area scheme, the Programme includes a package of incentives to assist in the creation of wildlife habitats, to provide better public access to farmland, to reduce livestock numbers on sensitive moorland sites, and to encourage organic farming methods. The proposed Programme will include the Countryside Commission for Wales's 'Tir Cymen', the Countryside Stewardship Scheme in Wales, which is already making good progress. £1.5 million is expected to be spent on Tir Cymen in 1993-94, covering 200 agreements and 24,200 hectares in the 3 pilot areas.

RESEARCH AND MONITORING

18.18 Over £400,000 has been allocated by the Welsh Office in 1993-94 for environmental research on issues of particular relevance to Wales: acid rain, radioactivity and water pollution. Of the 12 research projects completed in the last 12 months, the most significant was that on PCB contamination in the Panteg area of Pontypool (in the vicinity of the Rechem plant). The study's findings were generally reassuring.

Water Environment

18.19 Water quality in Wales continues to improve. In 1993, 84% of EC-identified Welsh bathing waters met the stringent standards set by the EC Directive; and Welsh Water's £200 million investment programme will mean that all EC-designated

Hedgerow at Brecon. Continued emphasis is being given to supporting farmers in their role as custodians of the Welsh countryside

A55 Conway Crossing - a major improvement fully reflecting environmental considerations

bathing waters in Wales will comply with the Directive by 1997. 94% of river lengths in the NRA's Welsh Region are also judged to be of good or fair quality. In addition, the latest report of the Drinking Water Inspectorate confirms the high public drinking water quality standards in Wales.

GREENING OF POLICIES AND PROGRAMMES

18.20 As well as the review of the Roads Programme and the new Agri-Environment Programme, other significant ways in which environmental considerations are being reflected in Government programmes in Wales during 1993-94 have included:

- the issue of planning guidance - for example, on renewable energy and on the environmental appraisal of development plans - which stresses the importance of environmental issues. New strategic planning guidance for the proposed unitary authorities in Wales is also in preparation;

- the Wales Tourist Board published in 1993 a draft strategy, *Tourism 2000,* which takes sustainability and tourism as a key theme; the Development Board for Rural Wales is developing a new 'green' business park at Machynlleth; the Countryside Council for Wales has published forward-looking green policy proposals in a discussion paper, *Threshold 21;* and the Welsh Development Agency has reviewed its environmental improvement programme.

LOOKING AHEAD

18.21 The Government's overall aim is to protect the environment of Wales, while enabling necessary economic development to proceed. To this end, an integrated, strategic approach to development and conservation will be fostered. Specifically, this will include:

- the removal of major dereliction;
- reviewing the effectiveness of designated areas in achieving environmental objectives;
- regular examination of the Roads Programme to ensure projects are fully justified;
- energy efficiency, especially in the public sector; and
- recycling and waste minimisation.

REF NO	SUMMARY OF PREVIOUS WHITE PAPER COMMITMENTS	ACTION TO DATE	COMMITMENTS TO FURTHER ACTION
497	Issue guidance on road design in lowland areas by end 1992 (29.4, SYR 370)	Consultants appointed to assist with preparation of design guide	New guidance to be published in spring 1994
498	Study to be undertaken of options for improving public transport on A470 corridor (SYR 371)	Study completed and summary published October 1993	Welsh Office to support follow-up study
499			Monitor effectiveness of relocated vegetation salvaged from ancient woodland sites as a potential mitigation measure for new road schemes. Publish findings of monitoring study, and develop guidelines for new road schemes by spring 1995
500	Consider the need for planning guidance on Green Belts in Wales in light of Assembly of Welsh Counties final report (FYR p168, SYR 372)	AWC submitted report on Strategic Planning Guidance in Wales, including Green Belts, to the Secretary of State in July 1993; under consideration	
501	Review pilot scheme (Tir Cymen) after 3 years and consider wider application (SYR 373)		
502	Protect countryside through designated areas and review Cambrian Mountains (Extension) and Lleyn Peninsula ESAs in 1992. Designate new ESAs (19.9, SYR 374)	Cambrian Mountains (Extension) and Lleyn Peninsula ESAs revised during 1993 to provide greater environmental benefits. Ynys Môn, Radnor, Preseli and Clwydian Range designated as new ESAs	Amalgamate Cambrian Mountains (Original and Extension) ESAs during 1994
503	Protect countryside through appropriate national and international designations. Designate 2 more RAMSAR sites; and reach decision on Menai Straits (19.9, SYR 375)	SSSIs increased to 870 and 2 more Ramsar sites designated. Completion of second round of consultations on proposed Menai Straits MNR	Review effectiveness of designations in achieving environmental objectives
504	Ensure that Countryside Council for Wales takes comprehensive view of nature conservation and countryside issues. Introduce new Hedgerow Scheme (19.11, SYR 376)	New Hedgerow Renovation Scheme introduced in autumn 1992	
505	Aim to introduce public rights of way network in Wales by 1995 (SYR 376)		
506	Ensure Cadw achieves enhanced protection for the built heritage (19.22, SYR 377)	Key targets met or exceeded	
507	Develop new Heritage Charter for Wales (SYR 377)	*Heritage Charter* published	
508	Continue to protect scheduled monuments and accelerate resurvey programme; increase the number of inspectors (19.20, SYR 378)	Continued progress in listing and scheduling of buildings and monuments	Listing re-surveys to be doubled (to 40) in 1994-95

18. THE ENVIRONMENT IN WALES

149

REF NO	SUMMARY OF PREVIOUS WHITE PAPER COMMITMENTS	ACTION TO DATE	COMMITMENTS TO FURTHER ACTION
509	Take action to increase awareness appreciation of historic buildings (SYR 378)	Education initiative to increase awareness of heritage under way New *Guidance on Archaeology and Planning* issued. Updated *Guidance on Historic Buildings and Conservation Areas* issued for consultation	Review effectiveness of new guidance and strengthen where appropriate
510	Continue discussions with cathedral authorities about the need for repair grants (19.21, SYR 379)		
511	Hold National Garden Festival at Ebbw Vale and ensure site plays major role in enhancing South Wales Valleys (FYR p169, SYR 380)	Garden Festival closed in October 1992. Festival achieved target of 2 million visitors	
512	Put into effect plans for appropriate after-use of Ebbw Vale site (SYR 380)	Work has already started on developing the after-use of the site	Support the creation of Wales' first new urban village on Festival site
513	Reclaim another 600 hectares of derelict land in 1992-93. Enhance existing urban development measures (SYR 381)	450 hectares reclaimed in 1992-93. Extra £17m provided for Landscape and Urban Development Wales in 1992-93. Further increase of £8m provided for 1993-94 and an additional 405 hectares reclaimed	Reclaim another 690 hectares in 1994-95
514	Support regeneration via the Urban Programme (19.14, SYR 382)	Further £6.3m approved for environmental schemes in 1993-94	Support will continue in 1994-95 under new Strategic Development Scheme
515	Regenerate South Cardiff area through Cardiff Bay Development Corporation (19.17, SYR 383)	Increased resource allocation from £35m to £45m in 1993-94	
516	Restore disused land and buildings via Urban Investment Grant (19.16, SYR 384)	£6.5m of UIG allocated for 1993-94. Expected to trigger £40m of private sector investment	
517	Carry out housing improvements, and provide additional resources for authorities adopting a strategic approach to renovation (19.15, SYR 385)	Increased resources made available in 1993-94 (£171m), including £22m for area based renewal schemes	
518	Meet targets for housing improvements and land clearance in Programme for the Valleys by March 1993 (19.18, SYR 386)	Objectives met New Programme launched April 1993	
519	Further development of Rural Initiative (FYR p170, SYR 387)	Large number of capital projects supported in 1993-94	Support to continue in 1994-95 under new Strategic Development Scheme
520	Publish results of survey of PCB contamination in Pontypool area in 1993 (SYR 388)	Report published April 1993	Publish results of further research in 1994
521	Fund research into environmental matters of relevance to Wales (FYR p170, SYR 389)	Review of environmental research priorities completed. Funding provided for new research on effects of acid rain in Wales	

REF NO	SUMMARY OF PREVIOUS WHITE PAPER COMMITMENTS	ACTION TO DATE	COMMITMENTS TO FURTHER ACTION
522	Monitor water quality objectives in Wales. Introduce statutory water quality objectives gradually from 1993. Ensure investment programmes are completed by 1995 (FYR p170, SYR 390)	Government's proposals for SWQO system published December 1992. Draft Regulations issued for comment October 1993	Continue the process of introducing SWQOs for individual stretches of river gradually during 1994

Continue to monitor and ensure that by 1995 current investment programmes are completed |
| 523 | Continue to support voluntary bodies (FYR p171, SYR 391) | Grant schemes, including 'Environment Wales', continue to provide funding | |
| 524 | Further development of environmental initiatives with business (FYR p171, SYR 392) | Environmental Managers Network launched

Four Business Action Groups established and more in development

Waste minimisation feasibility study being sponsored | Consider scope for further initiatives with industry |
| 525 | Continue to implement energy efficiency strategy (SYR 393) | Since publication of Energy Plan in 1991, progress made in all sectors. Many Welsh firms joined 'Making a Corporate Commitment' campaign. 3 new energy advice centres being established. Energy Roadshows launched for NHS in Wales and visited every Unit and Trust | |
| 526 | Promote environmental education as a cross-curricular theme (19.29, SYR 394) | Joint two-year programme in environmental education set up between Countryside Council for Wales and Curriculum Council for Wales

HMI (Wales) published occasional paper in January 1993 on *Environmental Education in Schools in Wales 1992* | |
| 527 | New guidance on environmental education for Wales to be issued autumn 1992 (SYR 394) | Advisory Paper on *Environmental Education* from the Curriculum Council for Wales issued autumn 1992 | |

19 THE ENVIRONMENT IN SCOTLAND

19.1 During 1993, the Secretary of State for Scotland and Sir Hector Monro, the Green Minister at The Scottish Office, have taken forward a wide range of initiatives to sustain and improve the natural and built heritage of Scotland. Although this chapter concentrates on purely Scottish developments, the Secretary of State remains conscious of the national and international dimensions. The Scottish Office has worked closely with other Government Departments in the preparation of the four post-Rio UK documents.

19.2 Scottish Natural Heritage (SNH) is now in its second year of operation. Its budget for 1993-94 is £36.1 million, which represents a further increase of some 5% on the previous year. The organisation set itself an ambitious list of 50 tasks to be carried out during its first year and 90% of them were completed. SNH's work during the year included the introduction of schemes to provide incentives to landowners to manage their land for its nature conservation and landscape value. SNH is also involved in around 100 research projects and has started to draw up inventories on aspects of the natural heritage such as uplands, peatlands and freshwater resources.

19.3 Historic Scotland, now an Executive Agency, is responsible for safeguarding the nation's built heritage. As well as providing advice and financial assistance to others on built heritage issues, Historic Scotland conserves and preserves over 300 monuments in State care. Following a five-year survey of the conservation needs of monuments in care, it has put in hand a revised Operational Plan covering the maintenance of the estate. It is currently running a three-year study to examine the nature conservation needs at each site. Visitors to monuments in care in 1992-93 totalled 2.3 million.

19.4 Work on implementing the EC Urban Waste Water Directive has been carried forward through a series of public consultations. The water and sewerage authorities, industry and the river purification authorities have been closely involved in this process. Costs will be considerable - in the order of £1.3 billion over the next 12 years - and every effort is being made to ensure that the environmental benefits represent value for money.

THE NATURAL ENVIRONMENT AND ITS PROTECTION

19.5 The Secretary of State for Scotland is currently considering SNH's advice on the designation of Natural Heritage Areas. SNH has also been asked to develop, with other agencies, management measures for Wester Ross and for the Ben Nevis/Glencoe/Black Mount area. SNH will also play an important role in the future management of the Cairngorms, Loch Lomond and the Trossachs.

19.6 SNH has embarked on a number of pilot initiatives to explore how the concept of sustainability might be put into practice. These include a sustainable agriculture project, a local authority pilot with Ettrick

The report of the Cairngorms Working Party included many wide ranging recommendations

and Lauderdale District Council, and a joint initiative with The Scottish Office Agriculture and Fisheries Department looking at sustainable systems of land and water use in Scotland. It also published in October 1993 a policy document setting out SNH's interpretation of sustainable development.

19.7 The report of the Cairngorms Working Party was published in March 1993. It makes proposals for a management strategy for the area and for an administrative mechanism - a partnership board - for delivering the strategy. The Scottish Office has consulted on the recommendations in the report and the Secretary of State is now considering his response. The report of the Loch Lomond and the Trossachs Working Party was published in July 1993. It, too, recommends a number of strategies and includes an administrative structure - a local authority joint committee - for implementing them. This report was also the subject of public consultation.

PARTICIPATION AND PARTNERSHIP

19.8 Expenditure by the Government and its agencies on the four Government-led Partnership Areas will amount to approximately £40 million in 1993-94. More than 1200 projects have been supported through the Urban Programme. Expenditure on these totalled £69 million in 1990-91, and for 1993-94 the Government has increased the funding available to £83

million. The Urban Programme is supporting 14 projects in the environmental improvement category.

19.9 The Government has also continued to provide support for voluntary environmental organisations operating in Scotland. Some 40 organisations received funding totalling £378,000 under the Special Grants (Environmental) Programme and UK2000 Scotland received £435,000. An independent review of the Government's support to this sector concluded that it met policy objectives and gave value for money.

ENERGY AND ENERGY EFFICIENCY

19.10 The Secretary of State for Scotland has announced the Government's intention to introduce a Scottish Renewables Obligation (SRO), which will require ScottishPower plc and Scottish Hydro-Electric plc to obtain more electricity from renewable sources. The first Order to be made under the SRO is expected to be for some 30-40MW of additional renewable capacity and will comprise five technology bands: wind; hydro-electric power; landfill gas from existing sites; municipal and industrial waste; and energy crops from agriculture and forestry wastes.

19.11 As part of a three-year pilot study involving the Energy Saving Trust, seven Local Energy Advice Centres were established in Scotland in 1993. Based in Aberdeen, Edinburgh, Inverness, Lerwick, Dundee and Strathclyde, these centres will provide advice and information on all aspects of energy efficiency to the domestic and small business sectors.

INTEGRATING ENVIRONMENTAL CONCERNS INTO POLICIES AND PROGRAMMES

19.12 Following an earlier consultation exercise, the Secretary of State for Scotland announced in February 1993 the Government's intention to proceed with its plans to establish a Scottish Environment Protection Agency. A Bill enabling preparatory work to be undertaken was

SNH published its own sustainable development document in October 1993

Urban regeneration in Whitfeld, Dundee

153

announced in the Queen's Speech in November 1993.

19.13 The Secretary of State indicated in March 1993 that he would not be proceeding with the introduction of registers of land subject to contaminative uses. The Government is not, however, abandoning its commitment to identifying, assessing and dealing with contaminated land in Scotland. A wide-ranging review of the powers and duties of public bodies to tackle contaminated land is taking place and the Government is currently considering the main issues surrounding contaminated land policy.

19.14 National Planning Policy Guidelines (NPPGs) have now been issued on business and industry and land for housing; further guidance on mineral workings, archaeology and the planning system is at the post-consultation stage. Following consultation, planning guidance on renewable energy will be issued shortly. In addition, draft NPPGs on retail developments, land for waste disposal, transport and skiing developments are being prepared for consultation.

19.15 The initiative on tourism and the environment, launched by the Government in February 1992, seeks to encourage the further development of Scottish tourism while ensuring that environmental resources are maintained for future generations. The key mechanisms for the implementation of the initiative are site-based Tourism Management Programmes (TMPs), formulated and initiated by locally-based bodies in conjunction with national agencies. Guidelines for the development of TMPs have been published and eight pilot schemes have been set up to refine the approach. A national task force has also started work on caravan parks, coastal erosion, beach pollution and tourist routes. The publication and widespread distribution of *Going Green - Guidelines for the Scottish Tourism Industry* is aimed at encouraging the tourist industry to adopt an environmentally sustainable approach to its activities. A marketing plan has been prepared and a development manager appointed.

19.16 Following the publication of The Scottish Office's review *Roads, Bridges and Traffic in the Countryside* in February 1992, a major conference was held in Dundee in December 1992 where HRH the Prince of Wales delivered the keynote address. Implementation of a number of the review's recommendations has already taken place.

19.17 A *Code of Practice on Conservation, Access and Recreation* was published in August 1993. Although primarily intended for use by the water, sewerage and river purification authorities, the Code provides guidance to all who carry out work or own or manage facilities with implications for the water environment.

19.18 In March 1993, the Government consulted on proposals for a Scottish Agri-Environment Programme, based on an EC Regulation agreed as part of the Common Agricultural Policy Reform package. The Programme was submitted to the Commission for approval in July 1993. It includes not only the Environmentally Sensitive Area (ESA) schemes but also new initiatives to encourage the conservation of heather moorland, the creation of new habitats through long-term set-aside, assistance for organic farming, and the management of land for informal recreation in ESAs and on set-aside land. These new schemes are designed to complement the existing ESAs, which have met with considerable success in controlling the effects of modern agricultural practices on habitats and landscapes. Five new ESAs have been designated and three of the original areas have been extended. This brings the number of ESAs in Scotland to ten, covering 19% of agricultural land.

19.19 The Scottish Office has held a series of training seminars for senior staff on policy appraisal and the environment. These are intended to ensure that policy decisions in all areas of its work properly reflect environmental considerations.

RESEARCH AND MONITORING

19.20 The Scottish Office Environment Department's new publication *Environment Department Research Programme and*

Priorities, issued in September 1993, describes the current research programme and identifies research priorities for the next few years. This publication demonstrates the Government's commitment to improving the availability of information which is used to inform policy decisions.

19.21 The Scotland and Northern Ireland Forum for Environmental Research (SNIFFER) published its first biannual newsletter in summer 1993, outlining developments in the environmental research programme in both countries. SNIFFER members include The Scottish Office Environment Department, the Department of Environment for Northern Ireland, the River Purification Boards and the Scottish water and sewerage authorities.

19.22 The three-year study of the ecology of seals and their interaction with prey species and fisheries in the Moray Forth has been reviewed. Further research into the dietary and population dynamics of seals in this area is continuing.

INFORMING AND INVOLVING THE PUBLIC

19.23 *Learning for Life*, the report of the Secretary of State's Working Group on Environmental Education, was published in April 1993. It examines current environmental education provision and initiatives and makes recommendations to extend good practice and improve co-ordination. Public consultation on the recommendations has been undertaken and the Secretary of State is considering his response.

19.24 Fifteen Scottish schools participated in the OECD Environment in Schools Initiative. A national conference on the project and an international conference on 'Values in Environmental Education' was held in Stirling in May 1993.

19.25 The Scottish Office and the Convention of Scottish Local Authorities

published a model local environment charter for Scotland in October 1993. The guidance is intended to encourage local authorities to produce local charters of their own.

ACTION FOR ALL

19.26 The Institute of Environmental Managers was formed in September 1992 with assistance from Scottish Enterprise and The Scottish Office, in response to increasing public demands. Based in Edinburgh, the Institute aims to become a UK-wide body. The Scottish Environment and Business Initiative, launched by the Prince of Wales in June 1992 to improve access to environmental information and opportunities within the Scottish business community, has made significant headway. The Initiative's *First Progress Report* was published in September 1993.

19.27 The Scottish Office has helped to fund pilot projects to extend the recent EC Eco-Management and Audit Scheme to local government in the UK; two seminars were held in February 1994. Ross and Cromarty and the City of Glasgow District Councils, and Fife Regional Council were the main pilot authorities in Scotland. The Scottish Office published a policy statement on Green Housekeeping in its own estate in January 1993.

Learning for Life proposes a framework for the development of environmental education over the next decade

BRAER

On 5 January 1993, the tanker Braer, carrying oil from Norway to Canada, went aground and broke up on the coast of Shetland. The accident gave rise to the largest oil spill ever in Scottish waters - a spill twice as large as that of the Exxon Valdez in Alaska in 1989, and the eleventh largest in history. Yet the effects, in the event, were far less serious than first feared.

The Government took immediate action in the face of this crisis. The Department of Transport and the Shetland Islands Council mobilised response teams as soon as the vessel was known to be out of control. Although communications were impeded by the savage weather, Scottish Office and Department of Transport Ministers were on hand to assess the situation the following day. Within days, a special unit had been set up to co-ordinate action within The Scottish Office. The Secretary of State for Scotland reported on the spill to a special meeting of EC Transport and Environment Ministers in February 1993.

The severe weather, coupled with the lightness of the oil, made this an unusual oil spill. There was no large slick or heavy coastal contamination, and wildlife casualties were much lower than had been feared. But oil was blown over the land and dispersed into the sea. Immediate tests by the authorities allayed fears of serious air pollution or damage to drinking water supplies, and checks on local people established there were no long term adverse effects on health. But contamination near the wreck led The Scottish Office to declare exclusion zones on land and at sea to ensure that affected produce did not come to market. While most of Shetland's major salmon farming industry remained unaffected, there was a severe impact on a number of salmon farms. Compensation payments have been made, and claims continue to be assessed, by the insurers and others.

The work of assessing the damage still continues under an Ecological Steering Group set up by the Secretary of State for Scotland soon after the incident. The Group has an independent Chairman, Professor William Ritchie of the University of Aberdeen. It contains distinguished scientists with an extensive knowledge of oil spills and representatives of the main agencies and interests involved with monitoring. The Steering Group published an interim report in June 1993 and is expected to make a final report in summer 1994.

The recovery of the Shetland environment from the physical effects of the spill has been as remarkable as the incident itself. The incident required a major Government response and efforts are continuing to ensure that the experience gained can be applied effectively in responding to any future emergencies.

... and in spring 1993

REF NO	SUMMARY OF PREVIOUS WHITE PAPER COMMITMENTS	ACTION TO DATE	COMMITMENTS TO FURTHER ACTION
528	Introduce first Scottish Renewable Order at the same time as the next Renewable Order under the NFFO in England and Wales (SYR 395)	Announced in July 1993 the intention to implement a Scottish Renewables Obligation. Tender packs issued to interested parties	Introduce in autumn 1994
529	Promote improved energy efficiency and savings in local authority housing in Scotland (FYR p174, SYR 396)	Project to monitor and evaluate energy efficiency schemes set up in February 1993 Introduced Housing Plan System in 1993 encouraging local authorities to draw up strategies and set targets for energy efficiency	Consider results of report due spring 1994
530	Set up a Scottish Natural Heritage agency (20.5, SYR 397)	SNH's second year priorities include following through the recommendations of the Secretary of State's Working Parties on the Cairngorms, Loch Lomond and the Trossachs and on environmental education	
531	Work with Scottish Natural Heritage, DOE and others to implement the EC Habitats Directive (SYR 397)	Consultation paper issued October 1993	Introduce by June 1994 all legislative measures necessary to implement EC Habitats Directive. Provide EC with a list of possible sites by June 1995. Agree with Commission sites to be designated by June 1998. Complete designation of all sites by June 2004
532			Work with SNH, DOE and others on the implementation of the Biodiversity Action Plan
533	Ask SNH to develop proposals for Natural Heritage Areas in areas of outstanding natural heritage importance in Scotland (SYR 398)	Asked SNH to develop criteria for designation of NHAs. These criteria are currently being discussed	Ensure publication of designation criteria by June 1994
534	Nominate the Cairngorms as a World Heritage Site. Respond fully to the Working Party's final report and prepare in 1993 the case for World Heritage Listing (20.23, SYR 399)	Report published March 1993. Public consultation exercise undertaken on recommendations	Respond in mid-1994
535	Consider and respond fully to the Trossachs and Loch Lomond Working Party's report (SYR 400)	Report published July 1993. Public consultation exercise undertaken on recommendations	Respond in mid-1994
536	Consider SNH's proposals on access to the Scottish countryside, expected early 1993 (SYR 402)	Public consultation exercise undertaken November 1992. Report published 1993	SNH to produce recommendations in 1994
537	Support urban regeneration initiatives and make available additional support for action programme in North Lanarkshire (20.25, SYR 403)	Additional resources of up to £25m made available in both 1992-93 and 1993-94	Make available further additional resources in 1994-95

REF NO	SUMMARY OF PREVIOUS WHITE PAPER COMMITMENTS	ACTION TO DATE	COMMITMENTS TO FURTHER ACTION
538	Regenerate some of the worst peripheral housing estates through Government-led partnership initiatives (20.29, SYR 404)	Programmes worth £40m started in 1993-94	
539	Continue support for comprehensive area-based regeneration strategies targeted on disadvantaged urban areas (SYR 405)	Approved four new Scottish Homes Smaller Urban Renewal Initiatives in 1993-94, making 11 in total	
540	Increase Urban Programme expenditure to £81m in 1992-93 and maintain the number of projects supported annually at around 1200 (SYR 406)	Approved 1200 projects in the most deprived urban areas in Scotland at a total cost of £81m in 1992, rising to £83m in 1993-94	Funding available to support projects to be increased to over £84m in 1994-95
541	Implement new guidelines under which Urban Programme will operate in 1993-94 (SYR 406)	Implemented	
542			Review urban regeneration policy during 1994 in the light of responses to the consultation paper *Progress in Partnership* to ensure that maximum value is achieved from available funding
543	Create new Scottish Environment Protection Agency. Announce outcome of consultation exercise and introduce legislation as soon as practicable (FYR p175, SYR 407)	Announcement of intention to establish SEPA made February 1993. Bill to introduce paving provisions announced November 1993	Set up Shadow Board by November 1994
544	Continue to give Historic Scotland the priorities of protecting the built heritage and increasing understanding and enjoyment (20.31, SYR 408)	£27.5m allocated in 1992-93 which, when added to £7.2m generated income, enabled scheduling of an extra 300 monuments, historic building repair grant payments of £10.3m, and a programme of conservation works	
545	Publish a Historic Scotland Charter (SYR 408)	Charter published April 1993	
546	Comprehensively review National Planning Guidelines and other planning advice (20.20, SYR 409)	Most of Planning and Compensation Act 1991 has now been implemented. Environmental Assessment requirements applied to Private Bill procedures. New controls introduced over hazardous substances. Continued to consult on priorities for review	
547	Prepare guidance on land use, planning and transport with regard to energy efficiency and environmental audits (SYR 409)		Propose to commission research on energy efficiency with regard to the planning system
548			Work with DOE on arrangements for national voluntary Eco-Management and Audit schemes for local authorities

REF NO	SUMMARY OF PREVIOUS WHITE PAPER COMMITMENTS	ACTION TO DATE	COMMITMENTS TO FURTHER ACTION
549	Consult on the introduction of registers of land which may be contaminated (SYR 409)	Announced wide-ranging review of contaminated land in March 1993 in place of register proposals	
550	Consult on measures aimed at preventing dereliction (SYR 409)	Results of DOE consultation exercise awaited	
551	Issue final versions of guidance on housing, business and industry, principles of the planning system, skiing, minerals and archaeology (SYR 410)	Final versions of guidelines on business and industry and land for housing published	Issue final versions of guidance on the planning system, skiing, minerals and archaeology during 1994
552			Issue final versions of guidance on renewable energy and draft guidelines on retail development, land for waste disposal and transport during 1994
553	Issue consultative draft guidance on freshwater fish farming (SYR 411)	Draft guidance under consideration	Issue draft guidance for consultation as soon as practicable
554	Consult on extent of permitted development in SSSIs (SYR 412)	Overtaken by consultation paper *Permitted Development, Environmental Assessment and Implementation of the Habitats Directive*, issued August 1993	
555	Consider arranging a seminar on rural housing design (SYR 413)	Seminar deferred. Guidance included in report on design of timber framed housing in the countryside	
556	Develop 'Green Clause' for use in contracts for the design, construction and maintenance of buildings in the Scottish Office Estate (SYR 413)	'Green Clause' incorporated	
557			Will distribute report on design of timber frame housing in the countryside by spring 1994
558	Monitor work of task force to implement national tourism management initiative. Identify and encourage local pilot projects. Monitor progress and encourage wider use of guidelines (SYR 414)	Published guidelines for Tourism Management Programmes and implemented eight local and four national pilot programmes. Issued guidance booklet on 'green' tourism practice and product development. Prepared marketing plan for Tourism and Environment Initiative	
559			Incorporate relevant objectives into national strategic plan for Scottish tourism and provide lead on training for sustainable tourism

19. THE ENVIRONMENT IN SCOTLAND

REF NO	SUMMARY OF PREVIOUS WHITE PAPER COMMITMENTS	ACTION TO DATE	COMMITMENTS TO FURTHER ACTION
560	Review by mid-1993 public exposure to lead in drinking water in the light of medical advice and assessments of water authorities' monitoring results (SYR 416)	Collected data on water quality with a view to carrying out review	Complete as soon as practicable
561	Encourage Environmental Health (Scotland) Unit to develop into a national centre of excellence in environmental health (20.50, SYR 417)	Unit merged with Communicable Diseases (Scotland) Unit in August 1993 to combine expertise in one organisation Issued guidance to health professionals on ultraviolet radiation and skin cancer	
562			Prepare guidance by mid-1994 for identifying and dealing with incidents of pollution of water by cyanobacteria (blue-green algae)
563	Consult on results of the Review of Roads, Bridges and Traffic in the Scottish Countryside. Plan conference in December 1992 (FYR p174, SYR 418)	Review published for consultation February 1992. Conference held December 1992	
564	Keep Code of Practice for farmers to reduce pollution from agriculture under review and consider revisions after two years (SYR 419)	Code of practice kept under review	Any revisions to be considered during 1994
565	Develop Environmentally Sensitive Areas. Put in place first round scheme in late 1992. Complete review of second round ESAs. Implement third round of designations (SYR 401,420)	Improved and extended three current ESAs and designated a further five new ESAs. Consulted on Scottish Agri-Environment Programme in March 1993	
566			Review progress and develop monitoring programme for ESA schemes
567			Develop Agri-Environment Schemes for introduction in 1994
568	Support River Purification Boards and local authorities in controlling discharges and improving the quality of rivers, lochs and bathing waters (20.40, SYR 421)	Capital expenditure provision for 1993-94 for local authorities' water and sewerage programme increased to £237m with further in-year supplement of £10.5m. Grant of £55m in support of 344 schemes, comprising 125km of sewers, 745 megalitres per day (Ml/d) of pumping station capacity, 270Ml/d of sewage treatment works capacity and 5km of long sea outfall Encouraged setting up of Build, Own and Operate Schemes by the private sector to provide additional treatment works and infrastructure	

REF NO	SUMMARY OF PREVIOUS WHITE PAPER COMMITMENTS	ACTION TO DATE	COMMITMENTS TO FURTHER ACTION
569	Identify waters affected or which could be affected by nitrates from agricultural sources by December 1993. Draw up programmes to reduce or prevent pollution by December 1995 (SYR 421)	Highlighted two water bodies as candidates for identification	If appropriate, formally identify these waters and notify EC of associated vulnerable zones by June 1994
570	Identify sensitive areas under EC Urban Waste Water Treatment Directive and introduce a programme for implementing Directive by December 1993 (20.41, SYR 422)	Continued to collect data for preparation of implementation programme. Reached general agreement on location of sensitive areas and high natural dispersion areas	Finalise programme and convey summary to EC by June 1994
571	Stop dumping of sewage sludge at sea by end 1998 (20.41, SYR 423)	Strategies for Strathclyde and Lothian developed; Strathclyde's based on re-use, Lothian's on incineration	
572			Working Group to report in 1994 on further development of groundwater protection policy
573	Develop integration of quality management procedures between river purification authorities and Pollution Inspectorate and finalise memorandum of understanding (SYR 424)	Memorandum agreed between most of RPAs and HMIPI	
574	Review operation of charging scheme under IPC (SYR 425)	Reviewed March 1993	Carry out review annually
575	Frame Regulations to control pollution from industrial oils and chemicals. Undertake public consultation on proposals (SYR 427)	Draft consultation paper on proposals for industrial oil controls drawn up with advice provided by water regulatory authorities	Consult in 1994
576	Encourage the relevant water and river purification authorities to adopt a voluntary code on conservation, recreation and access. Publish code by end 1992 (FYR p175, SYR 428)	*Code of Practice* published August 1993	
577	Review operation of charging scheme for discharges (SYR 429)	Review commenced late 1993	Define changes to scheme in 1994
578	Carry out research into key aspects of Scotland's environment, including 3-year assessment of relative contributions of rivers to total nutrient flux in Scottish coastal zone and review of arrangements for management of fisheries in 1993 (SYR 430)	Research continued into nutrient flux and sandeel stocks. Exercise to map Scotland's land cover completed in spring 1993	Arrangements of fisheries management to be reviewed 1994
579	Continue research on seal ecology in Moray Firth and review progress of current studies in 1993 (FYR p176, SYR 431)	Programme reviewed in 1993 – continuation of research project agreed	Publish guidance by mid-1994

REF NO	SUMMARY OF PREVIOUS WHITE PAPER COMMITMENTS	ACTION TO DATE	COMMITMENTS TO FURTHER ACTION
580	Publish guidance on siting of marine fish farms by end 1992 (20.13, SYR 433)	Guidance revised following consultation	Publish mid-1994
581	Give priority to environmental issues at all levels in Scottish educational system (20.51, SYR 434)	Encouraged 15 schools to participate in OECD Environment in Schools Initiative. Hosted 'International Values in Environmental Education' conference in Stirling in May 1993	
582	Present environmental education report to OECD and disseminate it in Scotland (SYR 434)	Report presented to OECD December 1993	Disseminate information as part of the programme for 5-14 year olds
583	Consider report of Environmental Education Working Group, expected late 1993 (FYR p177, SYR 435)	Report, *Learning for Life*, published April 1993. Consultation on recommendations undertaken	Respond mid-1994
584	Issue formal guidance for schools on environmental education for 5-14 year olds by end 1992 (FYR p177, SYR 436)	National guidelines issued March 1993	
585			Develop material in support of national guidelines on environmental education for 5-14 year olds in 1994
586	Continue to support environmental work by the voluntary sector. Continue to develop the effectiveness of the Special Grants (Environmental) Programme and UK2000 Scotland (20.20, SYR 437)	Reviewed support for Special Grants (Environmental) Programme and UK2000 Scotland	Consider review findings and implement where appropriate
587	Encourage recycling in Scotland. Develop initiatives in the light of local authority plans and research (FYR p177, SYR 438)	Recycling plans received from most Scottish local authorities. Supplementary Capital Consents issued for recycling. Research project funded Recycling credits increased with effect from 1 April 1994	
588	Devote up to £1m per year for Central Scotland Woodlands Initiative in addition to funding from existing assistance schemes (20.19, SYR 439)	Over £0.7m made available in 1992-93, which supported planting of 626,000 trees (of which 75% were native broadleaved species), and environmental work in 30 villages	Make available £0.8m in 1994-95 to support the Initiative
589	Improve Scottish drinking water quality. Monitor quality of public and private water supplies (SYR 441)	Reports for drinking water quality in Scotland for 1991 and 1992 published in February and December 1993 respectively	
590	Ensure that air emissions are more strictly controlled and that air quality continues to improve. Assess need for action in 1993 in the light of the South West Scotland air quality study. Increase the number of air monitoring stations (20.35, SYR 442)	Air quality study under way. Introduced monitoring in specific areas	Results of air quality studies to be assessed during 1994

20 THE ENVIRONMENT IN NORTHERN IRELAND

20.1 The Government's policy for Northern Ireland is to protect and enhance its diverse and relatively unspoilt environment. It is a significant aspect of the UK Strategy for Sustainable Development and of the other initiatives following from the Earth Summit.

HIGHLIGHTS

'Growing a Green Economy' initiative launched

Environment Service Report 1991-93 published

Policy statement on peatland conservation published

Management structures developed on Strangford Lough, The Mournes, Lough Neagh and the Lower Bann

INTEGRATED POLICY MAKING

The Environment and the Economy

20.2 A key element of this strategy is the integration of environmental policies with other areas of decision making. The Government's initiative, 'Growing a Green Economy', which was launched in March 1993, sets out an integrated approach to the economy and the environment.

20.3 The aim of this initiative is to encourage business to meet higher environmental standards in a cost effective way, and thus remain competitive in international markets. It highlights the challenges faced by local businesses in meeting these standards and the opportunities which can result from the growing demand for environmentally friendly products. Northern Ireland's image as an unspoilt area means that it is well placed to benefit from such an approach. A broad based advisory committee has been set up to promote this initiative within industry and commerce and to encourage local companies to take positive action to respond to the environmental challenge.

20.4 Integrated policy making underlies also the Government's Rural Development Programme. This is designed to promote the revitalisation of disadvantaged rural areas and gives help to local communities to bring forward regeneration plans.

Green Housekeeping

20.5 The practices followed by Government on its own property are an essential part of the commitment to an integrated approach to environmental issues. The Green Housekeeping Strategy for the Northern Ireland Civil Service identified a number of important areas including the use of energy and water, the management of waste and practical advice on individual action.

20.6 The Northern Ireland Central Government Estate achieved a 5% improvement in energy performance over the first two years of the national campaign to achieve a 15% energy saving by 1996. Among other specific initiatives is the creation of a nature reserve at HM Prison at Maghaberry, which was a result of the interest of staff. Part of the reserve will be open to the public.

The Use of Energy

20.7 The benefits of improved energy efficiency continue to be promoted under the strategy 'Energy for the 90s and beyond'. This has included:

*   advice to industry and commerce on energy efficiency techniques;
*   financial assistance under the Energy Management Assistance Scheme (take-up has greatly exceeded the target);

- a continuing publicity campaign;
- assistance to some 9000 low income families with insulating and/or draughtproofing their homes;
- the promotion of Combined Heat and Power; and
- the Non-fossil Fuel Obligation on Northern Ireland Electricity plc to secure an initial tranche of up to 15MW of generating capacity from renewable sources, with further tranches likely to reach 45MW by 2005.

Transport

20.8 Predictions for traffic growth in Belfast suggest that congestion and pressure on the environment will increase if measures are not introduced now to try to encourage greater use of public transport and promote a change in attitude to car usage. A review is currently under way, aimed at developing a framework against which future decisions can be taken. The main themes likely to be considered include:

- integrated policy making;
- maintenance of a pleasant and healthy environment;
- land use and transportation; and
- increased use of public transport, together with a reduction in car use during peak periods.

FORESTRY

20.9 In line with the Statement of Forest Principles agreed at the Earth Summit, the Government is managing forests in Northern Ireland to provide many sustainable uses. These include timber production and environmental, social and recreational activities.

20.10 Forestry offers an important alternative land use to conventional agriculture. The Government is committed to further afforestation, both by public and private sector participation, through forestry grant schemes. The policy is to ensure that tree planting is carried out on suitable sites and in an appropriate manner.

COUNTRYSIDE MANAGEMENT

20.11 The management of the countryside is central to sustainable resource use. Where an area is of high scenic value, has a rich and varied wildlife and displays many features of the cultural heritage, the Government may designate it as an Area of Outstanding Natural Beauty (AONB). Proposals for the management and development of these areas are drawn up by the Government in conjunction with District Councils, community groups, voluntary bodies and other interested parties. In this way, co-ordination with other related activities, such as agriculture and tourism, is achieved. The Government is committed to reviewing those AONBs established under previous legislation, with a view to re-designating them under the Nature Conservation and Amenity Lands (Northern Ireland) Order 1985. To date, four 'new-style' AONBs have been created and consultations are under way over two previously undesignated areas.

20.12 Other action taken or planned involves initiatives to encourage farmers to protect and enhance habitats, landscape and historic features. These include:

- extending two existing Environmentally Sensitive Areas (ESAs), designating one in Co. Fermanagh and the proposed designation of two more;
- schemes under the EC Agri-Environment Regulation (to be introduced in 1994) to protect and

Knockmore, Co. Fermanagh - one of two proposed new Areas of Outstanding Natural Beauty

enhance moorland and improve or create habitats outside ESAs;

• continuing the arterial drainage maintenance programme, using environmentally acceptable working methods.

HABITATS AND SPECIES

20.13 The protection of peatland, particularly in the form of raised and blanket bogs, is one of the main objectives for nature conservation in Northern Ireland. Measures already in place, or which are proposed for early implementation, will ensure that representative sites of peatland habitats are protected.

20.14 In keeping with the remainder of the UK, Northern Ireland is working towards fulfilling the requirements of the EC Habitats and Species Directive. Legislation is being prepared and will be completed by June 1994. The Government will ensure that potential Sites of Community Importance are declared as Areas of Special Scientific Interest by June 1995 and that Special Protection Areas under the EC Conservation of Wild Birds Directive are designated by June 1998. These sites will be Northern Ireland's contribution to the Europe-wide 'Natura 2000' network.

20.15 Since *This Common Inheritance* was published in 1990, the total area protected by Area of Special Scientific Interest (ASSI)

designation has increased more than sevenfold. The Government is committed to completing the survey and the declaration of ASSIs by 2001.

THE HISTORIC HERITAGE

20.16 The principle that rare and vulnerable resources require special protection applies equally to the historic heritage. A number of important steps have been taken over the past 12 months, including:

• further progress with the identification survey of historic monuments, which has, since 1990, covered some 3900 sites and monuments;
• completion of the third stage of the presentation programme at Carrickfergus Castle;
• a programme to celebrate the 800th anniversary of Grey Abbey;
• completion of the main survey of pre-1914 buildings and listing of additional buildings, to bring the total since 1990 to 600.

POLLUTION CONTROL

20.17 The improvement of water and air quality and the disposal and management of waste are crucial elements of the Government's policy to control the most harmful environmental effects of development. The priorities are to continue to tackle the problems of urban air quality, strengthen controls over water pollution, improve air and water quality monitoring and enhance the water pollution control incident response procedures.

20.18 Important changes in legislation are being prepared which will:

• establish a new system of industrial air pollution control;
• strengthen the standards of waste disposal and management;
• lead to better control of litter;
• improve the control of discharges of effluents to the aquatic environment.

20.19 Major research and monitoring

Monea Castle - one of the 3900 historic sites identified since 1990

programmes have been completed or are under way, including:

- studies of air quality in Belfast, Londonderry and Newry;
- monitoring concentrations of pollutants such as smoke and sulphur dioxide and nitrogen dioxide.

20.20 Comprehensive water quality management plans for the Erne, Lagan and Foyle catchments are being prepared and standards for effluent discharges from sewage treatment works operated by Government are being provided in a public register.

20.21 The Government will maintain and build on this action. Sewage treatment will be improved. The Government will continue to work with industry and the farming community to prevent damage to Northern Ireland's water.

AWARENESS, AND EDUCATION AND PARTICIPATION

20.22 The need to raise public awareness underlies the 1990 White Paper and subsequent reports and the initiatives which followed the Earth Summit.

20.23 The aim of formal environmental education is to give pupils a basic knowledge of what the environmental issues are, leading to an awareness of how those issues can affect their own lives. The education covers not only conservation issues, but also development. This will enable young people to make informed choices and decisions and to respond sensibly to problems with an environmental dimension. Schools, colleges and

universities are being encouraged to incorporate an environmental element into the non-statutory curriculum, for which a range of projects, competitions and other initiatives are available.

20.24 It is also important to give the public access to information about the environment, threats to it and action that needs to be taken. The Government's commitment to this was illustrated by the opening of the Monuments and Buildings Record to the public in October 1992, since when more than 700 enquiries have been received.

20.25 It is vital that the public is not only aware of environmental issues, but takes action, in partnership with Government, to deal with them. The value of this may be seen in the development of management structures for areas which, in terms of the conservation of natural resources, are extremely important: Strangford Lough, The Mournes, Lough Neagh and the Lower Bann.

A management structure has recently been developed for Lough Neagh

Belfast - where major research and monitoring into air quality is under way

REF NO	SUMMARY OF PREVIOUS WHITE PAPER COMMITMENTS	ACTION TO DATE	COMMITMENTS TO FURTHER ACTION
591	Adopt good conservation practices in the management of the Government's own estate (21.6, SYR 443)	Published *Policy Statement on Peatland Conservation*. Work commenced on identification and survey of Government-owned historic buildings at risk	Cease to use peat in open ground in Government estate. On completion of survey of Government-owned historic buildings at risk, recommendations to be prepared and strategy for implementation devised
592	Complete in March 1993 management plans for over half the 44 statutory Nature Reserves. Draw up plans covering the conservation and enhancement of estate lands (SYR 443)	Countryside Management System (CMS) further developed for Nature Reserves; by the end of 1992-93 23 plans were prepared using CMS. By March 1994, 32 management plans for Nature Reserves were completed and a system for the introduction of CMS to country park management plans was produced	CMS will now be extended to country parks
593	Introduce environmental auditing for all Forest Service operations (SYR 443)	Environmental auditing introduced for all Forest Service activities Statement published on the environmental criteria to apply to both public and grant aided afforestation	
594	Maintain hedges of Agricultural College farms in an environmentally friendly manner (SYR 443)	Measures implemented	
595	Provide advice, research and grant aid to farmers to reduce pollution from farms and encourage environmentally sensitive farming (21.6, SYR 444)	Continued to make grant aid for repair of farm waste containment facilities more widely available. Introduced a Countryside Management Code for protection of water	Introduce Countryside Management Codes for protection of air and soil. Undertake further intensive advisory campaigns covering all farms in targeted high risk river catchments. Resurvey the '1000' farms originally subjected to survey 5 years ago and assess changes in farm waste management brought about in the intervening period
596	Consider a proposed pilot farm waste management plan scheme (SYR 444)	Pilot scheme launched March 1993	
597	Review scope for increasing dry matter levels in silage and reduce quantity of polluting liquor (SYR 444)	Research commenced	
598	Designate further ESAs (SYR 444)	Two existing ESAs upgraded and extended and one new ESA designated	Two further ESAs to be designated (Sperrins and Slieve Gullion)
599			Three schemes to be introduced to encourage organic farming, the improvement of habitats alongside bodies of water and the protection and enhancement of moorland outside ESAs
600			New Agricultural Development Operational Programme 1994-99 to include improved incentives for farmers to protect and enhance environmental features on their farms

REF NO	SUMMARY OF PREVIOUS WHITE PAPER COMMITMENTS	ACTION TO DATE	COMMITMENTS TO FURTHER ACTION
601	Continue to support the creation of smoke control areas (21.16, SYR 445)	£1m grant-aid provided in 1993-94	Complete Smoke Control Programmes in Belfast and Newry
602	Prohibit the sale of unauthorised fuels in smoke control areas. Introduce primary legislation by 1993-94 (21.16, SYR 446)	Issued Consultation Paper on new regulatory proposals	Introduce by end 1994
603	Aim to double the use of unleaded petrol (21.17, SYR 447)	Commitment achieved	
604	Consider renewed campaign (SYR 447)	As commitment to double use of unleaded petrol has been achieved, renewed publicity campaign no longer considered necessary	
605	Seek to reduce public sector energy usage by 15% by 1995. Implement recommendations of consultant's report on review of energy management structures in Northern Ireland Central Government estate (21.31, SYR 448)	Introduced direct billing for single occupancy buildings within Government Office Estate. Ran a programme of training courses for premises offices. Recommendations implemented in stages during 1993	
606	Introduce a Non-Fossil Fuel Obligation (NFFO) in Northern Ireland (SYR 449)	NFFO involving initial tranche of up to 15 MW generating capacity from renewable sources introduced in April 1994	
607	Review the capacity for renewable energy in Northern Ireland, in light of the Non-Fossil Fuel Obligation. Report in autumn 1992 on the first phase of renewables study conducted by Northern Ireland Department of Economic Development and Northern Ireland Electricity plc (SYR 450)	Report on first phase published in August 1993. Report on second phase completed September 1993	
608	Establish a Northern Ireland Energy Efficiency Action Group (NIEEAG) (SYR 450)	NIEEAG established March 1993	NIEEAG to produce first action plan by June 1994
609	Continue to protect habitats by completing the survey and declaration of Areas of Special Scientific Interest and National Nature Reserves, and progress proposals on Strangford Lough (21.8, SYR 452)	Declared, by April 1994, a further 18 ASSIs bringing the total to 54 Publish a 'Guide to Designation' on the Strangford Lough proposed Marine Nature Reserve	To declare as ASSIs by 1995 two intact lowland raised bogs and four extensive areas of blanket bog
610			Submit to EC a list of sites to be considered as Sites of Community Importance under Habitats Directive by June 1995, having first declared them as ASSIs. Designate all Special Protection Areas under the HSD as ASSIs by June 1998
611	Declare by December 1992 an ASSI for Lough Neagh (SYR 452)	Declared December 1992	

169

REF NO	SUMMARY OF PREVIOUS WHITE PAPER COMMITMENTS	ACTION TO DATE	COMMITMENTS TO FURTHER ACTION
612	Complete the review of Areas of Outstanding Natural Beauty (21.10, SYR 453)	Review in progress	
613	Designate by late 1993 two Areas of Outstanding Natural Beauty in Fermanagh (SYR 453)	Continued discussion with interested parties over proposed designations	Designate during 1994
614			Designate AONB around Strangford Lough in 1995. Commence review of Sperrins AONB
615	Increase the number of conservation areas from 26 to 59 (FYR p181, SYR 454)	Designated a further 20 conservation areas, bringing the total to 46	
616	Conduct a series of river corridor surveys to pave the way for environmentally friendly methods of drainage maintenance (FYR p180, SYR 455)	318 km of watercourse have been surveyed to date	
617	Carry out post-works audits (SYR 455)	Post-works audits commenced	
618	Target Belfast as a key area for regeneration (FYR p180, SYR 456)	Research studies continuing. Tidal inlets on edge of landfill site remodelled. Computer modelling of movement of silts around harbour completed	
619	Purchase land for Bog Meadows scheme before work can take place on the ground (SYR 456)		
620	Further enhance Collin Glen Community Forest with additional planting (SYR 457)	Additional planting carried out	
621	Continue to support Community Economic Regeneration Scheme and Community Regeneration Improvements Special Programme (CRISP) (FYR p182, SYR 458)	Approved financial assistance for CRISP schemes in 28 towns	
622	Continue a major urban environmental improvement proposal in Londonderry. Support projects related to the town centre programme, a promotional strategy and a community action programme (FYR p180, SYR 459)	Continued to direct resources at the neediest areas of the city	
623	Fund research into environmental matters with particular relevance to Northern Ireland (FYR p181, SYR 460)	39 research projects in progress	
624	Survey important habitats including one of fens; complete Earth Sciences Site Conservation Review (SYR 460)	Earth Science Review commenced. Fen survey continuing. *Irish Red Data Book on Vertebrates* published December 1993	

REF NO	SUMMARY OF PREVIOUS WHITE PAPER COMMITMENTS	ACTION TO DATE	COMMITMENTS TO FURTHER ACTION
625	Prepare a central record of historic wrecks. Commission work in 1993-94 (SYR 461)	Initiated work on records of wrecks in Northern Ireland waters in October 1993	Complete by 1995
626	Prepare a strategy to reduce smoke and SO$_2$ levels in areas of previous breaches or at risk of breaches of the EC Directive on smoke and SO$_2$ (21.16, SYR 462)	Major detailed study under way. Preliminary reports received and study being taken to completion	
627	Extend the existing sampling programme for Northern Ireland coastal waters to those not included in the list identified under EC Bathing Water Directive (FYR p181, SYR 463)	Monitored a further 9 coastal bathing waters and 22 inland recreational waters	
628	Extend the monitoring of water quality to all main rivers and estuaries and to Strangford Lough, and increase by at least 80 the number of river quality monitoring stations by 1995 (21.22, SYR 464)	Introduced some 275 chemical and biological river monitoring stations and 29 estuarine sampling stations, thus covering most of the main river systems and estuaries (including Strangford Lough) in Northern Ireland	
629	Add a further 41 new chemical monitoring stations in 1993. Current 260 biological stations to be increased by 15% during 1992-3 (SYR 464)	Commitment completed 1993	
630	Further improve the River Lagan as a key element in the regeneration of the Belfast river front and dock area. Produce a Water Quality Management Plan for the Lagan by end 1993. Construct a new weir by January 1993 (21.19, SYR 465)	Started preparation of Plan for the Lagan catchment. Weir completed	
631	Improve sewage treatment and end sea disposal of sewage sludge (21.22, SYR 466)	Sludge disposal strategy established and development of programme continued	
632	Prepare an implementation programme in relation to the Urban Waste Water Treatment Directive by end 1993 (SYR 466)	Ongoing	Submit programme to EC
633	Aim to manage rivers and estuaries so that water quality is 'good' or 'fair' and continue to prosecute polluters (21.18, SYR 467)	Investigated pollution incidents, arranged clean-up operations and prosecuted offenders	
634			Consider the introduction of more effective enforcement powers to prevent water pollution from farms and industry
635	Complete by end 1993 management plans for River Erne and River Foyle catchments (SYR 467)	Water quality data collection for Erne and Foyle catchments complete. Draft background papers substantially complete	Complete by May 1994

REF NO	SUMMARY OF PREVIOUS WHITE PAPER COMMITMENTS	ACTION TO DATE	COMMITMENTS TO FURTHER ACTION
636	Introduce new maximum fines of £20,000 for river pollution (SYR 467)	Maximum fine increased from £2000 to £20,000	
637	Complete the listing of pre-1960 buildings of architectural and historic interest by 1994 (21.26, SYR 469)	Listed 600 buildings since the 1990 White Paper and grant-aided 850 repair and maintenance schemes in the same period	
638	Encourage the promotion of revolving funds (FYR p182, SYR 470)	Continued to provide financial support to revolving funds	
639	Consider a number of further projects under revolving funds scheme (SYR 470)	Further projects under consideration	
640	Complete identification survey of all historic monuments by 1995 (21.27, SYR 471)	Recorded a total of 3900 historic monuments since the 1990 White Paper	
641	Commit resources for a major scheme to improve the presentation of Carrickfergus Castle (21.27, SYR 472)	Completed third phase	Complete refinements in 1994
642	Provide by 1992 a publicly accessible Monuments and Buildings Record (21.27, SYR 473)	Record open to the public in October 1992	
643			Enhance the Record with projects targeting architectural and industrial records
644	Enhance the presentation of State Care Monuments (SYR 474)	Organised presentation programme to mark 800th anniversary of Grey Abbey in 1993	Complete three presentation schemes in 1994
645	Prepare further Best Practice Guides for industry and commerce; arrange a conference followed by a series of workshops on Combined Heat and Power; focus media advertising on an energy efficient house; arrange further specialist seminars for industry and commerce including EC Thermie programme; organise a heat recovery and energy management technique programme and a schools debating competition (SYR 475)	Launched series of measures including Best Practice Guides; specialist seminars; competitions for the industrial, commercial, domestic and education sectors; schools debating competitions; workshops on CHP; media advertising focused on an energy efficient house; and an Energy Management Assistance Scheme	Prepare by August 1994 further Best Practice Guide for industry and commerce

Arrange in 1994 two further workshops on CHP |
646			Organise, jointly with the Department of Transport, Energy and Communications in the Republic of Ireland, a conference on saving energy in buildings
647	Introduce revised arrangements under Home Energy Efficiency Scheme, where appropriate (SYR 476)	Taken decision to streamline existing arrangements for assistance with insulating and draughtproofing low income households	Complete consultations and introduce changes to arrangements in 1994
648			Explore with the Energy Saving Trust and other interested parties the scope for an extension of the Trust's activities in Northern Ireland

REF NO	SUMMARY OF PREVIOUS WHITE PAPER COMMITMENTS	ACTION TO DATE	COMMITMENTS TO FURTHER ACTION
649	Combat the problems caused by litter; carry out a Litter Action Plan (FYR p182, SYR 477)	Litter Action Plan implemented through Tidy Northern Ireland. Annual campaigns to be scheduled on national events. Baseline Litter Survey completed by Tidy Northern Ireland	
650	Introduce in 1993 a new Litter (Northern Ireland) Order and Code of Practice (SYR 477)	Consultation on draft Litter Order and Code of Practice delayed	Legislation and Code of Practice to be introduced during 1994
651	Continue to support environmental awareness in education (SYR 478)	Support continued	
652	Continue to promote the exploration of environmental issues in other educational themes (21.35, SYR 479)	Continued two-year project to develop a range of approaches to the topic in the classroom	Complete project
653			Enhance the protection of historic monuments under new Historic Monuments and Archaeological Objects Order 1994. Field monument wardens to monitor 400 scheduled sites
654			Make available archaeological information through publications: publish three books in 1994
655			Bring forward legislation for comprehensive controls for the protection of the environment through the safe management of waste
656			Bring forward legislation for a new system of industrial air pollution control
657			Conduct market research on smoking in public places

ANNEX A
CROSS REFERENCE OF SECOND AND THIRD YEAR REPORT COMMITMENTS

This table gives a cross reference between commitments listed in the Second and Third Year Reports. It also identifies commitments reported complete in the Second Year Report.

Second Year Report Commitments	Third Year Report Commitments	Second Year Report Commitments	Third Year Report Commitments
1	1,2,3,6,7,9,13,15,16,68	35	57
2	2	36	58
3	10	37	59
4	4,13	38	61
5	14,15,16	39	62
6	17	40	64,66
7	18	41	64
8	19,20	42	64
9	21,22	43	67
10	23	44	71
11	9,25	45	71
12	26	46	71
13	27	47	73
14	11	48	74
15	28	49	49
16	30	50	77
17	31,32	51	78
18	33	52	484
19	35,36,37	53	79
20	39	54	80
21	41	55	83
22	42	56	289
23	45	57	57
24	46	58	114
25	50	59	89
26	49	60	90
27	51	61	90
28	51	62	91
29	51	63	91
30	52	64	92
31	53	65	93
32	482	66	93
33	54	67	94
34	56	68	95

Second Year Report Commitments	Third Year Report Commitments	Second Year Report Commitments	Third Year Report Commitments
69	96,97,98	121	166
70	99	122	553,580
71	100	123	167
72	101	124	168
73	102	125	169
74	103	126	Reported complete 1992
75	104	127	170
76	105	128	158
77	106	129	184
78	107	130	172
79	108,110,111,112	131	173,174
80	113	132	175,176
81	115	133	178
82	116	134	179
83	118	135	181
84	118	136	182,185,186
85	11,119,120	137	187,189,192
86	121	138	Reported complete 1992
87	122	139	394,395
88	124	140	193,194
89	125	141	195
90	126,128,129	142	185,196
91	130,132	143	197,198
92	126	144	199
93	132	145	158
94	133	146	200
95	134	147	201,202
96	134	148	204,205
97	134	149	206
98	135	150	207
99	136,137	151	209,210
100	138	152	211
101	139	153	212
102	140,141	154	213,214
103	142	155	217,218
104	143	156	219
105	143	157	216
106	144	158	215
107	145	159	43,44
108	146	160	220
109	147,148	161	223
110	149	162	224,225
111	150,151,152	163	224
112	482	164	227
113	9,154	165	228
114	155	166	226
115	155	167	229
116	157	168	227
117	158	169	230
118	160,161	170	231
119	160,162,164	171	232
120	165	172	232,234

Second Year Report Commitments	Third Year Report Commitments	Second Year Report Commitments	Third Year Report Commitments
173	235	225	313
174	236,237,238	226	314
175	240	227	303
176	241,247,248,249	228	319
177	250	229	321
178	172	230	322
179	182,277	231	323
180	159	232	324
181	251	233	325
182	252,253	234	327
183	254	235	328
184	256	236	330
185	257	237	331
186	259,260	238	332,333
187	261	239	334
188	261	240	336
189	262	241	337
190	263	242	337
191	264,265	243	338
192	266,267,267	244	339
193	304	245	341
194	268,269	246	342
195	270,271	247	343
196	272,273	248	334
197	274	249	345,346
198	275,276	250	347
199	277	251	348,349
200	278	252	350
201	279	253	47
202	280	254	351,352
203	281	255	353,354,356,358,359,360
204	282,283	256	355,362
205	284,285	257	363
206	286	258	364
207	287,288	259	363
208	290	260	365
209	292	261	366,368,370
210	294	262	371
211	296	263	372,373,374
212	299	264	375
213	Reported complete 1992	265	368,376
214	300, 301	266	377
215	302	267	393
216	303	268	393
217	305	269	Reported complete 1992
218	306	270	379
219	307	271	380,381,382
220	304	272	383
221	192,308,309	273	384
222	310	274	378,383
223	311	275	386
224	312	276	387

Second Year Report Commitments	Third Year Report Commitments	Second Year Report Commitments	Third Year Report Commitments
277	388	329	449
278	390	330	450
279	396	331	449
280	390	332	451
281	390	333	452
282	397	334	453
283	399	335	455
284	400	336	456
285	401	337	457
286	402	338	458
287	403	339	459,460
288	404	340	461
289	406	341	462
290	404	342	463,464
291	405	343	466
292	408	344	466
293	364	345	467
294	408	346	469
295	409	347	470
296	411	348	471
297	412	349	472
298	412	350	474
299	412	351	475
300	413	352	Reported complete 1992
301	415	353	Reported complete 1992
302	415	354	477
303	415	355	481
304	415	356	482
305	417	357	Reported complete 1992
306	415,416	358	483
307	417	359	486
308	419	360	487
309	421	361	488
310	422	362	489
311	424	363	489
312	424,427,429,433	364	490
313	423,424	365	491
314	424,426	366	492
315	430	367	493
316	432	368	495
317	433	369	496
318	434	370	497
319	436	371	498
320	437	372	500
321	439	373	501
322	439	374	502
323	442	375	503
324	444	376	504,505
325	445	377	506,507
326	446	378	508,509
327	447	379	510
328	448	380	511,512

Second Year Report Commitments	Third Year Report Commitments	Second Year Report Commitments	Third Year Report Commitments
381	513	433	580
382	514	434	581,582
383	515	435	583
384	516	436	584
385	517	437	586
386	518	438	587
387	519	439	588
388	520	440	Reported complete 1992
389	521	441	589
390	522	442	590
391	523	443	591,592,593,594
392	524	444	595,596,597,598
393	525	445	601
394	526,527	446	602
395	528	447	603,604
396	529	448	605
397	530,531	449	606
398	533	450	607
399	534	451	608
400	535	452	609,611
401	565	453	612,613
402	536	454	615
403	537	455	616,617
404	538	456	618,619
405	539	457	620
406	540,541	458	621
407	543	459	622
408	544,545	460	623,624
409	546,547,549,550	461	625
410	551	462	626
411	553	463	627
412	554	464	628,629
413	555,556	465	630
414	558	466	631,632
415	558	467	633,635,636
416	560	468	638
417	561	469	637
418	563	470	638,639
419	564	471	640
420	565	472	641
421	568,569	473	642
422	570	474	644
423	571	475	645
424	573	476	647
425	574	477	649,650
426	Reported complete 1992	478	651
427	575	479	652
428	576		
429	577		
430	578		
431	579		
432	Reported complete 1992		

ANNEX B
RECENT PUBLICATIONS AND GUIDANCE

Worldwide Environmental Issues

• Sustainable Development: The UK Strategy.
HMSO, 1994. £22. ISBN O-10-124262-X.

• Climate Change: The UK Programme.
HMSO, 1994. £10. ISBN 0-10-124272-7.

• Biodiversity: The UK Action Plan.
HMSO, 1994. £18.50. ISBN 0-10-124282-4.

(Summary copies of these documents are available free of charge from DOE, PO Box 151, London E15 2HF.)

• Sustainable Forestry: The UK Programme.
HMSO, 1994. £6.50. ISBN 0-10-124292-1.

• A Guide to the Eco-Management and Audit scheme for UK local government.
HMSO, 1993. £33. ISBN 0-11-752719-X.

• The UK Environment.
HMSO, 1992. £14.95. ISBN 0-11-752420-4.

European Environmental Issues

• A Flourishing Partnership - The UK's Environmental Activities in Central and Eastern Europe. DOE, 1993.
Available free of charge from DOE, Room AG14, Romney House, 43 Marsham Street, London SW1P 3PY.

• Realising our Potential: A Strategy for Science, Engineering and Technology.
HMSO, 1993. £9.65. ISBN 0-10-122502-4.

UK Environmental Issues

• Annual Review of Government-funded Research and Development 1993.
HMSO, 1993. £28.50. ISBN 0-11-430083-6.

Global Atmosphere

• Motoring and the Environment. DOT, 1993.
Available free of charge from DOT, Public Enquiry Unit, 2 Marsham Street, London SW1P 3EB.

Business and Industry

• ACBE Third Progress Report. DOE, 1993.
Available free of charge from DOE, Room C16/11A, 2 Marsham Street, London SW1P 3EB.

Land Use and Planning

• Planning Policy Guidance note 4 (revised): Industrial and Commercial Development and Small Firms.
HMSO, 1992. £2. ISBN 0-11-752723-8.

• Planning Policy Guidance note 5 (revised): Simplified Planning Zones.
HMSO, 1992. £3.90. ISBN 0-11-752717-3.

• Planning Policy Guidance note 6 (revised): Town Centres and Retail Developments.
HMSO, 1993. £3.60. ISBN 0-11-752842-0.

• Planning Policy Guidance note 8 (revised): Telecommunications.
HMSO, 1992. £3.90. ISBN 0-11-752747-5.

• Planning Policy Guidance note 20: Coastal Planning.
HMSO, 1992. £4.50. ISBN 0-11-752711-4.

• Planning Policy Guidance note 21: Tourism.
HMSO, 1992. £4.50. ISBN 0-11-752726-2.

• Planning Policy Guidance note 22:
Renewable Energy.
HMSO, 1993. £4. ISBN 0-11-752756-4.

• Minerals Planning Guidance note 11: The
Control of Noise at Surface Mineral
Workings.
HMSO, 1993. £4. ISBN 0-11-752779-3.

• Regional Planning Guidance note 7:
Northern Region.
HMSO, 1993. £4. ISBN 0-11-752863-3.

• Development Plans: A Good Practice
Guide.
HMSO, 1992. £22. ISBN 0-11-752689-4.

• Environmental Appraisal of Development
Plans: A Good Practice Guide.
HMSO, 1993. £10. ISBN 011-752866-8.

• Planning, Pollution and Waste
Management.
HMSO, 1992. £12.50. ISBN 0-11-752668-1.

• The Effectiveness of Green Belts.
HMSO, 1993. £19. ISBN 0-11-752799-8.

• Reducing Transport Emissions through
Planning.
HMSO, 1993. £12.80. ISBN 0-11-752785-8.

• Development Control - A Charter Guide.
DOE, National Planning Forum and the
Welsh Office, 1993.
Available free of charge from DOE, PO Box
151, London E15 2HF.

• Planning and Pollution Controls. DOE,
1993.
Available free of charge from DOE, Room
C16/11, 2 Marsham Street, London SW1P
3EB.

• Motorway Service Areas (Circular 23/92).
HMSO, 1992. £0.90. ISBN 0-11-752706-8.

• Development and Flood Risk (Circular
30/92).
HMSO, 1992. £2.20. ISBN 0-11-752737-8.

• Listed Buildings and Conservation. DOE,
1993.
Available free of charge from DOE, Room
C16/11, 2 Marsham Street, London SW1P
3EB.

• MPG3 Open Cast Coal Mining. DOE,
1993.
Available free of charge from DOE, Room
C16/11, 2 Marsham Street, London SW1P
3EB.

• MPG6 Guidelines for Aggregate Provisions
in England and Wales. DOE, 1993.
Available free of charge from DOE, Room
C16/11, 2 Marsham Street, London
SW1P 3EB.

• Volume 10 of the Design Manual for
Roads and Bridges: The Good Roads Guide.
HMSO, 1993.

Countryside and Wildlife

• Code of Good Agricultural Practice on
the Protection of the Soil. MAFF, 1993.
Available free of charge from MAFF
Publications, London SE99 7TP.

• Countryside Survey 1990: Main Report.
DOE, 1993. £12.00
Available from Publication Sales Unit, Block
3, Spur 2, Room 1/2, Government Buildings,
Lime Grove, Eastcote HA4 8SE.

• The National Forest Strategy. Countryside
Commission, 1993.

• Forestry and the Environment Volume I
(Commons Environment Select Committee
Report).
HMSO, 1993. £18.50. ISBN 0-10-297493-4

• Forestry and the Environment Volume II
(Commons Environment Select Committee
Report).
HMSO, 1993. £38.50. ISBN 0-10-020073-7.

Towns and Cities

• Action for London's Trees. Countryside
Commission, 1993.
Available from Countryside Commission
Postal Sales, PO Box 124, Walgrave,
Northampton NN6 9TL. £7.50. ISBN 0-86-
170403-7.

• Trees in Towns.
HMSO, 1993. £12. ISBN 0-11-752845-5.

• Cycle Routes Programme. DOT, 1993.
Available from Transport Research
Laboratory Library, PO Box 304,
Wokingham, Berks RG11 6YU.

• Bypass Demonstration Project. DOT,
1993.
Available free of charge from DOT, Room
C10/18, 2 Marsham Street, London SW1P
3EB.

Heritage

• Draft Planning Policy Guidance note 15:
Historic Buildings and Conservation Areas.
DOE/DNH, 1993.

• Consultation Paper: Protection of
Conservation Areas. DOE/DNH, 1993.

(Both documents available free of charge
from Department of National Heritage,
Third Floor, 2-4 Cockspur Street,
London SW1Y 5DH.)

Air Quality

• Urban Air Quality in the UK. DOE, 1993.
Available free of charge from DOE, Room
B365, Romney House, 43 Marsham Street,
London SW1P 3PY.

• Diesel Vehicle Emissions and Urban Air.
DOE, 1993.
Available free of charge from DOE, Room
B365, Romney House, 43 Marsham Street,
London SW1P 3PY.

• Benzene - Report of EPAQS Panel on Air
Quality Standards.
HMSO, 1994. £5.95. ISBN 0-11-752859-5.

• Air Pollution and Tree Health in the UK -
Report of Terrestrial Effects Review Group.
HMSO, 1993. £20. ISBN 0-11-752636-3.

• Critical Loads: Concept and applications -
Report of Institute of Terrestrial Ecology.
HMSO, 1993. £30. ISBN 0-11-701666-7.

• Emissions of Volatile Organic Compounds
from Stationary Sources in the UK. DOE,
1993.
Available free of charge from Warren
Springs Laboratory, Gunnels's Wood,
Stevenage, Hertfordshire SG1 2BX.

• Reducing Emissions of Volatile Organic
Compunds and Levels of Ground Level
Ozone. DOE, 1993.
Available free of charge from DOE, Room
B364, 43 Marsham Street, London SW1P
3PY.

Water

• Development Below the Low Water
Mark: A Review of Regulation in England
and Wales. DOE, 1993.
Available from DOE, Room 912, Tollgate
House, Houlton Street, Bristol BS2 9DJ.

• Managing the Coast: A Review of Coastal
Management Plans in England and Wales.
DOE, 1993.
Available from DOE, Room 912, Tollgate
House, Houlton Street, Bristol BS2 9DJ.

• Fourth Report of the Group Co-
ordinating Sea Disposal Monitoring (Aquatic
Environment Monitoring Report No. 31).
MAFF, 1993.
Available from MAFF, Lowestoft, Suffolk.

• Monitoring and Surveillance of Non-
Radioactive Contaminants in the Aquatic
Environment and Activities Regulating the
Disposal of Waste at Sea 1991 (Aquatic
Environment Monitoring Report No.36).
MAFF, Directorate of Fisheries Research,
1993.
Available from MAFF, Lowestoft, Suffolk.

• UK Action Plan for the Phasing out and
Destruction of Polychlorinated Biphenyls
(PCBs) and Dangerous PCB Substitutes.
DOE, 1993.
Available free of charge from DOE, Room
B464, Romney House, 43 Marsham St,
London SW1P 3PY.

• Mapping the Distribution of Metal
Contamination in United Kingdom
Estuaries. Plymouth Marine Laboratory,
1992.
Available from Citadel Hill, Plymouth PL1
2PB.

• Review on the use of Sewage Sludge in
Agriculture. MAFF, 1993.
Available from MAFF Publications, London
SE99 7TP.

• Water Charges: The Quality Framework. DOE, 1993.
Available free of charge from DOE, Room A401, Romney House, 43 Marsham Street, London SW1P 3PY.

• Policy and Practice for the Protection of Groundwater. NRA, 1992. £15.
ISBN 1-873160-372.
Available from NRA, Rivers House, Waterside Drive, Aztec West, Almondsbury, Bristol BS12 1UD.

• Low Flows and Water Resources. NRA, 1993. £5. ISBN 1-873160-429.
Available from NRA, Rivers House, Waterside Drive, Aztec West, Almondsbury, Bristol BS12 1UD.

• Drinking Water 1992: a Report by the Chief Inspector of the Drinking Water Inspectorate.
HMSO, 1993. £25. ISBN 0-11-752853-6.

• Paying for Quality: The Political Perspective. OFWAT, 1993.

• Bathing Water Quality in England and Wales 1992. NRA, 1992. £3.
Available from NRA, Rivers House, Waterside Drive, Aztec West, Almondsbury, Bristol BS12 1UD.

• First Report by the Government's Standing Advisory Committee on Conservation, Access and Recreation in the Water Industry. DOE, 1993.
Available free of charge from DOE, Room A405, Romney House, 43 Marsham Street, London SW1P 3PY.

• Water Pollution Incidents in England and Wales 1992. NRA, 1993. £4.50. ISBN 1-87-316055-0.
Available from NRA, Rivers House, Waterside Drive, Aztec West, Almondsbury, Bristol BS12 1UD.

• Making Markets Work for the Environment.
HMSO, 1993. £10. ISBN 0-11-752852-8.

• Health Effects of Sea Bathing - Phase III. WRc, 1994. £65. Available from WRc plc, Henley Road, Medmenham, Marlow, Bucks SL7 2HD.

Waste, Recycling, Contaminated Land and Litter

• Council Regulation (EC) No 259/93 of 1 February 1993 on the supervision and control of shipments for waste within, into and out of, the European Community. EC, 1993.

Hazardous Substances and Genetically Modified Organisms

• Weed Control and Environment Protection.
HMSO, 1992. £6.00. ISBN 0-11-752708-4.

• The Regulation and Control of the Deliberate Release of Genetically Modified Organisms: DOE/ACRE Guidance Note No 1. DOE, 1993. £8.10.
Available from Publication Sales Unit, Block 3, Spur 2, Room 1/2, Government Buildings, Lime Grove, Eastcote HA4 8SE.

• Fast Track Procedures for Certain Releases: DOE/ACRE Guidance Note No 2. DOE, 1994. £5.25.
Available from Publication Sales Unit, Block 3, Spur 2, Room 1/2, Government Buildings, Lime Grove, Eastcote HA4 8SE.

• Advisory Committee on Hazardous Substances: First Annual Report 1991-92. HMSO, 1992. £10. ISBN 0-11-752638-X.

• Advisory Committee on Hazardous Substances: Second Annual Report 1992-93. HMSO, 1993. £13. ISBN 0-11-752858-7.

• Discussion Paper: Reducing Emissions of Hazardous Chemicals to the Environment. DOE, 1994.
Available free of charge from DOE, Room A324, 43 Marsham Street, London SW1P 3PY.

• Reduced Information Requirements for Releases of Plants under the GMO Regulations: DOE/ACRE Guidance Note No 3. DOE, 1994. £6.00.
Available from Publication Sales Unit, Block 3, Spur 2, Room 1/2, Government Buildings, Lime Grove, Eastcote HA4 8SE.

• The control of legionellosis including legionnaires' disease. Health and Safety Booklet: HS (G) 70. HSE, 1993.
Available from HSE Books, PO Box 199, Sudbury, Suffolk CO10 6FS.

Involving the Public

• Your Council and the Environment - The Model Local Environment Charter. DOE, 1993.
Available free of charge from DOE, PO Box 151, London E15 2HF.

The Environment in Wales

• Access to Environmental Information: Your Rights Explained. WO, 1993.
Available free of charge from Welsh Office, Environment Division 3, Cathays Park, Cardiff CF1 3NQ.

• Heritage Charter. CADW, 1993.
Available free of charge from Cadw, Welsh Historic Monuments, Brunel House, 2 Fitzalan Road, Cardiff CF2 1UY.

• Tourism 2000. Wales Tourist Board, 1994. £15.00. ISBN 1-85013-058-2.
Available from Wales Tourist Board, Brunel House, 2 Fitzalan Road, Cardiff CF2 1UY.

• Threshold 21. Countryside Council for Wales, 1993. ISBN 0-901087-327.
Available free of charge from Countryside Council for Wales, Plas Penrhos, Ffordd Penrhos, Bangor, Gwynedd LL57 2LQ.

• Policy and Perspectives for Welsh Countryside. Countryside Council for Wales, 1992. ISBN 0-901087-319.
Available free of charge from Countryside Council for Wales, Plas Penrhos, Ffordd Penrhos, Bangor, Gwynedd LL57 2LQ.

• Wind Turbine Power Stations. Countryside Council for Wales, 1992. ISBN 0-901087-300.
Available free of charge from Countryside Council for Wales, Plas Penrhos, Ffordd Penrhos, Bangor, Gwynedd LL57 2LQ.

The Environment in Scotland

• Local Environment Charter for Scotland. SO, 1993.

• Tourism and the Scottish Environment - A Sustainable Partnership. SO/Scottish Tourist Board, 1992.

• Going Green-Guidelines for the Scottish Tourism Industry. SO/Scottish Tourist Board, 1993.

• Tourism Management Initiative - Guidelines for the Development of Tourism Management Programmes. SO/Scottish Tourist Board, 1993.

• An assessment of the potential renewable energy resource in Scotland. Highlands and Islands Enterprise, 1993.
£15. ISBN 0-7058-1685-0.

• Progress in Partnership - A consultation paper on the future of urban regeneration policy in Scotland. SO, 1993.

• First Progress Report of the Scottish Environment and Business Initiative. SO, 1993.

• Learning for Life - A National Strategy for Environmental Education in Scotland. The Report of the Working Group on Environmental Education to the Secretary of State for Scotland. SO, 1993. £5.00.

• Common Sense and Sustainability - A Partnership for the Cairngorms. The Report of the Cairngorms Working Party to the Secretary of State for Scotland. SO, 1993.

• The Management of Loch Lomond and the Trossachs. The Report of the Loch Lomond and the Trossachs Working Party to the Secretary of State for Scotland. SO, 1993.

• The Habitats Directive - Consultation Paper. SO, 1993.

• Bathing Waters in Scotland - Monitoring in 1992: Summary of Results. SO, 1993.

• Abstraction Controls: A System for Scotland. SO, 1993.

• Code of Practice on Access, Conservation and Recreation for Water and Sewerage Authorities and River Purification Authorities. SO, 1993.

• Protecting Scotland's Water Environment. SO/Scottish River Purification Boards' Association, 1992.

• The Environment Department Research Programme of Priorities. SO, 1993. ISBN 0-7480-0802-0.

• National Policy Guideline (NPPG)2 - Business and Industry. SO, 1993.

• NPPG3 - Land for Housing. SO, 1993.

• NPPG1 - Planning System. SO, 1994.

• Planning Advice Note (PAN)38 - Structure Plans: Housing Land Requirements. SO, 1993.

• PAN39 - Farm and Forestry Buildings. SO, 1993.

• PAN40 - Development Control. SO, 1993.

• PAN41 - Development Contrary to Development Plans. SO, 1994.

• Good Air Quality in Your Home. SO, 1992.

• Raising the Standard for the Built Heritage: A Charter on Performance Standards by Historic Scotland. SO, 1993.

• Memorandum of Guidance on Listed Buildings and Conservation Areas 1993. SO, 1993. £6.00.

• Scotland's Listed Buildings: A Guide to their Protection. SO, 1993.

The Environment in Northern Ireland

• Environment Service Report. DOE (NI), 1993.

• Growing a Green Economy: A Strategy for the Environment and the Economy in Northern Ireland. Department of Economic Development, 1993.

• Conserving Peatland in Northern Ireland. DOE (NI), 1993.

• The Householder's Guide to Radon. DOE (NI), 1993.

• Water Pollution - The Cost. DOE (NI), 1993.

• Radon in Dwellings (Northern Ireland) - Second Report. DOE (NI), 1993.

• Consultation Paper: A Future Strategy for Waste. DOE (NI), 1993.

• Consultation Paper: Air Quality. DOE (NI), 1993.

• Consultation Paper: Ban on the Sale of Smokeless Fuels in Smoke Control Areas. DOE (NI), 1993.

• Consultation Paper: Limiting the Sulphur Content of Domestic Fuel. DOE (NI), 1993.

• Review of the Water Act (NI) 1972. DOE (NI), 1993.

(All the above documents available free of charge from DOE (NI), Environment Service, Calvert House, 23 Castle Place, Belfast BT1 1FY.)

• River and Estuary Quality in Northern Ireland. HMSO, 1993. £11.95. ISBN 0-337-08313-04

• Afforestation: The DANI statement on Environmental Policy. DANI, 1993. ISBN 1-85527-1117.

• Code of Good Agricultural Practice for the Protection of Water. DANI, 1993. (Both documents available free of charge from DANI, Dundonald House, Stormont Estate, Belfast.)

ANNEX C
USEFUL ADDRESSES

GOVERNMENT DEPARTMENTS/AGENCIES

Ministry of Agriculture, Fisheries and Food
Environmental Protection Division
Nobel House
17 Smith Square
London SW1P
tel 071 238 3000

Ministry of Defence
Main Building
Whitehall
London SW1A 1HE
tel 071 218 9000

UK Ecolabelling Board
Eastbury House
30-34 Albert Embankment
London SE1 7TL
tel 071 820 1199

Department for Education
Sanctuary Buildings
Great Smith Street
London SW1P 3BT
tel 071 925 5000

Employment Department
Caxton House
Tothill Street
London SW1H 9NF
tel 071 273 3000

Department of the Environment
2 Marsham Street
London SW1P 3EB
tel 071 276 3000

Foreign and Commonwealth Office
Environment Section
King Charles Street
London SW1A 2AH
tel 071 270 3000

Department of Health
Richmond House
79 Whitehall
London SW1A 2NS
tel 071 210 3000

Home Office
Main Building
50 Queen Anne's Gate
London SW1H 9AT
tel 071 273 3000

Department of National Heritage
2-4 Cockspur Street
London SW1Y 5DH
tel 071 211 6000

Overseas Development Administration
94 Victoria Street
London SW1E 5JL
tel 071 917 0709

Department of Social Security
Richmond House
79 Whitehall
London SW1A 2NS
tel 071 210 5000

Department of Transport
Public Enquiries Unit
2 Marsham Street
London SW1P 3EB
tel 071 276 0800

Her Majesty's Treasury
Parliament Street
London SW1P 3AQ
tel 071 270 3000

Department of the Environment for Northern Ireland
Environment Service
Calvert House
23 Castle Place
Belfast BT1 1FY
tel 0232 230560

The Scottish Office
Environment Department
St Andrews House
Edinburgh EH1 3DD
tel 031 556 8400

Welsh Office
Cathays Park
Cardiff CF1 3NQ
tel 0222 825111

The Countryside Commission
John Dower House
Crescent Place
Cheltenham GL50 3RA
tel 0242 521381

Energy Efficiency Office
2 Marsham Street
London SW1P 3EB
tel 071 276 6200

English Heritage
Fortress House
23 Savile Row
London W1X 1AB
tel 071 973 3000

Forestry Commission
231 Corstorphine Road
Edinburgh EH12 7AT
tel 031 334 0303

Health and Safety Executive
Baynards House
1 Chepstow Place
Westbourne Grove
London W2 4TF
tel 071 243 6000

National Rivers Authority
30-34 Albert Embankment
London SE1 7TL
tel 071 820 0101

English Nature
Northminister House
Peterborough PE1 1UA
tel 0733 340345

Her Majesty's Inspectorate of Pollution
Romney House
43 Marsham Street
London SW1P 3PY
tel 071 276 3000

Rural Development Commission
11 Cowley Street
London SW1P 3NA
tel 071 276 6969

Scottish Natural Heritage
12 Hope Terrace
Edinburgh EH9 2AS
tel 031 447 4784

Historic Scotland
20 Brandon Street
Edinburgh
EH3 5RA

Cadw (Welsh Historic Monuments)
Brunel House
2 Fitzalan Road
Cardiff CF2 1UY
tel 0222 465511

Council for the Protection of Rural Wales
Ty Gwyn
31 High Street
Welshpool
SY21 7JP

Countryside Council for Wales
Plas Penrhos
Fford Penrhos
Bangor LL57 2LQ
tel 0248 370444

SAVING ENERGY

Neighbourhood Energy Action
St Andrew's House
90/92 Pilgrim Street
Newcastle Upon Tyne
NE1 6SG
tel 091 261 5677
fax 091 261 6496

For information on financial
and practical assistance
available to those on low
incomes contact your local
electricity and gas supplier.

NHS CENTRE FOR GREENING THE NHS

Dr J.A. Muir Gray
Director of Health Policy
and Public Health
Oxford Regional Health Authority
Old Road
Headington
Oxford OX3 7LF
tel 0865 226738

RECYCLING

Waste Watch
Hobart House
Grosvenor Place
London SW1X 7AE
Tel 071 245 9998
For general recycling enquiries
ring Wasteline on
071 245 9718

BUILT HERITAGE

Joint Committee of the National Amenity Societies
St Anns Vestry Hall
2 Church Entry
London EC4V 5HB
tel 071 236 3934

Civic Trust
17 Carlton House
Terrace
London SW1Y 5AW
tel 071 930 0914

National Trust
36 Queen Anne's Gate
London SW1H 9AS
tel 071 222 9251

TRANSPORT

Environmental Transport Association
The Old Port House
Heath Road
Weybridge KT13 8RS
tel 0932 828882

RAC
Public Policy Division
114 Rochester Row
London SW1P 1JQ
tel 071 233 5711

AA
Norfolk House
Priestley Road
Basingstoke
Hants RG24 9NY
tel 0256 493014

GARDENING

The Henry Doubleday Research Association
Ryton Organic Gardens
Ryton-on-Dunsmore
Coventry CV8 3LG
tel 0203 303517

Mr David Carter
The National History Museum,
Cromwell Road
London SW7 5BD
tel 071 938 9452 (for information on
insects and wildlife)

ENVIRONMENT AND COUNTRYSIDE

The Royal Society for the Protection of Birds
The Lodge, Sandy
Bedfordshire SG19 2DL
tel 0767 680551

The RSNC Wildlife Trusts Partnership
The Green, Witham Park
Lincoln LN5 7JR
tel 0522 544400

or your local Wildlife Trust

**British Trust for Conservation
Volunteers**
36 St Mary's Street
Wallingford OX10 OEU
tel 0491 39766

Groundwork Foundation
85/87 Cornwall Street
Birmingham B3 3BY
tel 021 236 8565

**Council for the Protection of Rural
England**
Warwick House
25 Buckingham Palace Road
London SW1W OPP
tel 071 976 6433
fax 071 976 6373

RSPCA
Causeway
Horsham
West Sussex
RH12 1HG
tel 0403 264181
fax 0403 241048

Friends of the Earth
26-28 Underwood Street,
London N1 7JQ
tel 071 490 1555

AIR AND NOISE

**The National Society for Clean Air
and Environmental Protection**
136 North Street
Brighton BN1 1RG
tel 0273 326313

**The Atmospheric Research and
Information Centre**
Dept. of Environmental and Geographical
Sciences
Manchester Metropoltan University
Chester Street
Manchester M1 5GD
tel 061 247 1590
fax 061 247 6332

**Global Climate Change Information
Centre**
Atmospheric Research & Information
Centre
Manchester Metropolitan University
Chester Street
Manchester M1 5GD
tel 061 247 1593

**MRC Institute for Environment
and Health**
University of Leicester
P O Box 138
Lancaster Road
Leicester LE1 9HN

National Air Quality Report
summary of current air quality
measurements and advice on what to do if
air quality becomes poor
tel 0800 556677

LITTER

Tidy Britain Group
The Pier
Wigan
WN3 4EX
tel 0942 824620
fax 0942 824778

**BUSINESS AND ENVIRONMENTAL
WORK**

ETIS: Support for UK industrial research

EUROENVIRON: Support for research
and development in Europe.

DEMOS: Support for demonstration
projects.

Further information about these schemes
can be obtained from:

ETIS
Chris Regan,
Department of Trade and Industry
tel 071 215 1051

John Thompson,
Department of the Environment
tel 071 276 8318

EUROENVIRON
Anne Hill,
Department of Trade and Industry
tel 071 215 1054

DEMOS
Mr D C Johnson,
Department of Trade and Industry
tel 071 215 1065

Better Environment Awards for Industry
Information about this scheme can be obtained from:

Myra Henderson
Royal Society of Arts
(also known as Royal Society for the Encouragement of Arts, Manufactures and Commerce)
8 John Adam Street
London WC2N 6EZ
tel 071 930 5115

Business and the Environment Programme
Information about this programme can be obtained from:

Edwin Datschefski
The Environment Council
21 Elizabeth Street
London SW1W 9RP
tel 071 824 8411

Business in the Environment
8 Stratton Street
London W1X 5FD
tel 071 629 1600
fax 071 629 1834

ENVIRONMENTAL EDUCATION

Council for Environmental Education
University of Reading
London Road
Reading RG1 5AQ
tel 0734 756061

National Association for Environmental Education (UK) (NAEE)
Wolverhampton University
Walsall Campus
Gorway
Walsall
West Midlands WS1 3BD
tel 0922 31200
fax 0922 323177 (marked for the attention of NAEE)

Environmental Education Adviser's Association (EEAA)
c/o Richard Moseley
Education Department
Dalvenie House, County Hall
Truro
Cornwall TR1 3BA
tel 0872 74282 ext 3429
fax 0872 70340 (please state Dalvenie on faxes)

National Association for Urban Studies (NAUS)
Architecture Workshop Ltd
Blackfriars
Monk Street
Newcastle-upon-Tyne NE1 4XN
tel 091 232 8183

VOLUNTARY WORK

A wide range of groups undertake environmental voluntary work from national groups like the Royal Society for Nature Conservation and the British Trust for Conservation Volunteers (see above) to local groups.

For further information contact organisations direct or seek information from:

The National Council for Voluntary Organisations
Regent's Wharf
8 All Saints Street
London N1 9RL
tel 071 713 6161
fax 071 713 6300

Community Service Volunteers
17 Midland Road
St Philips
Bristol BS2 OJT
tel 0272 411114

GENERAL INFORMATION

Environmental Contacts : a Guide for Business
(who does what in Government
Departments) available from
Department of Trade and Industry
Direct Marketing Centre
Bowen Industrial Estate
Bargoed CF8 9EP.
tel 0443 821877

Who's Who in the Environment
produced by The Environment Council,
(see above)

Further information on specific
environmental questions may be obtained
from:

Douglas Matthews
Department of the Environment
Room A127
Romney House
43 Marsham Street
London SW1P 3PY

ANNEX D
GREEN MINISTERS

DEPARTMENT	MINISTER
Agriculture, Fisheries and Food	The Rt Hon Mrs Gillian Shephard MP
Chancellor's Departments	The Rt Hon Sir John Cope
Defence	The Viscount Cranborne
Education	Robin Squire MP
Employment	The Lord Henley
Environment	The Rt Hon John Gummer MP
Foreign and Commonwealth Office	The Hon Mark Lennox-Boyd MP
Health	Baroness Cumberlege CBE
Home Office	Peter Lloyd MP
Law Officers'	Sir Derek Spencer QC MP
Lord Chancellor's	John M Taylor MP
National Heritage	Iain Sproat MP
Northern Ireland Office	Tim Smith MP
Overseas Development Administration	Baroness Chalker
Public Service and Science	David Davis MP
Scottish Office	Sir Hector Monro MP
Social Security	The Viscount Astor
Trade and Industry	Patrick McLoughlin MP
Transport	The Rt Hon John MacGregor OBE MP
Welsh Office	The Rt Hon John Redwood MP

ANNEX E
PHOTO CREDITS

INTRODUCTION

P4   The UK - Taking Rio Forward - Crown Copyright, Robin Nowacki

P5   Blackmore Vale, Dorset - B & C Alexander, Still Pictures

WORLDWIDE ENVIRONMENTAL ISSUES

P7   Beaked Heliconium - Sue Cunningham Photographic

P8   Sarawak Rainforest - Nigel Dickinson, Environmental Picture Library
'Partnership for Change' Conference - Crown Copyright, DOE

P9   Desert Reforestation - Jorgen Schytte, Still Pictures

P10   Black Rhino - Martin Wright, Still Pictures

EUROPEAN ENVIRONMENTAL ISSUES

P19   Ham Castle, Belgium
Central Copenhagen, Denmark - Jorgen Schytte, Still Pictures

P20   Scrap Iron Factory, Slovakia - Irene Lengui, Environmental Picture Library

P21   Rila Monastery, Bulgaria - John Mason, Ardea

UK ENVIRONMENTAL ISSUES

P25   Satellite Picture of UK - DRA, Still Pictures

P26   Shell Refinery - Hellier Mason, Still Pictures

P28   Pollution Inspector - Mark Edwards, Still Pictures

GLOBAL ATMOSPHERE

P35   Methane Extraction - Shanks & McEwan (Southern) Ltd.
Ocean Heat Balance Image - SERC/RAL/ESA

P36   Halon Recycling - Kiddi-Graviner
Sonde Measuring Ozone - P.Bucktrout, British Antarctic Survey

ENERGY AND THE ENVIRONMENT

P43   Combined Heat & Power Engine - ETSU, DTI

P44   DOE Brochures - Crown Copyright, DOE

P45   Wind Farm - ETSU, DTI

BUSINESS AND INDUSTRY

P53   Washing Machine - Hoover Ltd.

LAND USE AND PLANNING

P57   Top : Bentall Centre, Kingston - The Bentall Centre, Barry R.Bulley
Bottom: Market Stall, Kingston - Council Planning Department, Laurence Photography

P58   Rail Transporting Aggregate - Mendip Rail Ltd.

COUNTRYSIDE AND WILDLIFE

P65   Butterfly - English Nature
Thwaite, Yorkshire - Countryside Commission

P66   Cockaynes Wood, Essex - Rural Action

P67   Wild Plants - Bob Gibbons, Holt Studios

P68   Forestry Map - Countryside Commission

TOWNS AND CITIES

P77   Lavender Pond - Crown Copyright
Contaminated Land Site - Environmental Picture Library

P78   The Clarences, Stockton-on-Tees - Crown Copyright, DOE
Fly Tipping - Martin Bond, Environmental Picture Library

P79   UK Traffic - Mark Edwards, Still Pictures

Printed in the United Kingdom for HMSO
Dd 5062305, 5/94, C60, 51-4190, 39462, Ord 286712.